HENRY PURCELL

GARLAND COMPOSER
RESOURCE MANUALS
(Guy A. Marco, General Editor)
(VOL. 18)

GARLAND REFERENCE LIBRARY
OF THE HUMANITIES
(VOL. 885)

GARLAND COMPOSER RESOURCE MANUALS

General Editor: Guy A. Marco

HENRY PURCELL
A Guide to Research

Franklin B. Zimmerman

GARLAND PUBLISHING, INC. • NEW YORK & LONDON
1989

Library of Congress Cataloging-in-Publication Data

Zimmerman, Franklin B.
    Henry Purcell (1658/9–1695): a guide to research / Franklin B.
Zimmerman.
        p. cm.— (Garland composer resource manuals; 18) (Garland
reference library of the humanities; vol. 885)
    Bibliography: p. 326
    Includes index.
    ISBN 0-8240-7786-5 (alk. paper)
    1. Purcell, Henry. 1659–1695—Bibliography. I. Title.
II. Series. III. Series: Garland composer resource manuals; v. 18.
ML134.P95Z55 1989
780'.92'4—dc19   88-23677
                                                              CIP
                                                               MN

Printed on acid-free, 250-year-life paper
Manufactured in the United States of America

780.0711
Puc
2.m

CONTENTS

C. The Music

PREFACE

The purpose of this manual is to provide for the reader a numbered list of Purcell's complete works, a compilation of hitherto unpublished prefaces and dedications to his published works, an account of Purcell's life and times, information on editions of his music, and a selective bibliography with commentary. It is intended for students and lovers of music who wish to know more about the creations, and the life and the times of this man who, more successfully than anyone else, provided solutions for problems inherent in the musical art, as practiced in English-speaking cultures. Purcell always composed in an engaging manner. Often, he wrote with extraordinary inspiration.

Some of the chapters that make up this volume bring new information or new order to what we know of Purcell. Others shed new light on his life and works. These factors, it is hoped, will be useful and interesting to the reader involved with Purcell's music, whether as performer, scholar or music lover. The classified list of works also brings additional items to the Purcell canon, at the same time rearranging the old list published by Macmillan & Co. twenty-four years ago in London, when this author's *Analytical Catalogue of Purcell's Complete Works* first appeared. I believe this present list to be more complete and up-to-date than any other now available. Each entry bears the original work-number as then assigned, except in the few instances where changes have been necessary. For each item, the primary modern source of any given work is identified.

Purcell's life story is all the more fascinating because of an aura of mystery surrounding it. That story is briefly summarized in this guide, both to relieve the somewhat austere presentation of other data relevant to Purcell's works, and to show at least some of the major works within the context of Purcell's life and times.

Reproduction of prefatory and dedicatory material from early editions of Purcell's music appearing during or shortly after his lifetime have been included in this compilation for similar reasons. Apart from providing information on the music of Purcell and his contemporaries, these contain interesting points of human or historical interest, affording modern Purcellians better understanding of the immediate foreground of his creations. These materials are followed by a selective list of published collections of Purcell's works, with inventories of the pieces they contain, followed by another list of modern editions of individual works from the Purcell canon.

The guide ends with a selective bibliography, providing brief commentary on major studies of various aspects of Purcell's life and works, followed by an index of persons and places and subjects. Bibliographical items have been selected on the basis of intrinsic value, relevance and currency. A few that do not seem to measure well in these regards have been listed with negative commentary, or with no commentary at all.

For assistance and advice, which have been most helpful in the compilation of this guide, I am particularly grateful to Marie Ellen Larcada and Maureen Buja, of Garland Publishing, Inc. Both have rendered assistance beyond the call of duty to make this publication possible. I am also grateful to Paul Whitehead, a doctoral candidate at the Universtiy of Pennsylvania, for yeoman service throughout the study.

Referring again to purposes mentioned in the first paragraph above, it is this author's hope that each of the above described features will prove somehow useful in the reader's pursuit of the never-ending delight that Purcell's music can afford.

Garland Composer
Resource Manuals

In response to the growing need for bibliographic guidance to the vast literature on significant composers, Garland is publishing an extensive series of research guides. The series, which will most likely appear over a five-year period, encompasses almost 50 composers; they represent Western musical tradition from the Renaissance to the present century.

Each research guide offers a selective, annotated list of writings, in all European languages, about one or more composers. There are also lists of works by the composers, unless these are available elsewhere. Biographical sketches and guides to library resources, organizations, and specialists are presented. As appropriate to the individual composers, there are maps, photographs, or other illustrative matters, and glossaries and indexes.

ABBREVIATIONS AND CONVENTIONS

D=Dubious or doubtful ascription
K.M.=La Fontaine, Henry Cart de, *Kings Musick*
mnp=music not printed
N=Newly discovered entry
NYPL=New York Public Library
O.U.P.=Oxford University Press
P. Soc. Ed.=Purcell Society Edition
Pur. Soc. Ed.=Purcell Society Edition
S=Spurious or supposititious ascription
W.A.M.=Westminster Abbey Muniments.

HENRY PURCELL

CLASSIFIED LIST OF THE COMPLETE WORKS OF HENRY PURCELL

SACRED VOCAL WORKS

ANTHEMS (Nos. 1-N70)

1. Awake, put on thy strength (XIV, 41)
2. Behold, I bring you glad tidings (XVIII, 1)
3. Behold, now praise the Lord (XIIIA, 49)
4. Be merciful unto me (XXVIII, 28)
5. Blessed are they that fear the Lord (XXVIII, 42)
6. Blessed be the Lord (XVIII, 60)
7. Blessed is he that considereth the poor (XXVIII, 71)
8. Blessed is he whose unrighteousness is forgiven (XIIIA, 71)
9. Blessed is the man that feareth the Lord (XXVIII, 83)
10. Blow up the trumpet in Sion (XXVIII, 96)
11. Bow down Thine ear, O Lord (XIII, 103)
12. Give sentence with me, O God (XXXII, 117)
13A. Hear me, O Lord, and that soon (XIIIA, 87)
13B. Hear me, O Lord, and that soon (XIIIA, 90)
14. Hear my pray'r, O God (XXVIII, 125)
15. Hear my prayer, O Lord (XXVIII, 135)
16. In Thee, O Lord, do I put my trust (XIV, 53)

65. Why do the heathen so furiously rage? (XVII, 1)
N66. If the Lord himself (fragment)
N67. I will love Thee, O Lord (XXVIII, 157)
N68. Praise the Lord, ye servants (fragment)
N69. The Lord is King and hath put on glorious apparel (XXXII, 30)
N70. I will love Thee, O Lord (Oxford, Bodleian Fragment)

CANONS   (Nos. 101-N110)
101. Alleluia ('Canon 4 in 2, *recte et retro*'; XXXII, 174)
102. Domine non est exaltatum (Incomplete; XXXII, 172)
103. Gloria Patri et Filio (XXXII, 163)
104. Gloria Patri et Filio ('Canon 3 in 1'; XXII, 159)
105. Gloria Patri et Filio ('Canon 4 in 1 *per arsin et thesin*' ; XXXII,161)
106. Glory be to the Father ('Canon 4 in 1'; XXXII, 168)
107. God is gone up ('Canon 7 in 1, unison'; XXXII, 170)
108. Laudate Dominum ('Canon 3 in 1'; XXXII, 170)
109. Miserere mei ('Canon 4 in 2'; XXXII, 171)
N110. Alleluia ('Canon 5 in 1'; Michael Broome, *A Collection of Psalm Tunes*, 1728)

CHANTS   (Nos. 120-125)
120. *Chant No. 1 in a minor* (XXXII, 174)
121. *Chant No. 2 in G Major* (XXXII, 173)
122. *Chant No. 3 in G Major* (XXXII, 174)

HYMNS, PSALMS, AND SACRED PART-SONGS (Nos. 130-144)

SERVICES   (Nos. 230-232)

230. *Service in B-flat Major* Morning, Communion,
     and Evening (XXIII, 1)
231. *Evening Service in g minor* (XXIII, 80)
232. *Te Deum and Jubilate in D-Major* (XXIII, 90)

SECULAR WORKS

CATCHES   (Nos. 240-292)

240. A health to the nut-brown lass (XXII, 5)
241. An ape, a lion, a fox and an ass (XXII, 1)
242. As Roger last night (XXII, 1)
243. Bring the bowl and cool Nantz (XXII, 1)
244. Call for the reck'ning (XXII, 2)
245. Come, let us drink (XXII, 2)
246. Come, my hearts, play your parts (XXII, 3)
247. Down with Bacchus (XXII, 3)
248. Drink on, till night be spent (XXII, 4)
249. Full bags, a brisk bottle (XXII, 18)
250. God save our sov'reign Charles (XXII, 4)
251. Great Apollo and Bacchus (XXII, 4)
252. Here's a health, pray let it pass (XXII, 5)
253. Here's that will challenge all the Fair (XXII, 5)
254. He that drinks is immortal (XXII, 4)
255. If all be true that I do think (XXII, 6)
256. I gave her cakes and I gave her ale (XXII, 6)
257. Is Charleroi's siege come too? (XXII, 6)
258. Let the grave folks go preach (XXII, 7)
259. Let us drink to the blades (XXII, 7)
260. My lady's coachman John (XXII, 8)
261. Now England's great council (XXII, 8)
262. Now we are met and humours agree (XXII, 9)

292. Young John, the gard'ner (XXII, 18)

ODES, BIRTHDAY SONGS, WELCOME SONGS, AND OTHER OCCASIONAL VOCAL WORKS (Nos. 320-344)

320. Arise, my muse (XI, 36)
321. Celebrate this festival (XXIV, 36)
322. Celestial music did the gods inspire (XXVII, 29)
323. Come ye sons of art away (XXIV, 87)
324. Fly, bold rebellion (XV, 116)
325. From hardy climes (XXVII, 1)
326. From those serene and rapturous joys (XV, 1)
327. Great parent, hail (XXVII, 59)
328. Hail, bright Cecilia (VIII, 1)
329. Laudate Ceciliam (X, 44)
330. Light of the world (Missing)
331. Love's goddess sure was blind (XXIV, 1)
332. Now does the glorious day appear (XI, 1)
333. Of old when heroes thought it base (I, 1)
334. Raise, raise the voice (X, 26)
335. Sound the trumpet, beat the drum (XVIII, 121)
336. Swifter, Isis, swifter flow (XV, 24)
337. The summer's absence unconcerned we bear (XV, 83)
338. Welcome, glorious morn (XI, 72)
339. Welcome to all the pleasures (X, 1)
340. Welcome, Vicegerent of the mighty King (XV, 1)
341. What shall be done in behalf of the man (XV, 52)
342. Who can from joy refrain? (IV, 1)

513. There ne'er was so wretched a lover (XXII, 120)
514. Though my mistress be fair (XXII, 23)
515. Trip it in a ring (XXII, 132)
516. Underneath this myrtle shade (XXII, 100)
517. Were I to choose the greatest bliss (XXII, 86)
518. What can we poor females do? (XXII, 104)
519. When gay Philander left the plain (XXII, 20)
520. When, lovely Phyllis, thou art kind (XXII, 30)
521. When Myra sings (XXII, 109)
522. When Teucer from his father fled (XXII, 48)
523. While bolts and bars my days control (XXII, 130)
524. While you for me alone had charms (XXII, 146)
525. Why, my Daphne, why complaining? (XXII, 93)
N526. To this place we've now come ('94 Songs by Henry Purcell, D. Purcell, Blow *et altri.*')

THREE- AND FOUR-PART SONGS AND LARGER VOCAL WORKS (Nos. 541-548)

541. Hark, Damon, hark (XXVII, 93)
542. Hark how the wild musicians sing)XXVII, 109)
543. How pleasant is this flow'ry plain (XXII, 74)
544. If ever I more riches did desire (XXVII, 118)
545. In a deep vision's intellectual scene (XXVII, 140)
546. 'Tis wine was made to rule the day (XXII, 177)
547. We reap all the pleasures (Fragmentary: XXVII, 156)

548. When the cock begins to crow (XXII, 181)

INCIDENTAL MUSIC (Nos. 570-614N)

570. *Abdelazer, or The Moor's Revenge* (XX, 1)
571. *A Fool's Preferment, or The Three Dukes of Dunstable* (XX, 11)
572. *Amphitryon, or The Two Sosias* (XX, 21)
573. *Aureng-Zebe, or The Great Mogul* (XX, 42)
574. *Bonduca, or The British Heroine* (XVI, 45)
575. *Circe* (XVI, 95)
576. *Cleomenes, the Spartan Hero* (XVI, 120)
577. *Distressed Innocence, or The Princess of Persia* (XVI, 122)
578. *Don Quixote, The Comical History of* (XVI, 132)
579. *Epsom Wells* (XVI, 221)
580. *Henry the Second, King of England* (XX, 38)
581. *King Richard the Second, or The History of the Sicilian Usurper* (XX, 43)
582. *Love Triumphant, or Nature Will Prevail* (XX, 70)
583. *Oedipus* (XXI, 1)
584. *Oroonoko* (XXI, 38)
585. *Pausanias, the Betrayer of His Country* (XXI, 44)
586. *Regulus, or The Faction of Carthage* (XXI, 51)
587. *Rule a Wife and Have a Wife* (XXI, 85)
588. *Sir Anthony Love, or The Rambling Lady* (XXI, 87)
589. *Sir Barnaby Whigg, or No Wit Like a Woman's* (XXI, 103)
590. *Sophonisba, or Hannibal's Overthrow* (XXI, 109)

613. *Tyrannic Love, or The Royal Martyr* (XXI, 135)

N614. *'The Stairre Case Overture.'* (Yale & Bamb. MSS)

OPERA, SEMI-OPERAS ('AMBIGUES'), MASQUE (Nos. 626-632)

626. *Dido and Aeneas* (III)
627. *The Prophetess, or The History of Dioclesian* (IX)
628. *King Arthur, or The British Worthy* (XXVI)
629. *The Fairy Queen* (XII)
630. *The Indian Queen* (XIX)
631. *The Tempest, or The Enchanted Isle* (XIX,111)
632. *Timon of Athens, the Man-Hater* (II)

KEYBOARD WORKS: HARPSICHORD (Nos. 641-671)

641. *Air in G Major* (VI, 49)
642. *Almand and Corant in a minor* (Pauer, 152, 4)
643. *Almand with Division in G Major* (VI, 47)
644. *Corant in G Major* (VI, 48)
645. *Ground in Gamut* (VI, 33)
646. *Lilliburlero. A New Irish Tune* (VI, 31)
647. *March in C Major* (VI, 28)
648. *March in C Major* (VI, 28)
649. *Minuet in a minor* (VI, 29)
650. *Minuet in a minor* (VI, 29)
651. *Minuet in G Major* (VI, 51)
652. *Prelude in A minor* (VI, 40)
653. *Rigadoon in C Major* (VI, 32)
654. *Sarabande with Division in a minor* (VI, 35)

655. *Scotch Tune 'A New Scotch Tune'* in G Major (VI, 30)
656. *Sefauchi's Farewell* (VI, 32)

SUITES

660. *Suite in G Major: Prelude, Alemand, Corant, Saraband* (VI, 1: I)
661. *Suite in g minor: Prelude, Alemand, Corant, Saraband* (VI, 2: II)
662. *Suite in G Major: Prelude, Alemand , Corant* (VI, 6: III)
663. *Suite in a minor: Prelude, Alemand, Corant, Saraband* (VI, 10: IV)
664. *Suite in B-flat Major: Almand, Corant, Saraband* (Pauer, 156-7, 166)
665. *Suite in C Major: Prelude, Almand, Corant, Saraband, Jigg* (Dart: *Musick's Handmaid*, 21-2.)
666. *Suite in C Major: Prelude, Almand, Corant, Saraband* (VI, 13: V)
667. *Suite in D Major: Prelude, Alemand, Hornpipe* (VI, 16: VII)
668. *Suite in d minor: Almand, 'Bell Barr,' Corant, Hornpipe* (VI, 18: VII)
669. *Suite in F Major: Almand, Corant, Minuet* (VI, 20: VIII)
670. *The Queen's Dolour* (Barclay Squire, N. 22)
671. *Prelude for Ye Fingering* (Howard Ferguson)

TRANSCRIPTIONS   (Nos. T675-T699)

T675. *Air in d minor* (VI, 37)
T676. *Air in d minor* (VI, 41)
T677. *Canary in B-flat Major* (MS Drexel 5609)

T678. *'Cibell,' Trumpet Tune, called The Cibell* (VI, 27)

T679. *Chacone with canon, in a minor* (Br. Library copy, *A Choice Collection of Lessons for the Harpsichord*)

T680. *Chacone in g minor* (VI, 24)

T681. *Ground in c minor* (VI, 39)

T682. *A New Ground in e minor* (VI, 30)

T683. *Hornpipe in B-flat Major* (British Library Add. 22099)

T684. *Hornpipe in d minor* (VI, 38)

T685. *Hornpipe in e minor* (VI, 47)

T686. *Jig in g minor* (VI, 26)

T687. *March in C major* (VI, 23)

T688. *Minuet in d minor* (VI, 32)

T689. *New Minuet in d minor* (VI, 29)

T690. *Overture in c minor* (Pauer, 160)

T691. *Overture in D Major* (Pauer, 164)

T692. *Overture in D Major* (Pauer, 162)

T693. *Overture, Air and Jig in gamut-flat* (VI, 56)

T694. *Song Tune in C Major* (VI, 28)

T695. *Song Tune in C Major* (Dart, *Musick's Handmaid*)

T696. (?) *Suite in d minor* (*The Lady's Banquet,* 1706)

T697. *Trumpet Tune in C Major* (VI, 27)

T698. *Trumpet Tune in C Major* (VI, 24)

T699. *Air in C Major* (*The Harpsichord Master,* 1697)

ORGAN (Nos. 716-721)

716. *A Verse in F Major* (VI, 36)

717. *Voluntary in C Major* (VI, 35)

718. *Voluntary in d minor* (VI, 61)
719. *Voluntary for Double Organ* (VI, 64)
720. *Voluntary in G Major* (VI, 63)
721. *Voluntary on the 100th Psalm in A Major* (VI, 59)

STRINGS; FANTASIAS AND RELATED FORMS (Nos. 730-756)

730. *Chacony à 4 in g minor* (XXXI, 61)
731. *Fantasia '3 Parts upon a Ground,' à 4, in g minor,* (XXXI, 52)
732. *Fantasia à 3 in d minor* (XXXI, 1)
733. *Fantasia à 3 in F Major* (XXXI, 3)
734. *Fantasia à 3 in g minor* (XXXI, 5)
735. *Fantasia à 4 in g minor* (XXXI, 7)
736. *Fantasia à 4 in B-flat Major* (XXXI, 10)
737. *Fantasia à 4 in F Major* (XXXI, 13)
738. *Fantasia à 4 in c minor* (XXXI, 16)
739. *Fantasia à 4 in d minor* (XXXI, 19)
740. *Fantasia à 4 in a minor* (XXXI, 22)
741. *Fantasia à 4 in e minor* (XXXI, 25)
742. *Fantasia à 4 in G Major* (XXXI, 38)
743. *Fantasia à 4 in d minor* (XXXI, (31)
744. *Fantasia à 4 in a minor* (XXXI, 94)
745. *Fantasia upon one note à 5 in F Major* (XXXI, 34)
746. *In nomine à 6 in g minor* (XXXI, 37)
747. *In nomine à 7 in g minor* (XXXI, 39)
748. *Pavan à 3 in A Major* (XXXI, 46)
749. *Pavan à 3 in A-re flat* (XXI, 44)
750. *Pavan à 3 in B-flat* (XXXI, 49)
751. *Pavan à 3 in Gamut* (XXXI, 42)
752. *Pavan à 4 in g minor* (XXXI, 49)

N755. *Pavan à 4 in f minor* (Yale Music MS Osborn
515)

N756. *Pavan in f minor* (Yale Music MS Osborn 515)

SONATAS AND RELATED FORMS
(Nos. 770-780)

770. *Overture and Suite Fragment in G Major*
(XXXI, 68)

771. *Overture in d minor* (XXXI, 76)

772. *Overture à 5, in g minor* (XXXI, 93)

N773. *Prelude for Solo Violin in g minor* (XXXI,
93)

N774. *'Mr. Purcell's Jig'* (*Apollo's Banquet*, 1687)

N775. *Overture à 4 in C Major* (Yale Music MS
Osborn 515) (Bass part only)

N776. *Overture in C Major* (Yale Music MS Osborn
515) (Bass part only)

780. *Sonata for Violin in g minor* (XXXI, 95)

SONATAS OF THREE PARTS (Nos. 790-801)

790. *Sonata I in g minor* (V, 1)

791. *Sonata II in B-flat Major* (V, 9)

792. *Sonata III in d minor* (V, 18)

793. *Sonata IV in F Major* (V, 27)

794. *Sonata V in a minor* (V, 35)

795. *Sonata VI in C Major* (V, 42)

796. *Sonata VII in e minor* (V, 51)

797. *Sonata VIII in G Major* (V, 61)

798. *Sonata IX in c minor* (V, 71)

799. *Sonata X in A Major* (V, 82)

800. *Sonata XI in f minor* (V, 88)

801. *Sonata XII in D Major* (V, 96)

SONATAS OF FOUR PARTS (Nos. 802-811)
802. *Sonata I in b minor* (VII, 1)
803. *Sonata II in E-flat Major* (VII, 13)
804. *Sonata III in a minor* (VII, 23)
805. *Sonata IV in d minor* (VII, 34)
806. *Sonata V in g minor* (VII, 46)
807. *Sonata VI in g minor* (VII, 57)
808. *Sonata VII in C Major* (VII, 70)
809. *Sonata VIII in g minor* (VII, 82)
810. *Sonata IX in F Major* (VII, 93)
811. *Sonata X in D Major* (VII, 106)

TRUMPET AND STRINGS (No. 850)
850. *Sonata in D Major* (XXXI, 86)

WIND CONSORT (No. 860)
860. *March and Canzona in c minor* (XXXI, 92)

DIDACTIC EXAMPLES (Nos. 870-871)
870. *Counterpoint and Canon*
    A. *Examples in two parts* (XXXI, 101-2)
    B. *Examples in three parts* (XXXI, 102-4)
    C. *Examples in four parts* (XXXI, 104)
871. *Miscellaneous Exercises*

DOUBTFUL ASCRIPTIONS TO PURCELL

ANTHEMS
    D1. Awake up my glory
    D2. Glory be to God on high
    D3. O be joyful
    D4. O God, they that love Thy name (XXXII, 120)

D5. O pray for the peace
D6. Peace be within thy walls
D7. Sing we merrily unto God
D8. Turn Thee again, O Lord

CANONS AND CHANTS

D15. Alleluia
D21. Glory be to the Father
D22. Laudate Dominum (Canon 3 in 1)
D30. Single Chant (in A Major)
D31. Single Chant (in C Major)
D32. Chant (in G Major)
D33. Chant (in g minor)
D34. Chant (in g minor)
D35. Venite (Chant in G Major)
D36. Chant (in g minor)
D37. Chant (in B-flat Major)
D38. Chant (in g minor)

HYMNS AND PSALMS

D40. Far from me be all false ways
D41. O God, sole object of our love
D42. O that my grief was throughly weigh'd
D43. Put me not to rebuke, O Lord
D44. The gracious bounty of our Lord
D45. *Walsall*
D46. *Westminster Abbey*

SACRED SONGS AND DUETS

D69. Arise, great dead, for arms renown'd
D70. Arise, my darken'd melancholy soul
D71. It must be done, my soul
D72. My op'ning eyes are purg'd

D73. O give thanks
D74. O praise the Lord, laud ye the name
D75. Praise the Lord, O my soul, and all that is within me
D76. The Lord, ev'n the most mighty
D77. The night is come
D78. Soon as the morn salutes your eyes

SERVICE MOVEMENTS
D90. Sanctus
D91. Te Deum in C

CATCHES
D100. Fie, nay prithee John
D101. Hail, happy words, abodes of peace
D102. Let's live good honest lives
D103. Say, good master Bacchus
D104. Since women so false and so jiltish are grown
D105. The glass was just tim'd
D106. Tom, making a mantua for a lass
D107. Well rung, Tom boy

ODES
D120. *'Address of the Children of the Chapel Royal to the King and their master, Capt. Cooke, on his Majesty's birthday, A.D. 1670, composed by master Henry Purcell, one of the children of the said chapel.'*

SOLO SONGS
D130. A quire of bright beauties
D131. As unconcern'd and free as air
D132. Away, fond love, thou foe to rest

D133. How peaceful the days are
D134. In Cloe's sparkling eyes
D135. Musing, I late on Windsor terras sate
D136. Of noble race was Shinkin (thrum)
D137. One long Whitsun holiday
D138. Sunny, rich and fantastic; The old tumbler
D139. Vacant
D142. O that my grief was throughly weigh'd
D143. Put me not to rebuke, O Lord
D144. What ungrateful devil makes you come
D143. When first Dorinda's piercing eyes
D144. While Phyllis is drinking
D145. Young Strephon he has woo'd me

THREE-PART SONG
D171. A poor blind woman that has no sight at all

INCIDENTAL MUSIC
D200. (?) *Neglected Virtue, or The Unhappy Conqueror*
D201. *Unidentified Play*

KEYBOARD WORKS
D218. *Almand in a minor*
D219. *Almand and Borry (rather, Gavotte and Saraband) in D-sol-re#*
D220. *Gavotte in G Major*
D221. *Ground in c minor*
D222. *Ground in d minor*
D223. *Jig in g minor*
D224. *Minuet in d minor*
D225. *Minuet in e minor*
D226. *Overture in A Major*

D227. *Rigadoon in d minor*
D228. *Suite in g minor*
D229. *Toccata in a minor*
D230. *Trumpet Minuet*
D231. *Trumpet Minuet*
D240. *Prelude in C Major*
D241. *Voluntary and Adagio in C Major*
D242. *'The Voluntary Composed by Mr. H. Purcell'*
(fragment)

FANTASIAS, SONATAS, AND RELATED FORMS FOR STRINGS

D250. *Fantasia à 4 in C Major*
D251. *Sonata Fragment in c minor*
D252. *Sonata Fragment in c minor*
D253. *Tinker's Dance*
D254. *Mr. Mountfort's Farewell*
D255. *(?) Jig in G Major*
D256. *(?) Jig in g minor*
D257. *(?) Jig in F Major*

INCIDENTAL MUSIC

D571/9. *Here's a health to the King (A Fool's Preferment)*

SPURIOUS ASCRIPTIONS

SACRED VOCAL WORKS

S1. By the waters of Babylon (P. Humfrey)
S2. Christ is risen (E. White)
S3. Come, honest Sexton (M. Locke)

S4. God sheweth me His goodness (William Norris)

S5. Great is the Lord (? H. Loosemore)

S6. Hosannah to the Prince of light (? H. Loosemore)

S7. How pleasant is Thy dwelling place (Henry Carey)

S8. I am the Resurrection (J. Weldon)

S9. I heard a great voice (W. Croft)

S10. My heart rejoiceth (W. Norris)

S11. O come, loud anthems (M. Cooke)

S12. O God, wherefore art Thou (J. Blow)

S13. O Lord God of my salvation (V. Richardson)

S14. O Lord, rebuke me not (J. Weldon)

S15. O miserable man (D. Purcell)

S16. O that mine eyes would melt into a flood (H. Loosemore)

S17. The Lord my pasture shall prepare (H. Carey)

S18. To celebrate Thy praise, O Lord (H. Carey)

S19. Turn Thou us, O good Lord (G. Jeffries)

SECULAR VOCAL WORKS

S50. A lass there lives upon the green (R. Courteville)

S51. Cease the rovers (D. Purcell)

S52. Come pull away boys (G. Holmes)

S53. Fill all the glasses (J. Eccles)

S54. Had she not care enough (J. Savile)

S55. Hang sorrow (W. Lawes)

S56. Hark the bonny Christ Church bells (H. Aldrich)

S57. How happy are they (J. Marsh)

S58. How well doth this harmonious meeting prove (H. Bond)

S59. Lightly tread, 'tis hallowed ground (M. Wise)

S60. Ode to an expiring frog (A. Hutchings)

S61. Old Chiron thus preached (M. Wise)

S62. Say what you please (W. Turner)

S63. Since Cloris the pow'rs (Gresham MS)

S64. The owl is abroad (J.C. Smith)

S65. Was ever Nymph like Rosamund (T. A. Arne)

S66. Why does the morn (J. Blow)

S67. Hark, Harry, 'tis late (J. Eccles)

S68. Forth from my dark and dismal cell (Anon., 1661)

S69. Sweet Tyraness, I now resign (ssb; H. Purcell, Sr.)

S70. Sweet Tyraness, I now resign (sopr.; H. Purcell, Sr.)

DRAMATIC MUSIC
S100. *Macbeth* (R. Leveridge)

INSTRUMENTAL MUSIC
S120. *Air in D Major* (J. Clarke)

S121. *Cibell* (Lully)

S122. *Purcell's Ground,* or *'The Welsh Ground.'*

S123. *Jig in g minor* (Morgan)

S124. *Trumpet Tune* (J. Clarke)

S125. *Trumpet Voluntary* (J. Clarke)

S126. *Verse in the Phrygian Mode* (N. Lebégue)

HENRY PURCELL:
A BIOGRAPHICAL SKETCH

Henry Purcell, known even in his own lifetime as the "Orpheus Britannicus," was born in 1659,[1] presumably in the City and Liberty of Westminster. At least that was the neighbourhood in which his father, Henry the elder, earned a living as singer and Master of the Choristers at St. Peters, Westminster, during the period in which his famous son was born. In that fashionable surburb of London, young Henry Purcell lived and worked, dying on the eve of St. Cecilia's Day, November 21, 1695, at slightly less than 37 years of age.[2]

The exact date on which he was born remains unknown. But an early engraved portrait printed as frontispiece to *The Sonatas of Three Parts*[3] in June 1683,[4] describes him as being then twenty-four years of age. Therefore his actual birthday must have fallen sometime between late November and early June, or perhaps May, allowing a month for the trio sonatas to have been in the press.[5] Whatever the precise date of his birth may have been, it is clear that young Henry was born and reared in a professional musical environment.[6] He may have been born in the singing-men's quarters in the Dean's Yard, Westminster Abbey,[7] where his future wife, Frances, was to live for several years after his death,[8] but during his boyhood and until the death of his father on August 11, 1664, the family lived in one of the houses on the south side of Great Almonry (near Tothill Street). Within a few years of his father's passing, Purcell became a member of the Children of the Chapel Royal, training and studying daily at nearby St. Peters, Westminster. Shortly thereafter, in 1669, his mother, Elizabeth, moved to a house nearby in Tothill Street South. There she was to end her days, having outlived her celebrated son by some four years when she died in 1699.[9]

Very likely, Henry Purcell, the younger, was already established as a chorister in the Chapel Royal when his mother moved to her new home. W. H. Cummings conjectured that young Purcell had been adopted after his father's death in the summer of 1664 by his uncle, Thomas Purcell, Gentleman of the Chapel Royal and Groom of the Robes. If there was a formal legal adoption, no actual records have been found. In a letter to John Gostling written in 1679, Thomas refers to Henry as his son. But surely, this is misleading, for, as we shall see, all the evidence clearly shows Henry the elder to have been the father of the famous composer.[10] After acting in *loco parentis* for nearly fifteen years, Thomas might have referred quite naturally to Henry as his son. But such usage would have been warranted only if he had actually adopted him after his brother's untimely death. For proof that he was the son of Henry the elder, we have, as mentioned above, the testimony of John Hingeston's will, wherein the younger Henry is identified as the son of Elizabeth Purcell, wife to the elder Henry.[11] There is also Thomas Ford's "An account of Musicians & their works," which states quite definitely:

> Purcell, Henry. Son of Hen: Purcell.
> Gent. of Chapel, who died Aug. 11, 1664;
> scholar to Dr. Blow and to Dr. Christopher
> Gibbons, Master of the Children and organist
> to Charles II and William III and organist of

St. Peters', Westminster. He died Nov. 21, 1695.[12]

The music historians Burney, and Hawkins, who knew personal acquaintances of Purcell, name Henry the elder as father, and identify Thomas as the uncle. Since the only evidence supporting any other family relationship derives from the above-cited passage in Thomas's letter to John Gostling, further pursuit of alternate hypotheses is scarcely profitable.

Of Purcell's education very little is known. That he attended St. Peters' School may be assumed from the fact that he received a mourning ring from Richard Busby, the headmaster. That he felt his schooling inadequate we know from his own statement in the preface to the above-mentioned trio sonatas of 1683.[13] Precisely when he entered the Choir of the Chapel Royal as a chorister is uncertain. But he cannot have done so before the year 1665, when he was six,[14] and probably did so later. His earliest training as a chorister would have taken place under the civil war veteran, Captain Henry Cooke, an excellent singer and composer who had studied in Italy. Indeed, tradition has it that Purcell finished his first composition under Cooke's tutelage, providing a musical setting for *An Address of the Children of the Chapel Royal to the King, and their Master, Captain Cooke, on His Majesties Birthday, A.D. 1670.*[15] But final proof that this was indeed Purcell's composition must await more conclusive evidence.

After Cooke's death in 1672,[16] Purcell's musical training continued under Pelham Humfrey, a former chorister and Cooke's successor as Master of the Children. Interestingly enough, Humfrey, at that time held a joint appointment with his charge's uncle, Thomas Purcell, as Composer-in-Ordinary for the Violins.[17] Purcell's tutelage with Humfrey was quite short, however, for the latter died on July 14, 1674, at the age of 27. Thereafter, Purcell's musical training became the responsibility of John Blow, who remained a faithful and supportive friend even after young Purcell had surpassed him as a famous composer. During much if not all of this time, Purcell also learned from Matthew Locke, a friend and mentor until he died in 1677. Apart from stylistic affinity and the touching elegy Purcell composed on Locke's death, evidence confirming this friendly relationship is limited to one document. This is a letter from Locke to "Dear Harry," which reveals that he and young Henry were close friends:

> Dear Harry,
>   Some of the gentlemen of His Majesty's Musick will honour my poor lodgings with their company this evening, and I would have you come and join them. Bring with thee, Harry, thy last anthem, and also the canon we tried over together at our last meeting. Thine in all kindness,
>   M. Lock
>   Savoy, March 16.[18]

As an organist Purcell had studied under the guidance of Dr. Christopher Gibbons, the only teacher mentioned by Anthony à Wood in his entry for Purcell:

> Born in London—He, Dr. Child, and Dr. Blow all organists to King William and Queen Mary. PURCELL, HENRY, originally one of the Children in the King's Chapel Royal. Bred under Dr. Chr. Gibbons, I think, afterwards organist to King Charles

2nd, William III. Organist at St. Peter's
Church at Westminster.[19]

Thomas Ford's entry is more succinct, as we have seen
above.

Apart from musical training and performance, Purcell's
activities as a chorister included rigorous schooling that
continued until shortly before December 17, 1673, when a
warrant was issued for his dismissal. No doubt Henry
Purcell departed because his voice had broken, but we need
not suppose that his allowances were cut off at that time.
Frequent entries in the Chapel Royal accounts show that
former choristers continued to receive financial support and
clothing until placed elsewhere.

Nor did Purcell's schooling end with his dismissal from
the choir in 1673. In 1678 his name appeared on the roster
of Westminster School as one of the "Bishop's Boys." It
was written into the space in which that of Charles Purcell, a
brother or cousin and former scholar, had been partially
erased "Bishop's Boys" held scholarships covering tuition
and costs, under a dispensation from a former Bishop
Williams, of Lincoln.[20] It may be conjectured that Purcell,
like many of his elder musical colleagues, already was
practicing the professional pluralism then so popular in and
around the English. In any case, his scholarship no doubt
provided for Purcell's continued training after dismissal
from the Chapel Royal. Or, it is possible that the young
genius had been associated with the school for some time,
and received this preferment only upon the disappearance of
Charles Purcell. That he came under the direct influence of
Richard Busby, the famous "flogging master" at St. Peter's
is more than probable, for Busby later remembered him in
his will with the thoughtful gift of a mourning ring.[21]

As we have seen, Purcell's official career as a composer may have already begun with a composition for King Charles II and for his choir-master, Captain Cooke. However, both the anecdote and the work itself are in considerable doubt. On June 10, 1673, it is nevertheless quite certain that he officially became assistant to John Hingeston, Keeper and Repairer of the Instruments at the Chapel Royal. The rubric "without fee" seems not to have been followed religiously, for there are frequent entries in the Treasurer's accounts for the years 1675 through 1680 recording payments to Purcell for tuning the organ, copying music, and for other small tasks.[22]

In 1677, upon the death of his mentor, Matthew Locke, Purcell was appointed Composer-in-Ordinary for the Chapel Royal Violins, an appointment that no doubt facilitated the early flowering of his creative genius in the remarkable fantasias which began to appear shortly afterward. Two years later John Blow graciously handed over to him the position Purcell was to enjoy for the rest of his life as Organist at Westminster Abbey. Thus, even before reaching the age of twenty, young Henry Purcell's resumé—had he had such—would have listed no less than five different professional musical activities including those of chorister, copyist, composer, instrument-keeper, and organist. Probably he played other instruments as well, as we know from the two portraits of him as violist—or "tenorist"— which have survived.[23]

Then Purcell's lifestyle changed, quite suddenly it seems. Sometime around 1680 or 1681 he married. His bride's Christian name was Frances, and there is evidence, circumstancial to be sure, that she was the daughter of a prominent and wealthy citizen of Westminster, Captain John Baptist Peters.[24] Altogether, six children were born to the couple; of these, only Frances, Edward, and Mary Peters survived their father, the latter by only a few weeks.[25]

Even before this time Purcell's fame had begun to spread beyond the confines of Westminster. He entered the world of theatrical music in London with pieces such as *The Stairre-Case Overture,* and attracted all London music publishers with his songs, most especially with his inspired and touching elegy on the death of his worthy master, Matthew Locke, *What shall we do, now he is gone?*[26] By the end of 1680 he had finished almost all the finely wrought fantasias for three, four, and five viols, and the *In nomines* for six and seven instruments. In these elegant, yet deeply conceived musical creations, Purcell single-handedly revived two of England's oldest instrumental chamber traditions, climaxing them with masterworks of such power and beauty as former generations in England had never known. At the same time, Purcell revealed his dual orientation as both a guardian of the rich treasures of England's musical past, and as harbinger of the new harmonic and tonal music of the future, which reflected not only the latest musical trends in France and Italy, but also the adventurous harmonic practices of his own country.

His native English orientation also is manifested in his early anthems, welcome songs and birthday odes, despite obvious foreign influences which nevertheless reveal his close acquaintance with contemporary masters in France and Italy, such as Lully, Bassani, Gratiani and the little-known, but highly competent composer of Italian trio sonatas, Lelio Colista. But Purcell's own very modern style is clearly in the ascendant in the theatrical songs, dialogues, and incidental music for the London stage. His music for Nathaniel Lee's *Theodosius* (1680), Nahum Tate's *King Richard II* (1681), and Thomas D'Urfey's *Sir Barnaby Whigg* (1681) soon created his reputation as foremost musical innovator in England's theatrical world.

Purcell's modern style shone forth also in the frankly Italianate trio sonatas, with which he was preoccupied during this early theatrical period. This magnum opus, a set of twelve, found its way into print in 1683. Like the fantasias and *In nomines* of the immediately preceding period, these more modern chamber pieces, in which Purcell avowedly "imitated the most fam'd Italian masters," were soon established as nonpareil within their genre, not only among English composers, but throughout Europe. Already it was clear that Purcell was no mere insular music master.

Meanwhile, his uncle Thomas Purcell had died on July 31, 1682, leaving vacant several important musical positions at court. He had been very active as Gentleman of the Chapel Royal, as an official composer in "The Private Music," as a leader of the Corporation of Musicians, and as an important figure in the theatrical and concert world. His death also created an opening among King Charles's Grooms of the Robe—a vacancy soon filled by his son Francis. Just a week after the burial of his uncle Thomas on August 2nd, Purcell celebrated the birth of a second son, John Baptist, who, however, survived little more than two months of infancy.

Even while involved with these family events, Purcell had to contend with a new and worrisome business at the Abbey. On February 4, 1683, he was obliged publicly to take the sacrament before witnesses in Westminster Abbey. Possibly this was merely a formal observance of the infamous Test Act—a formality required because he had succeeded Edward Lowe as Organist to the Chapel Royal, on July 14, 1682.[27] On the other hand, he may have been called in because of a suspicion that he had entertained Catholic sympathies, as did several associates, the Duke of York, and even King Charles II himself. Just at this time, what with Titus Oates's flamboyant revelations about a Catholic plot to take over the nation,[28] and such actual events as the Rye House Plot,[29] public feelings against the Catholics ran high. Whigs missed no opportunity to expose and damage the opposition. Possibly, Purcell had fallen victim to their zeal.

Nevertheless, he continued to produce new compositions throughout 1683, as if totally unaffected by all these events. After seeing the *Sonatas of III Parts* through the press in June of 1683, he managed within the next few months to compose eight songs for the fourth book of *The Choice Ayres and Songs,* seven more for the fifth book in the same series, and the royal ode of thanksgiving for the King's providential delivery from the Rye House Plot, ("Fly, bold rebellion," Z324). He also composed an ode celebrating the marriage of Princess Anne to Prince George of Denmark ("From hardy climes," Z325) and set three odes for the newly established St. Cecilia's day celebrations.[30] In 1684 he was involved in a widely discussed organ competition between Bernard Smith and Renatus Harris,[31] and at last, upon John Hingeston's death, he was paid a salary and livery annually thereafter for his duties as Keeper of the Instruments. He saw the new St. Cecilia Ode, "Welcome to all the pleasures," through the press, composed several new catches, including "My wife has a tongue as good as e'er twang'd,"[32] which has given rise to absurd tales of his domestic infelicity on the part of latter-day gossips. He also finished an impressive number of songs and dialogues, in addition to another royal ode, *From those serene and rapturous joys* [Z326] to welcome Charles II back from Windsor in the Fall.

The text of this ode, written by Thomas Flatman, seemed most appropriate to the King's happy and comfortable position at the beginning of 1685. His hard-won political strengths had helped him to establish a solid financial basis for the first time since he had ascended the throne, and at last he was able to adopt a benevolent attitude toward his enemies. The arts flourished, commerce developed mightily, and the nation seemed on the verge of golden prosperity. The tenor of life at court in those halcyon days is reflected in another quaint incident—a royal boating trip—which may be quoted directly from Sir John Hawkins's *History of Music:*

> Charles the Second had given orders for building a yacht, which as soon as it was finished he named the *Fubbs* in honour of the Duchess of Portsmouth, who, we may suppose, was in her person rather full and plump. . . . Soon after the vessel was launched the King made a party to sail in the yacht down the river and around the Kentish coast; and to keep up the mirth and good humour of the company, Mr. Gostling was requested to be of the number. They had got as low as the North Foreland, when a violent storm arose, in which the King and the Duke of York were necessitated, in order to preserve the vessell, to hand the sails and work like common seamen. By good providence, however, they escaped to land: but the distress they were in made an impression on the mind of Mr. Gostling which was never effaced. Struck with a just sense of the deliverance, and the horror of the scene he had but lately viewed, upon his return to London he selected from the Psalms those passages which declare the wonders and terrors of the deep and gave them to Purcell to compose as an anthem, which he

did, adapting it so peculiarly to the compass
of Mr. Gostling's voice, which was a deep
base, that hardly any person but himself was
then, or has since, been able to sing it; but the
King did not live to hear it.[33]

Quite suddenly, King Charles died of an apoplectic
stroke on February 3, 1685.[34] As the nation mourned,
Purcell was commissioned to write another of his touching
funeral laments, *If pray'rs and tears* [Z380], a warmly
evocative setting of an anonymous text, with an affective
subtitle: "Sighs for our late sovreign King Charles ye 2[d]."

The death of the King at first brought no apparent change
in Purcell's official position, for all his plural responsibilities
flowed on apace. Musically, however, Purcell's
compositions began about this time to show new strength of
inspiration, modernistic tonal style, and more impressive
structural design. The official anthem for James II's
coronation on April 23rd, *My heart is inditing* [Z30] breathes
an air of courtly grandeur in the Lullian manner: this
splendid ceremonial style suggested that Purcell had truly
reached his period of mastery. From contemporary
descriptions we see that it was an awesome occasion,[35] and
Purcell's anthem "performed by the whole Consort of
Voices and Instruments" was beautifully timed to be heard
immediately after the coronation of Queen Mary of Modena,
thus providing a thrilling climax for the entire event.

The new king soon showed that he neither shared in nor
aspired to the political wisdom his elder brother had
demonstrated to such good effect over the past two decades.
Whereas Charles II had wisely hidden his monarchial
persuasion, James II, overestimating his own strengths by
far, decided that he single-handedly could turn the tide of
enthusiasm for parliamentary government that had run so

strongly and so clearly throughout the seventeenth century. Pompously, if blindly, he immediately set about this impossible task. Beginning at the coronation itself, and continuing in the ceremonies with music and fireworks on the Thames before Whitehall, he openly espoused the cause of monarchy by divine right, oblivious to the massive opposition he would surely encounter.

King James's earliest overt blunder was to allow rescheduling of the performance of Louis Grabu's and Dryden's "opera," *Albion and Albanius*. Though clearly modelled after the Lullian form and perhaps acceptable in its instrumental portions, dramatically speaking, the work was inept—certainly nothing more than a "vast piece of royal flattery."[36] It was expressly revived to bolster the case for divine right for the Stuarts. Opening early in June at Dorset Garden, it ran for only six performances before the appearance of Argyll's armies in the north and Monmouth's forces in the west called a halt to James's and Grabu's foolish and bloated allegory. The insurrection, however, was quelled in less than a month, with Monmouth captured and brutally beheaded.

Purcell had auspiciously celebrated the new King's reign with the above-mentioned coronation anthem, and with his first official royal ode, "Why are all the muses mute?" in which he portrayed James II as Caesar. Then, upon Monmouth's death, he found himself setting the following outrageous lyrics to another sort of allegory, again relating to the problem of Stuart succession:

> A grasshopper and a fly,
> In summer hot and dry,
> In eager argument were met
> About priority.
> Says the fly to the grasshopper:

"From mighty race I spring,
Bright Phoebus was my dad, 'tis known,
And I drink and eat with a King."
Says the grasshopper to the fly:
"Such rogues have oft appear'd,
Your father might be of high degree,
But your dam on a midden was rear'd."
Cho: So rebel Jemmy Scott,
That fain a King had been,
His father might be the Lord knows what
But his mother we knew a quean,
A quean, a quean, a quean.[37]

This little satire, subtitled "A [*sic*] Allegory" in the original print, brought out the comic dramatist in Purcell. Nowhere among his short topical pieces do we find a scenario more clearly drawn, images more vividly created, or melodic and harmonic devices more trenchantly wedded to the text. The satire was wickedly double-edged, poking fun at Monmouth and James II with equal abandon. (One wonders if this was a safe venture for a royal composer to have indulged in.) To represent James, Duke of Monmouth, as a fly of questionable lineage was a telling stroke, particularly just then, when the whole medieval notion of spontaneous generation had been so thoroughly debunked by William Harvey.[38] But to depict the King as a grasshopper was nothing short of *lèse-majesté*. However, had King James taken note of the ridiculous figure he cut—and here one should comment that the caricature pairing the diminutive Jemmy Scott as a fly with the angular King James II as a grasshopper was most apt—he might have changed his own conduct, thereby changing history. Instead, he clung stubbornly to his outmoded notions, while the throne upon which he sat swayed more and more alarmingly, toppling in little more than two years' time.

Meanwhile, Purcell continued to develop his new expansive style, revealing new-found strength in such serious compositions as the magnificent birthday ode, *Sound the trumpet, beat the drum* [335] for James II's birthday on October 14, 1687, and the anthem *Blessed are they that fear the Lord* [Z5]. John Gostling's copy of the latter bears the interesting rubric "Composed for the Thanksgiving appoint'd to be observed in London and 12 miles around and upon the 29th following over England for the Queen's being with child." Once again, Purcell was involved with a topical subject relating to the central issue of Catholic succession: Was this child actually the offspring of James II and Mary of Modena, or a babe brought into the lying-in room in a warming-pan to befool those in attendance?[39] Like other problems of royal succession elsewhere in Europe, this was to cause bloodshed among members of various English factions several times before it was finally laid to rest.

Purcell's stylistic development was not restricted to these forms, however, as may be seen in his twenty-nine songs published in the four books of *The Theatre of Music,* printed by John Playford and published by his son, Henry, during the years 1685 and 1686, or in the catches and duets that appeared in the same period. One of Purcell's most impressive masterpieces was the pastoral threnody *Gentle shepherds, you that know* [Z464], set to verses penned by Nahum Tate. According to William Cummings, the piece was occasioned by the sudden, tragic death not of "Honest John Playford," but rather of his son, John, Jr.[40] Evidence as to the truth of this assertion is not available at present, but the text itself seems quite appropriate to the passing of a young person. Pending further evidence, Cummings's opinion may be accepted as valid.

Purcell's anthems and sacred songs appearing in Henry Playford's *Harmonia Sacra,* along with several masterful anthems such as *O, sing unto the Lord* [Z44] and *The Lord is King, the earth may be glad* [Z54], all reveal him in full mastery of the late, expanded style mentioned above. Clearly, he had reached a new plateau, stylistically speaking.

For Purcell himself the signal event of the year was the birth of his daughter Frances, one of three children who survived him. But he was also surely pleased that, with the fall of James II at the end of 1688 and the establishment of William and Mary as monarchs of Great Britain, he received a new appointment at court as Gentleman of the Private Music. Seemingly, this was a sinecure, adding to his fees without heavily increasing his responsibilities. From a charming anecdote first reported by Hawkins, we learn that his new duties involved performing chamber works for Queen Mary. The story can best be told in Hawkins's own words, quoted from a passage tracing the history of the old Scots tune, "Cold and raw":

> This tune was greatly admired by Queen Mary . . . and she once affronted Purcell by requesting to have it sung to her, he being present: the story is as follows. The queen having a mind one afternoon to be entertained with music, sent to Mr. Gostling, then one of the chapel, and afterwards subdean of St. Paul's, to Henry Purcell and Mrs. Arabella Hunt, who had a very fine voice and an admirable hand on the lute with a request to attend her; they obeyed her commands; Mr. Gostling and Mrs. Hunt sang several compositions of Purcell, who accompanied them on the harpsichord; at length the queen

beginning to grow tired asked Mrs. Hunt if
she could not sing the old Scots ballad 'Cold
and raw.' Mrs. Hunt answered yes, and sang
it to her lute. Purcell was all the while sitting
at the harpsichord unemployed, and not a
little nettled at the queen's preference of a
vulgar ballad to his music, determined that
she should hear it upon another occasion: and
accordingly in the next birthday song, viz.,
that for the year 1692, he composed an air to
the words, "May her bright example chace
Vice in troops out of the land," the bass
whereof is the tune Cold and raw.[41]

Hawkins's *History* was also the source of another
anecdote, this one casting Purcell in much less favorable
light. According to Hawkins,[42] in 1689 Purcell entered into
dispute with Dr. Sprat, Dean of Westminster, over his right
to the money taken for admission into the organ loft at the
Coronation of William and Mary. Purcell was summarily
ordered to turn over the entire sum, which amounted to
£478.14.5. Subsequent inquiry, however has shown that
Purcell was innocent of any wrongdoing in this incident.[43]

These events coincided with Purcell's rise to
preeminence as the foremost composer for the stage in
London. His popularity in this realm grew quickly as he
began to compose operas and semi-operas. His first operatic
venture was to set Nahum Tate's libretto *Dido and Aeneas*
[Z626] as an opera, with a great deal of dance intermixed, to
satisfy the needs of the royal choreographer Josias Priest,
who had an active dance program at a boarding school for
young ladies in Chelsea. These elements were not
uncommon in seventeenth-century opera, particularly in

France, so it seems clear that Purcell and Tate had studied the field carefully. What was unusual about Purcell's approach to *Dido and Aeneas* was that he should have attempted to perform such a work with amateurs, an attempt that is all the more astonishing in view of the superb quality of the music itself. Actually, there is no evidence, only an unsupported tradition, that the first performance was an amateur affair. Nothing would have prevented Josias Priest, or Purcell himself, from hiring professional performers.

Although quite short, the opera had more dramatic power than any work heard to date—indeed, on any stage in Europe up to that time. Its four principal characters—Dido, Aeneas, Belinda, and the Sorceress—are clearly drawn and convincing. The dramatic pace, which is greatly abetted by the seventeen intercalated dances, moves quickly and forcefully to the denouement. And the melodic beauty and general musical inspiration are profoundly moving. Topically suited to the Glorious Revolution, *Dido and Aeneas* is one of the masterworks of the age.

Each year thereafter until his death, Purcell mounted one major operatic event for the London stage. In contemporary terminology, these actually were called "semi-operas," since dialogue, dance, and pantomime were included in their performance. First, in 1690, came *The Prophetess; or The History of Dioclesian* [Z627], a work of great topical significance, since its plot paralleled the events bringing about the fall of the Stuarts—even to James II's attempted recoup in Ireland, which was so effectively put down by King William and General Ginkel. Musically, *Dioclesian* was a resounding success,[44] being the first example of Purcell's new brilliant orchestral style, replete with trumpets and drums, which characterizes all his productions during the reign of William and Mary.

His next venture, *King Arthur* [Z628], was less successful, perhaps due to an incomprehensible story line. Dryden wrote the libretto as a sequel to his earlier opera, *Albion and Albanius,* with an even more thickly obfuscated plot. But Purcell's music is all clarity and delight, expressed again in his resplendent late style. This, added to the fact that "it was excellently adorned with scenes and machines . . . and dances made by Mr. Jo: Priest,"[45] brought great success to Purcell, Dryden, Josias Priest, and to the company. Unfortunately Purcell's autograph score was lost,[46] so that no further performances were possible until the work was reconstructed for a performance at the Drury Lane Theatre in 1770.

Purcell's opera for the next season, the longest of his works in this genre, was reported as follows by Peter Motteux in *Gentleman's Journal* for May 1692:

> The opera of which I have spoken to you in former hath at last appeared, and continues to be represented daily; it is called *The Fairy Queen* [Z629]. The drama is originally Shakespeare, the music and decorations are extra-ordinary. I have heard the dances commended, and without doubt the whole is very entertaining.

Aesthetically, the production seems to have been a great success, but financially, it did not do so well, as Downes observes:

> in ornaments was superior to the other two; especially in clothes for all the singers, and dancers, scenes, machines and decoration, all most profusely set-off; and excellently

> performed, chiefly the instrumental and vocal
> part composed by the said Mr. Purcel and
> dances by Mr. Priest. The Court and the
> town were wonderfully satisfied with it; but
> the expenses in setting it out being so great,
> the company got very little by it.[47]

Purcell evidently did not think it too long, for he added two very lengthy arias for a production in the following season, "Ye gentle spirits"[48] and "O, let me weep" *(The plaint)*. The latter is not very successful in production, for it belongs neither to the plot nor to the musical flow. It is a lovely piece, perhaps best left to be performed in the concert hall as a recital song.

Purcell's last semi-opera, *The Indian Queen* [Z630], is filled with irrational and paradoxical qualities. Musically it is one of the most imaginative, dramatic, and expressive of all Purcell's stage works. His penchant for the occult and the mystical, demonstrated from the very beginning of his career,[49] found profoundly effective expression here. In terms of composition and style, it is modern beyond belief. However, dramatically speaking, it is the most old-fashioned of all his major works, harking back to the early Restoration period when the London stage was showing the first feeble signs of its coming restitution.

The controversy over which of its joint authors—Sir Robert Howard and John Dryden—actually was responsible for the play can be rather easily solved, I think, by recourse to simple stylistic comparison of their known works. A great deal of the text of the play is fusty stuff, safely attributable to Sir Robert Howard; the lyrical portions along with the adaptations which turned the play into an opera, show a mellifluent and skillful quality, nowhere else achieved by Howard, and bearing stylistic signs of Dryden's handiwork.

The original plot was bizarre, and filled with historical inaccuracies: Howard set the play against a background of wars between Mexico and Peru as if these were neighboring principalities. Such total disregard for history and geography would have been totally uncharacteristic of Dryden. Nor would Dryden have created the improbable cardboard villainess Queen Zempoalla, depicted in the original play. The vast amount of bombast with which the original was stuffed is also uncharacteristic of Dryden.

However, as Curtis Price suggests,[50] his might well have been the skillful hand that revised the play as an opera for the production of 1695, for which Henry Purcell provided music. He set all but the additional act, which death prevented him from completing, and which consequently was passed on to his brother, Daniel. Whatever the truth here, Purcell rose magnificently to the challenge. Indeed, he somehow managed to turn the weaknesses of the original play into sources of remarkable musical power, with new musical characterizations, awesome scenarios, and orchestral music that mark the pinnacle of his career as a dramatic composer. As with Wagner's *Götterdämmerung,* one feels on hearing *The Indian Queen* that there had been a quantum leap in compositional skill, as shown in brilliant solo characterizations, highly affective ensembles and choruses, and orchestral passages that transcend in pure musical inspiration any earlier creations.

During the last five or six years of his life, Purcell's creative development manifested itself not only in the English semi-opera, but in many other forms as well. Of the forty-three plays for which he provided incidental music, all but half a dozen were written during this final period. These too reflect the rapid maturation and fulfillment of style which are so impressive in the semi-operas, as do several anthems, numerous songs and dialogues, and odes and welcome songs. In the last-named genre, his five birthday odes for Queen Mary [Z320, 321, 331, 332, and 338] and his last great St. Cecilia Ode, "Hail, bright Cecilia" [Z328] reveal Purcell's creative forces in the fullness of their power and perfection. In the latter, a tour-de-force of instrumental and vocal virtuosity, Purcell is said to have sung the counter-tenor solo, "Tis Nature's voice," with the "incredible graces" he himself had written.[51] Whatever the truth of this assertion, the work itself stands as a monument to the seventeenth-century English ode, foreshadowing the mighty secular odes that Handel was to create in London by mid-eighteenth century.

Amidst all this remarkable creative flow, Purcell died on the eve of another annual St. Cecilia's Day celebration, which he had done so much to maintain and enrich as one of the founder-members of the London St. Cecilia Society. The exact cause of death is not known, though Westrup's conjecture that he may have been consumptive is perhaps as likely as any. Hawkins explains that he died from over-exposure to the cold having been locked out by Mrs. Purcell because of his carousing. But this tale may be dismissed for what it is: mere gossip.

From the hastily scrawled signature in his will, and from the obvious haste in which this document was drawn up, it would seem that death came unexpectedly.[52] And yet from the annotations to two songs,[53] Altisidora's "From rosy bowers," *Don Quixote* III [Z578] and "Lovely Albina's come ashore" [Z394], we know that Purcell had been ill for quite some time before his death.

Buried in Westminster Abbey, near the organ he once played and took care of, Purcell still lives in the memory of his countrymen and of some few beyond the seas, as "the British Orpheus." His reputation on the Continent had impressed no less a musician than Archangelo Corelli who,

according to Cummings, was actually on his way to England to visit Purcell personally when news of his death turned him back.[54] Elsewhere on the continent, Purcell was equally popular, witness the following statement from *Mackays's Journey Through England,* of 1722:

> The English affect more the Italian than the French music, and their own compositions are between the gravity of the first and the levity of the other. They have had several great masters of their own. *Henry Purcell's* works in that kind are esteemed beyond Lully's everywhere.[55]

In recent years, the kind of lip service this sort of memory has always evoked has begun to give way to genuine musical interest. Gradually, Purcell's music has been brought back to life through the diligent efforts of the Purcell Society, and through the fine work of such scholars as Sir Jack Westrup, Heather Professor of Music at the University of Oxford, Denis Arundell, Eric Walter White, the late R. Thurston Dart, Dr. Margaret Laurie, Professor Michael Tilmouth, Katherine Rohrer, and Curtis Price, along with a host of others too numerous to mention here.[56] Indeed, this Purcellian revival may well have been a significant and influential force in the British musical renaissance that has grown so impressively in the last half century, as well as an important factor in the broad and lively growth of a great musical public in England, which for too long has been thought of abroad as "the land without music." In short, the Purcell heritage remains one of England's greatest musical assets.

Notes

1. The date of birth usually recorded before the appearance of J. A. Westrup's seminal biography in 1941 was 1658. As the reader will discover below, this may turn out to be the correct date.

2. See *The Flying Post*, November 23-26, 1695.

3. See *infra*, Chapter 3, 1683c.

4. Reproduced in F. B. Zimmerman, *Henry Purcell (1659-1695): His Life and Times* (University of Pennsylvania Press, 1983), p. 358.

5. The reasoning here is complicated, and since it has been misinterpreted by others, needs to be clarified: When he died, Purcell was in his thirty-seventh year, that is to say, beyond his thirty-sixth birthday. We know that his thirty-seventh birthday would have fallen some time after November 21, 1695. In the preface to the twelve trio sonatas, we are told that Purcell was twenty-four years old about the time these were published in June of 1683. This tells us that his twenty-fourth birthday had taken place some time before June, or perhaps even before May. The sonatas were advertised as "completely finish'd" in *The London Gazette* for May 24, 1683, and it is very likely that there was some delay between the time that the portrait engraving was finished and the publication actually appeared. Thus he was actually born sometime between November 21, 1658, and May or June of 1659.

6. J. A. Westrup deduced that Henry was son to Thomas Purcell on the basis of a letter to John Gostling, which is quoted below. His conjecture, however, is fairly disproven by the will of John Hingeston, dated December 12, 1683, which bequeathed £5 "to my Godson Henry Pursall (son of Elizabeth Pursall)," and by numerous other documents. For a full discussion of Purcell's genealogy, see F. B. Zimmerman, *Henry Purcell (1659-1695): His Life and Times* (2nd revised edition, 1983), Appendix II, pp. 331-347.

7. The reasoning here is negative. Since birth records were kept fairly regularly in most parish churches, since these records have been thoroughly searched revealing no trace of Purcell's birth outside Westminster Abbey, and, since birth records were not kept in the Abbey, there is reason to believe that Purcell was born there.

8. See p. 144, item 1699a, and p. 145, c1700.

9. W.A.M. Chapter Minutes, 1662-85 (December 31, 1669).

10. The letter, now housed in the Nanki Library in Shirikawa, Japan, was addressed to Mr. John Gostling, Chaunter of the quire of Canterbury Cathedral:

> SIR,
> I have received the favor of yours of the 4th with the inclosed for my sonne Henry: I am very sorry wee are like to be without you soe long as yours mentions: but 'tis very likely you may have a summons to appeare among us sooner than you imagine; for my sonne is composing wherin you will be chiefly concern'd. However, your occasions and tyes where you are must be considered and your conveniences ever complyde withall: in the meantime assure yourself I shall be carefull of your concernes heir [i.e., 'here'] by minding and refreshing our master's memory of his Gratious promis when there is occasion. My wife returns thanks for the compliment with her servis: and pray you give both our respects and humble services to Dr. Belk and his Lady, and beleeve that I am, Sir, your affectionate and humble servant.
>
>   T. Purcell.
> Dr. Perce is in toune but I have not seen him since. I have perform'd ye compliments to Dr. Blow, Will Turner, etc.
>
> F faut: and E lamy are preparing for you.

11. Dated December 12, 1683.

12. Oxford, Bodleian MS Mus.e.17, ff. 39v and 40.

13. Speaking of himself, Purcell wrote: "He is not asham'd to own his unskilfulness in the Italian Language; but that's the unhappiness of his Education, which cannot be accounted his fault, however he thinks he may warrantably affirm, that he is not mistaken in the power of the Italian Notes, or elegancy of their Compositons, which he would recommend to the English artists" (*Sonatas of Three Parts*, 1683).

14. In *Henry Purcell* (London: Sampson, Low, Marston & Co., Ltd., [1903]), p. 17, W. C. Cummings states positively that he became a chorister at age six, without, however, citing any evidence.

15. The late Edward F. Rimbault, music antiquarian, claimed to own an autograph copy of this work, but this appears to have been lost. Cummings (*Henry Purcell*, p. 20) even goes so far as to state that

Rimbault's copy was in the hand of Pelham Humfrey. Rosamund McGuiness, in her doctoral dissertation, f. 20, suggests that the ode "See, Mighty Sir, the Day appears" (attributed to Humfrey in British Library MS Additional 33287, fol. 69) might be the work in question. Somehow, the whole matter remains shadowy and uncertain.

16. Henry Cooke evidently had become ill some time previously, for he resigned as Marshall of the Corporation of Musicians some time before June 24, 1672, when Thomas Purcell was elected in his place, according to Cummings (*op. cit.*, p. 16).

17. K. M., p. 255

18. The original seems to have disappeared, but Cummings states definitely that he "was indebted to the late Dr. Rimbault for a copy." Additional evidence supporting a close relationship with young Henry is found in the fact that his father had participated as a performer in Davenant's *The Siege of Rhodes*, for which Matthew Locke was a principal composer. According to Pepys's entry for February 21, 1660, he met "Mr. Locke and Pursell, Masters of Music, at Westminster Hall," thus indicating yet another tie between Locke and the Purcell family.

19. Oxford, Bodleian, MS. Wood D 19 (9).

20. A "Bishop's Boy," or Lord's Scholar was one who held an exhibition under the benefaction of Rev. John Williams, bishop of Lincoln and later archbishop of York. Those who qualified might continue as scholars at St. John's College, Cambridge, but it is clear that Purcell did not take up this option.

21. The mourning ring can be traced in Frances Purcell's will as late as February 7, 1706. See F. B. Zimmerman, *op. cit.*, p. 283.

22. See W.A.M. Treasurer's accounts 33709, 10, 12, 13, 14, etc.

23. See F. B. Zimmerman, *op. cit.*, pp. 356-357.

24. See Westminster Abbey Registers, p. 72.

25. See F. B. Zimmerman, *op. cit.*, *passim*.

26. It is said that Purcell himself composed the poem before setting it. *Ibid.*, p. 397.

27. His sixth professional appointment, as recorded in *The Chequebook* for July 11, 1682. Purcell's new duties were a matter of longestablished record, as we know from the sixteenth of the articles set down by George, Lord Bishop at the beginning of Charles II's reign, on December 19, 1663:

16. Of the three organists, two shall ever attend, one at the organ, the other in surplice in the quire, to bear a part in the psalmody and service. At solemn times they shall all three attend.

28. Titus Oates actually had brought his allegations before Parliament on October 21, 1678. By 1682, the tale of conspiracies on the part of Catholics to take over the nation by violence had spread such fear among Protestants as to nurture James Monmouth's and Shaftbury's plans to subvert the Stuart monarchy through Protestant sucession. So Purcell's test actually occurred at the height of the eight-year struggle between the Catholic and Protestant factions, during which time the whole nation seethed with political and religious unrest.

29. Although by the beginning of February 1683, the political situation had grown quiet enough for Monmouth to be released on bail—it is interesting that this event coincided almost exactly with Purcell's "test,"—within a few short months the Rye House Plot was discovered, an event which had the nation on tenterhooks until September 1683, when the suppression of the plot was celebrated with a public thanksgiving, for which Purcell was commissioned to write the above-mentioned ode, *Fly, bold rebellion* [Z324].

30. Purcell's three odes provided the bulk of the music performed for this inaugural occasion, including: *Welcome to all the pleasures* [Z339], *Laudate Ceciliam* [Z329] and, most probably, *Raise, raise the voice* [Z334].

31. The "Battle of the Organs" climaxed in a public hearing in Temple Church, Renatus Harris having chosen Giovanni Battista Draghi as his champion, Smith falling back on the resources of Henry Purcell and John Blow. The champions played on alternate days, and there seems to have been much skullduggery, including actual damage inflicted on the instruments themselves. After several years of controversy, George Jeffreys, later infamous as the Judge of the Bloody Assizes, awarded the palm to Smith, Blow and Purcell.

32. Subtitled "The Scolding Wife." See Z594.

33. *Op. cit.*, vol. 2, p. 693.

34. One wonders if the strain and hardship experienced on the ill-fated boating trip, described above, may have had an adverse effect on the King's health.

35. See, particularly, F. Sandford, *The History of the Coronation of the Most High, Most Mighty and Most Excellent Monarch, James* II and *Queen Mary* (London, 1687-88).

36. See Cummings, *op cit.*, p. 406.

37. This little scene is pure caricature, deriding both Charles II and James II, as indeed the entire Stuart family.

38. *De Generatione Animalium* (London, 1652). By curious coincidence, Harvey had actually been warden of Prince Charles and Prince James for several years before the execution of their father, King Charles I.

39. This possibility again is cited by Hawkins, although historians view it as the purest gossip.

40. Cummings, *op. cit.*, p. 46. Unless there were two younger members of the Playford family named John, Cummings mistook the nephew, John II, as a son. The nephew was a music printer, not a publisher, and old "Honest John's" publishing house was passed on to his son, Henry, not to John II as Cummings seems to indicate.

41. John Hawkins, *History of the Science and Practice of Music* (London: Novello, 1853), vol. II, p. 564.

42. *Op. cit.*, p. 745.

43. F. B. Zimmerman, *op. cit.* pp. 166-68.

44. According to John Downes (*Roscius Anglicanus*, p. 42) "It gratify'd the expectation of Court and City; and got the author great reputation."

45. As we are informed by John Downes in *Roscius Anglicanus*, p. 42.

46. It may have turned up at Oxford during the nineteenth century, for a catalog entry for an autograph score of the opera is recorded as part of the Music School Collection in the Bodleian as late as 1855.

47. *Op. cit.*, p. 42.

48. Curtis Price argues that this song may have been added after the songs had been printed, but before the actual performance in 1692. His reasoning, based on the notion that the tonality of this song, d-minor,

provides an excellent transition between the G-Major movements which precede and follow it, is sound.

49. For a few examples, see *Jehova, quam multi* [Z135], *Plung'd in the confines of despair* [Z142]; *Saul and the witch of Endor* [Z134] and *The Libertine Destroyed* [Z600].

50. Curtis Price, *Henry Purcell and the Restoration Stage*, p. 126.

51. Again, the evidence is not altogether clear. *Gentleman's Journal* for November 1692 announced that the ode "was admirably set to music by Mr. Henry Purcell, and perform'd twice with universal applause, particularly the second stanza, which was sung with incredible graces by Mr. Purcell himself." The syntax leaves room for doubt: Did Purcell actually sing the stanza, or merely write the graces? The question is all the more troublesome in that in Purcell's own hand the name of Mr. Pate is entered in the autograph score. Two Thomas Cross's prints support the notion that Purcell was the original virtuoso, but these may merely have followed after the error that first crept into the *Gentleman's Journal*. The puzzle cannot be solved on the basis of evidence presently available, but in the author's opinion, it is unlikely that Purcell could have maintained and practiced such virtuosity as a vocal soloist along with all else he had to do. It is also improbable that he could have done so without a great deal of contemporary commentary about his dual talent.

52. He left everything to his wife, Francis, and to his surviving children.

53. "From rosy bowers" is described in its first print as "the last piece set to musick by the late famous Mr. Henry Purcell," and "Lovely Albina's come ashore" is subtitled "The last song that Mr. Purcell set before he died." Elsewhere the latter song is identified as having been written "during his sickness."

54. Cummings, *op. cit.*, p. 89.

55. P. 138.

56. See Bibliography.

TEXTUAL MATTER FROM EDITIONS
OF PURCELL'S MUSIC, 1667-1700

Entries in this section of the guide consist of title-pages and forematter from English musical publications of the last third of the seventeenth century, with emphasis, of course, on those involving Purcell's compositions. Each entry begins with year of publication and the name of printer or publisher, in boldface, and first line or title, subtitle, in italics, followed by all remaining information, in ordinary typeface. Each entry ends with boldface numbers identifying works ascribed to Purcell in the publication represented. See pp. 163-210 for the complete list of works to which these numbers have been assigned. Misspellings and typographic errors have been tacitly corrected, although customary seventeenth-century orthographies have not been changed, even for the sake of consistency. To present these entries in quasi-facsimile, capitalization and punctuation have been preserved as shown in original documents, except that here again, typographical errors have been tacitly corrected. The style of this section therefore differs markedly from that used throughout the rest of the guide.

It has been the author's aim to provide accurate and complete text of every musical source published during Purcell's lifetime, omitting only a few passages having nothing to do with music, these identified by comment. Coverage of publications appearing after his death in 1695 is more selective. The author will be pleased if readers will notify him directly of any mistakes, either of omission or commission, which may be discovered.

Notes are provided to clarify obscure references and to identify briefly important figures in English musical life during the period in question. To conserve on space, only lesser known persons have been so documented, and commentary on other points of interest has been kept to a minimum.

For permission to publish the various excerpts appearing below I am grateful to the Trustees of the British Library, to the Syndics of the Fitzwilliam Museum, to the Regents of the Bodleian Library, and to the New York Public Library and the Library of Congress. I take pleasure also in acknowledging the able assistance of Paul Whitehead, doctoral candidate at the University of Pennsylvania, for his much valued assistance and advice on the details of this compilation, and also for assistance with other components of the guide.

The Texts

1667: John Playford
Catch that Catch Can, or The Musical Companion.
Containing catches and rounds for three and four voyces. To
which is now added a second book containing dialogues,
glees, ayres and ballads, &c. some for two, three, foure
voyces. Printed by W. Godbid for J. Playford: London,
1667.[1] **S54 S69**

1669: John Playford
*Select Ayres and Dialogues. To Sing to the Theorbo-Lute or
Basse-Viol.* Composed by Mr. Henry Lawes, late servant to
His Majesty in his publick and private musick: And other
excellent masters. The Second Book. Printed by William
Godbid for John Playford, and are to be sold at his shop in
the Temple, near the church dore. 1669.

1673a: John Playford
The Musical Companion, in Two Books. The first book
containing catches and rounds for three voyces. The second
book containing dialogues, glees, ayres and songs for two,
three and four voyces. Collected and published by John
Playford, practitioner in musick. London, printed by W.
Godbid for John Playford, at his shop in the Temple near the
Church, 1673.

Title-page: To all Ingenuous Lovers of Musick
The former Impression of this book finding so general
acceptance, both encouraged me to adventure another
edition; in which I have made it my care not only to amend
some defects, which were in the last, but indeed almost to
new model the whole: First by selecting out of it only such
songs as were most approved of, and by adding a

considerable number which were not printed in that book. Secondly by placing all for two voyces together: next, those for three: and lastly, those for four. And thirdly, printing the several parts in such a method as all may sing by one book. Lastly, the songs for two three and four parts are all printed in the G-sol-re-ut cliff, for the more convenient singing either of boys or men. The whole book, as it is now publish'd, I may truly say, the like (for so great a variety of musick) hath not been extant in this nation, nor any other (that I have seen) beyond the seas; the so much cry'd up Italian and French ayres being here imitated, if not equallized in this kind: Nor could I ever yet be convinc'd but that we have at this day as able professors of musick of our own nation, as any foreigners: For the musick is the same (abating the language) both for cords, discords, passions, spirits and humours: Where then is their excellency? Were we not generally too apt to disesteem the labours & parts of our own (though otherwise elaborate & ingenuous) country-men? It may well be perceiv'd by the much variety herein that my desire is to give contentment to the skillful and judicious; and if these my endeavours for the publick good of my countrey, prove pleasant and delightful to them, they still shall keep him in pains to please them, who subscribes himself their wellwisher John Playford.[2] **S69 253**

1673b: John Playford
Choice Songs and Ayres for One Voyce to sing to a Theorbo-Lute, or Bass-viol. Being most of the newest ayres, and songs sung at court and at the public theatres. Composed by several gentlemen of His Majesties Musick. The First Book. London. Printed by W. Godbid and are to be sold by John Playford near the Temple Church.[3] **S68**

f. 2 To the lovers of musick. Gentlemen & ladies, musick is

of different effects, and admits of as much variety of fancy to please all humours as any science whatever. It moves the affections, sometimes into sober composure, and other-times into an active jollity. These songs and ayres are such as were lately composed, and are very suitable and acceptable to the genius of these times. Many of the words have been already published, which gave but as little content to divers ingenious persons, who thought them as dead, unless they had the airy tunes to quicken them; to gratify whom, was a great inducement to me for their publication. The transcription of most of these songs were presented to the gentlemen who compos'd the musick, and by them allowed to be made publick. And herein likewise, to do their authors' right, my care and oversight of the press was [*sic*] not wanting; but notwithstanding all my diligence, some few errata's have past, both in the words and musick; which I desire the ingenious peruser to correct. These being accepted will encourage a second attempt in this kind, with an endeaver to remedy what shall be any way objected against this edition, Yours, N. D.

1675: J. Playford
Choice Ayres, Songs, & Dialogues to sing to the Theorboe-lute, or bass-viol. Being most of the newest ayres, and songs, sung at court, and at the publick theatres. Composed by several gentlemen of His Majesties musick, and others. The second edition, corrected and enlarged. Printed by W. Godbid,[4] and are to be sold by John Playford, near the Temple Church. 1675.

f.2 To the lovers of musick. Gentlemen & ladies, musick is of different effects, and admits of as much variety of fancy to please all humours as any science whatever. It moves the affections, sometimes into sober composure and other-times into an active jollity. These songs and ayres are such as were lately composed, and are very suitable and acceptable to the genius of these times. Many of the words have been already published, which gave but as little content to divers ingenious persons, who thought them as dead unless they had the airy tunes to quicken them; to gratify whom, was a great inducement to me for their publication. Your kind acceptance and general good liking of the former impression of this book has both encouraged and obliged me to present you with a second; wherein I have taken care to correct those errors that before escaped in the musick untaken notice of; and have likewise added several stanzas of verses to the songs that then wanted them; as also thirty five new ayres, songs and dialogues, never till now printed; most of which, (as well as those in the first edition) were transcribed from the original copies of the authors, and by them allowed to be made publick. By your approbation of this, you will engage to the publication of more of this kind, Your servant. J.P.[5] **436 S68**

1676: J. Playford
Choice Ayres and Songs to sing to the Theorbo-lute, or bass-viol. Being most of the newest ayres and songs, sung at court, and at the publick theatres. Newly reprinted with large additions. London, printed by William Godbid, and are sold by John Playford near the Temple Church. 1676.

f.2 The preface is the same as that in the edition of 1675, as far as the middle of line 17, ending "songs that then wanted them." Thereafter it reads: "as also now added above forty new ayres, songs and dialogues, never before printed; not doubting, but that the excellency of the whole work, as it is now published, is such, as will be kindly received by all true and ingenious lovers of musick; which is the endeavour of

him, who is your most hearty servant, John Playford." **436**
D132 S68

1678: J. Playford
Musick's Hand-Maid; New Lessons and Instructions for the
virginals or harpsichord. London, Printed for J.
Playford, and are sold at his shop near the Temple-church. 1678. [No
authentic Purcell works.]

1678: Banister & Low
New Ayres and Dialogues composed for Voices and Viols,
of two, three, and four parts: together with lessons for viols
or violins, by John Banister, one of the Gentlemen of his
majesties private musick, and Thomas Low, one of the
vicars choral of Saint Paul's, London. London: printed by
M.C. for H. Brome, at the Gun near the west end of St.
Paul's. MDCLXXVIII.

f.5 To the worthily honoured Roger L'Estrange, Esq;[6] Sir,
were I not well assured your innate candour will excuse the
rudeness of this dedicatory address, I would have made
some excuse for my presumption. But when I seriously
consider how true a votary you have been to the liberal arts,
and sciences, and how fair a proficient both in the theorie
and practical part of this harmonious and seraphick science, I
have been more easily induced to present you with these
musical composures, being no stranger to your name and
family, which for some centuries of years have born the stile
and title of Barons of this Realm. Neither have you
degenerated from your progenitors in your zeal and loyalty,
to the King and Church. But lest I should transgress the
bounds of my epistle, and your patience, I will couch all in
this compendious request, that you would vouchsafe to
shelter these composures under your kind protection, and to

own the presenter of them for, Sir, your most faithfull
honorer and obediently devoted servant, Cl. J.[7]

f.6 The Praise of Musick. Praise, pleasure, profit, is the
threefold band which ties men's minds faster than Gordion's
Knot.

f.7 To the Reader: A man without science, is like a realm
without a king, saith Aristotle. Melody is good to pacifie the
angry, to comfort the sorrowful, and to assuage all passions.

f.10 To conclude, music is good or bad, as the end to which
it tendeth. Among those things wherewith the mind of man
is wont to be delighted, I can find nothing that is more great,
more healthful, more honest than musick: the power whereof
is so great that it refuseth neither any sex nor age and (as
Macrobius saith) there is no breast so savage and cruel,
which is not moved with the touch of this delight. For it doth
drive away cares, perswade men to gentleness, represseth
and stirreth anger, nourisheth arts, encreaseth concord,
inflameth heroical minds to gallant attempts, curbeth vice,
breedeth virtues and nurseth them when they are born and
composeth men to good fashions. Vale. **363 387 397 418
419 433**

1679: J. Playford
*Choice Ayres & Songs to sing to the Theorbo-Lute or Bass-
Viol.* Being most of the newest ayres and songs, sung at
court, and at the publick theatres. Composed by several
Gentlemen of His Majesties Musick, and others. The Second
Book. London, printed by Anne Godbid,[8] and are to be sold
by John Playford, at his shop near the Temple Church,
1679.

To all lovers of musick. Gentlemen & Ladies, your kind acceptance of my former collection of the newest and best modish songs and ayres that were then in town, has encouraged me to undergo the pains and charge of publishing this second book, wherein you are presented with most of the choicest new-mode songs, that were composed since that time by several eminent masters of his Majesties musick. I shall not apologize for their excellency, the authors' names, which you will find added to most of them, are sufficient to declare it; and for those that want the reputation of their authors, whose names (through ignorance) are omitted, the esteem given them by the most skillful musicians, supplies that defect. Most of the songs and ayres herein contained I received exact copies of from the hands of their authors, to whom I acknowledge my self much obliged, for their assistance in promoting this work. And it has been my extraordinary care, to do them the justice, and give you the satisfaction, of having them truly corrected and well printed; for which, your approbation will be a sufficient recompense, and a farther incouragement to me to present you hereafter with more of this nature, and in the mean time to remain, Your obliged servant, John Playford. **356 386 468 470 471 D133 S58**

1680: R. Bentley and M. Magnus
Theodosius: or, The Force of Love, A Tragedy. Acted by their Royal Highnesses Servants, at the Duke's Theatre. Written by Nat. Lee. With musick betwixt the acts. (The note "by Henry Purcell" has been entered in a contemporary manuscript note).
   Nec mimus periculam ex magna
   Fama quam ex mala. Tacit.
London, printed for R. Bentley and M. Magnus, in Russel-street, near Covent Garden. 1680.

To her Grace, the Duchess of Richmond. Madam, the reputation that this play received on the stage, some few errors excepted, was more than I could well hope from so censorious an age, from whom I ask but so much necessary praise as will serve, once or twice a year at most, to gain their good company, and just keep me alive.

> *There is not now that Mankind that was then,*
> *When as the the sun and man did seem to strive*
> *(Joynt-Tenants of the world) who should survive:*
> *When if a slow-pac'd star had stol'n away*
> *From the observers marking, he might stay*
> *Two or three hundred to see't agen,*
> *And then make up his Observation pain.*
>
> Dr. Donn.

For, 'tis impossible in our limited Time (and I bring his opinion to back my own, who is without comparison the best writer of the age) to present our judges a poem half so perfect as he could make it. I must acknowledge Madam, with all humility, I ought to have taken more time and more pains in this tragedy, because it is dedicated to your Grace, who, being the best judge, (and therefore can when you please make us tremble) yet with exceeding mercy have pardon'd the defects of Theodosius, and given it your entire approbation. My genius, Madam, was your favorite when the poet was unknown, and openly received your smiles before I had the honour to pay your Grace the most submissive gratitude for so illustrious and advantageous a protection. To let the world too know that you do not think it beneath you to be officiously good, even from the extremest heights to discern the lowest creatures, and give them all the noblest influence you can, you brought her Royal Highness just at the exigent time, whose single presence on the poet's day is a subsistence for him all the year after.

Ah, Madam, if all the short-liv'd happiness that miserable poets can enjoy consist in commendation only; nay, if the most parts are content with popular breath, and even for that are thankfull: how shall I express my self to Your Grace, who by a particular goodness, and innate sweetness, merely for the sake of doing well, have thus rais'd me above my self, to have your grace's favor, is, in a word, to have the applause of the whole court, who are its noblest ornament, magnificent and eternal praise. Something there is in your meen so much above that we vulgarly call charming, that to me it seems adorable, and your presence almost divine, whose dazzling and majestick form is a proper mansion for the most elevated soul: and let me tell the world, nay, sighing speak it to a barbarous age (I cannot help calling it so, when I think of Rome and Greece). Your extraordinary love for heroick poetry is not the least argument to shew the greatness of your mind, and fulness of perfection. To hear you speak with that infinite sweetness and chearfulness of spirit that is natural to your Grace is, methinks, to hear our tutelar angels; but to behold you too, is to make prophets quite forget their heaven, and bind the poets with eternal rapture.

> *Her pure and eloquent blood*
> *Spoke in her cheeks,*
> *And so distinctly wrought,*
> *That one might almost say,*
> *Her body thought.*
> *You for whose body God made better clay,*
> *Or took soul's stuff such as shall late decay,*
> *Or such as needs small change at the last day.*
>
> Dr. Donn.

Ziphares and Semandra were first your Grace's two favourites; and though I ought not, Madam, to praise your wit by your judgement of my painting, yet I must say such characters every dawber cannot draw. It has been often observed against me that I abound in ungovern'd fancy; but I hope the world will pardon the sallies of youth: Age, despondence and dulness come too fast of themselves. I discommend no man for keeping the beaten road; but I am sure the noble hunters that follow the game, and must leap the hedges and ditches sometimes and run at all, or never come in to the fall of the quarry. My comfort is, I cannot be so ridiculous a creature to any man as I am to myself: for, who should know the house so well as the good man at home? who when his neighbours come to see him, still sets the best rooms to view; and if he be not a willful ass, keeps the rubbish and lumber in some dark hole, where no body comes but himself, to mortifie at melancholy hours. But how then, madam, in this unsuitable condition, how shall I answer the infinite honours, and obligations your grace has laid upon me? Your Grace, who is the most beautiful ideal of love and glory: who, to that divine composition, have the noblest and best-natur'd wit in the world? All I can promise, madam, and be able to perform, is that your Grace shall never see a play of mine that shall give offence to modesty and vertue; and what I humbly offer to the world, shall be of use at least, and I hope deserve imitation: which is, or ought to be, I am sure, the design of all tragedies and comedies both ancient and modern. I should presume to promise my self too some success in things of this nature, if your Grace (in whom the charms of beauty, wit and goodness seem reconcil'd) at a leisure hour would condiscend to correct with your excellent judgement, the errors of, madam, your Grace's most humble, most obedient, and devoted, servant, Nat Lee. **606/1, 2, 8, 9, 5, 6(mnp)**

1681: John Playford

Choice Ayres and Songs to sing to the Theorbo-Lute, or bass-viol: being most of the newest ayres and songs sung at court, and at the publick theatres. Composed by several Gentlemen of His Majesties Musick, and others. The third book. London, printed by A. Godbid and J. Playford Junior, and are sold by John Playford, at his shop near the Temple Church; and John Carr, at his shop at the Middle Temple-Gate, 1681.

f.2 To all lovers of musick. Gentlemen, this third book, or collection of new ayres and songs had come to your hands some months sooner, had I not been prevented by long sickness; however I hope it will not now be unwelcome. I need not here commend the excellency of their composition, the ingenious authors names being printed with them, who are men that understand to make English words speak their true and genuine sence both in good humour and ayre; which can never be performed by either Italian or French, they not so well understanding the proprieties of our speech. I have seen lately published a large volume of English songs, composed by an Italian master, who has lived here in England many years; I confess he is a very able master, but being not perfect in the true idiom of our language, you will find the air of his musick so much after his country-mode, that it would sute far better with Italian then English words. But I shall forbear to censure his work, leaving it to the verdict of better musical judgements; only I think him very disingenious and much to blame, to endeavour to raise a reputation to himself and book, by disparaging and undervaluing most of the best English masters and professors of musick. I am sorry it is (in this age) so much the vanity of some of our English gentry to admire that in a foreigner, which they either slight, or take little notice of in one of their own nation; for I am sure that our English masters in musick (either for vocal or instrumental musick) are not in skill and judgement inferiour to any foreigners whatsoever, the same rules in this science being generally used all over Europe: But I have too far digress'd and therefore beg your pardon. This book being bound up with the two others formerly published, will make a compleat Volume. To conclude, I desire you to think, that I have herein as much studied your satisfaction as my own interest, and kindly to receive this collection, from, Gentlemen, your hearty servant, John Playford. (from my house in Arundel Street near the Thames side. Novemb. 2. 1680). **357 374 388 407 416 432 606/5, 8, 9.**

1682: Blagrave
Wit and Drollery. Jovial poems corrected and ammended with new additions. *Ut Nector Ingenium.* London, printed for Obadiah Blagrave, at the Bear in St. Paul's Church Yard, 1682. **253(mnp) 571/6(mnp) 606/9(mnp)**

1683b: J. Playford
Choice Ayres and Songs to sing to the Theorbo-lute, or bass-viol: being most of the newest ayres and songs sung at court, and at the publick theatres. Composed by several gentlemen of His Majesties Musick, and others. The fourth book. London, printed by A. Godbid and J. Playford, Junior, and are to be sold by John Playford, at his shop near the Temple Church; and John Carr, at his shop at the Middle-Temple Gate, 1683.

f.2 To all lovers and understanders of musick. Gentlemen, this fourth book has met with the same fate as my former, not to come abroad at the time proposed; but the fault is not altogether mine; for I have met with great disappointments in this collection, large promises, and but slender performances; and had it not been for the assistance of some worthy gentlemen, my very good friends, (whose kindness I shall always acknowledge) I might have despair'd of my undertaking. Most of the songs have had the approbation of (and are composed by) the best masters in musick, so that my commendation can add little to their value: However it is probable some ignorant persons may unjustly censure them, like a certain pretender to musick, (who boasted himself a scholar of Mr. Birchenshaw's)[9] who publicly declar'd that in my last book there was but three good songs, the rest being worse than common ballads sung about the streets by footboys and link-boys; but (as Solomon, the wisest of men, has it) the way of a fool is right in his own eyes, and he that despiseth his neighbour is void of wisdom. As for such gentlemen who really understand musick, I doubt not but [that] they will give this as, they have done the former, a better reception; and that to them it will appear, that my design is more the public good, than my own private gain. I have with no small pains and care printed the songs as true as possible from the best copies, and have not imposed trash upon the buyer, like the publishers of the late collection of songs in octavo, wherein (besides the bad collection) there is scarce one line of musick true in the whole book. There has been a great deal of care to do this book well, and therefore I hope it will be so accepted, which will oblige, gentlemen, your servant, John Playford. **[12] 195 370 411 415 435 581 S66**

1683c: I. Playford and I. Carr
"Violino Primo"
Sonnata's of III Parts; two viollins and basse: to the organ or harpsecord. [By Henry Purcell] Composer in ordinary to his most sacred majesty, and organist of his Chappell Royall.

London, printed for the author: and sold by I. Playford and
I. Carr at the Temple, Fleet Street. 1683. Tho. Cross,
Junior, sculpt.

To the King: May it please your Majesty I had not assum'd
the confidence of laying ye following compositions at your
sacred feet; but that (as they are the immediate results of your
Majesties royall favour, and benignity to me, which have
made me what I am) so, I am constrain'd to hope, I may
presume, amongst others of your Majesties ever-obliged and
altogether undeserving subjects, that your Majesty will with
your accustom'd clemency, vouchsafe to pardon the best
endeavours of your Majesties's most humble and obedient
subject and servant, H. Purcell.

f.4 To the Reader. Ingenuous reader, Instead of an elaborate
harangue on the beauty and the charms of music (which after
all the learned encomions that words can contrive)
commends it self best by the performance of a skilful hand,
and an angelical voice: I shall say but a very few things by
way of preface, concerning the following book, and its
author: for its author, he has faithfully endeavor'd a just
imitation of the most fam'd Italian masters; principally to
bring the seriousness and gravity of that sort of musick into
vogue, and reputation among our country-men, whose
humor, 'tis time now, should begin to loath the levity, and
balladry of our neighbours: The attempt he confesses to be
bold, and daring, there being pens and artists of more
eminent abilities, much better qualify'd for the imployment
than his, or himself, which he well hopes these his weak
endeavours, will in due time provoke, and enflame to a more
accurate undertaking. He is not asham'd to own his
unskilfulness in the Italian language; but that's the
unhappiness of his education, which cannot justly be

accounted his fault, however he thinks he may warrantably affirm, that he is not mistaken in the power of the Italian Notes or elegancy of their compositions, which he would recommend to the English artists. There has been neither care, nor industry wanting, as well in contriving, as revising the whole work; which had been abroad in the world much sooner, but that he has now thought fit to cause the whole thorough bass to be engraven, which was a thing quite besides his first resolutions. It remains only that the English practitioner be enform'd that he will find a few terms of art perhaps unusual to him, the chief of which are these following: *Adagio and Grave,* which import nothing but a very slow movement: or *Presto Largo, Poco Largo,* or *Largo* by itself, a middle movement: *Allegro,* and *Vivace,* a very brisk, swift, or fast movement: *piano,* soft. The Author has no more to add, but his hearty wishes, that this book may fall into no other hands but theirs who carry musical souls about them; for he is willing to flatter himself into a belief that with such his labours will seem neither unpleasant, nor unprofitable. Vale.[10] **790-801**

1683e: *Ibid.* **790-801**

1683f: John Clarke
[*The Second Part of Youth's Delight on the Flagelet, or The Young Gentlewoman's Recreation;* being a choice collection of songs, tunes and ayres, composed by several able masters, and set to the flagelet. By the author of the first part. Printed for John Clarke: London, 1683[11]] **606/5, 8**

1683g: D. Brown
The Newest Collection of the Choicest Songs, as they are sung at court, theatre, musick-schools, balls, &c. London, printed by T. Haly for D. Brown, at the Black Swan and

Bible without Temple-Bar, and T. Benskin, in St. Bride's
Church-Yard, Fleet-Street. 1683 **292** (in B-flat, printed as a
song).

1683h: Hunt and Salter
*The Genteel Companion, being exact directions for the
recorder:* with a collection of the best and newest tunes and
grounds extant. Carefully composed and gathered by
Humphry Salter. London, Printed for Richard Hunt and
Humphry Salter, at the Lute in St. Paul's Church-Yard,
1683.

A2: To all Ingenious Lovers of Musick:
   I might as well endeavour to perswade, that the Sun is a
glorious, and beneficial Planet; as take pains to illustrate
musick with my imperfect praises; for every reasonable
man's own mind will be its advocate. Musick, belov'd of
Heaven, for it is the business of Angels; Desired on Earth as
the most charming pleasure of man. The world contains
nothing that is good, but what is full of harmonious
concord, nor nothing that is evil, but it is opposite, as being
the ill favour'd production of discord and disorder. I dare
affirm, those that love not music (if there be any such) are
dissenters from Ingenuity, and rebels to the monarchy of
reason. Of the kinds of musick, vocal has always had the
preference in esteem: and by consequence the recorder (as
approaching nearest to the sweet delightfulness of the voice)
ought to have the first place in opinion as we see by the
universal use of it confirm'd.
   For the assistance and improvement of all the lovers of
it, I have with great care made this collection of the best and
newest tunes extant; and for the advantage of beginners, that
have not the help of a master to instruct them, I have placed
in the beginning some easy tunes with dots under the violin

notes, by which means they may confirm themselves in the manner of playing every note.

1684a: Playford

A Musical Entertainment perform'd on November XXII. 1683, it being the Festival of St. Cecilia, a great patroness of music; whose memory is annually honour'd by a public feast made on that day by the masters and lovers of music, as well in England as in foreign parts. *"Musica laetificat cor."* London, printed by J. Playford, Junior, and are to be sold by John Playford near the Temple Church, and John Carr at the Middle-Temple Gate, 1684.

To the Gentlemen of the Musical Society, and particularly the Stewards for the year ensuing: William Bridgeman, Esq.; Nicholas Staggins, Doctor in Music; Gilbert Dolben, Esq., and Mr. Francis Forcer.

Gentlemen,

Your kind approbation and benign reception of the performance of these musical compositions on St. Cecilia's day, (by way of gratitude) claim this dedication: which likewise furnishes the author with the opportunity of letting the world know the obligations he lies under to you; and that he is to all lovers of music, a real friend and servant, Henry Purcell. **339**

1684b: J. Playford, Jr.

Choyce Ayres and Songs to Sing to the Theorbo-Lute or Bass-viol: being most of the newest ayres and songs sung at court, and at the publick theatres. Composed by several gentlemen of His Majesty's Musick, and others. The fifth book. London, printed by J. Playford Junior . . . sold by J. Playford . . . John Carr . . . London, 1684.

To all lovers and understanders of musick. Gentlemen, this fifth book of new songs and ayres had come sooner (by three months) to your hands, but the last dreadful frost put an embargo upon the press for more than ten weeks; and, to say the truth, there was an unwillingness in me to undertake the pains of publishing any more collections of this nature: But at the request of friends, and especially Mr. Carr, who assisted me in procuring some of these songs from the authors, I was prevailed with: Yet indeed the greatest motive was, to prevent my friends and country men from being cheated with such false wares as is daily published by ignorant and mercenary persons, who put musical notes over their songs, but neither minding time nor right places turn harmony into discord: Such publications being a scandal and abuse to the science of musick, and all ingenious artists and professors thereof. This I conceive I was bound to let my reader understand; and that in what hitherto I have made public of this nature, my pains and care has ever been not only to procure perfect copies, but also to see them true and well printed: But now I find my age, and the infirmities of nature, will not allow me the strength to undergo my former labours again, I shall leave it to two young men, my own son, and Mr. Carr's son, who is one of His Majesty's musick, and an ingenious person, whom you may rely upon, that what they publish of this nature shall be carefully corrected and well done, my self engaging to be assisting to them in the overseeing the press for the future, that what songs they make public be good and true musick, both for them [sic] the credit of the authors, and to the content and satisfaction of the buyers; which that they may never be otherwise, is the desire of, gentlemen, your most faithul servant, John Playford. **359 362 372 384 424 466 519**

1684c: John Patrick

A Century of Select Psalms, and portions of the Psalms of David, especially those of praise . . . For the use of the Charterhouse, London. By John Patrick, preacher there. London: printed by M.F. for R. Royston, Bookseller to the King['s] most excellent majesty. . . 1684. **132(mnp) 133(mnp) 136(mnp) 137(mnp) 138(mnp) 141(mnp) 142(mnp) 143(mnp)**

1685a: N.T. [Nathaniel Thompson]

A Choice Collection of 180 Loyal Songs, all of them written since the two late plots, (viz.) The Horrid Salamanca Plot in 1678 and the Fanatical Conspiracy in 1683. Intermixt with some new love songs. With a Table to find every Song. To which is added, The Musical Notes to each Song. The Third edition with many Additions. [London], printed by N.T. at the entrance into the Old-Spring-Garden near Charing-Cross, 1685. Price Bound 2 s.

To the Reader.

Amongst the several means that I have been of late years to reduce the deluded Multitude to their just Allegiance, this of Ballads and Loyal Songs has not been of the least influence. While the Fergusons, and heads of the factions were blowing up sedition in every corner of the countrey, these flying choristers were asserting the rights of monarchy, and proclaiming loyalty in every Street. The misinform'd rabble began to listen; they began to hear to truth in a song, in time found their errours, and were charm'd into obedience. Those that despise the reverend prelate in the Pulpit, and the grave judge on the bench; that will neither submit to the laws of God or man, will yet lend an itching ear to a loyal song, nay, and often become a convert by it, when all other means prove ineffectual. Divine

Herbert has it excellently exprest, where he says,
  A Verse may find him who a Sermon flies,
  And turn Delight into a Sacrifice.
It cannot be imagined how many scatter'd flocks this
melodious tingling hath reduced to their princely hives, who
otherwise had never been brought under the discipline of
obedience or government.

And, without ostentation I may say, I printed my newspapers and divers other pamphlets (that always vindicated
the King and government) to undeceive the people, who
were daily impos'd upon by Curtis, Smith, Harris, Care,
Vile, Baldwin, Janeway, &c. when no body else would or
durst. For this the malice of the Factious Party swell'd so
high against me, that They, with the assistance of a certain
instrument, (who swore through two Brick-walls before
Oates appear'd) caused me to be imprison'd six times, so
that for above six years I was never free from trouble,
having seldom less than 3 or 4 indictments at a sessions [*sic*]
against me; at other times informations in the Crown-Office,
which villainous contrivances of their agents, cost me at least
500£. in money, besides the loss of my trade and reputation;
the principal çrimes they alledged against me, were, Let
Oliver now be forgotten, a Song; A Hue and Cry after T.
Oates when turn'd from Whitehall; The Character of an
Ignoramus Doctor; A Dialogue between the Devil and the
Doctor; The Prisoner's Lamentation for the loss of Sheriff
Bethel; All which phamphlets tended to no other evil, than
the laying open the villanies of Oates and the rest of his
perjur'd disciples: And when these things were almost
blown over, this Varlet quarrels again with Oates's
Manifesto; because it so plainly discovers the impossibilities
and contradictions of Oates in the whole course of his
evidencing: But (thanks be to God) *Tempora mutantur* &c.
and truth daily shines more and more. For now this villain is

detected, and turn'd out of his imployment with disgrace, and consequently made incapable of doing further mischief to any of his Majesties loyal subjects: But to give him his due, he drein'd their Purses, for in 9 Months time they publickly gave him above 80£. besides many private gratuities, with hearty thanks for his good service, often affirming he did the cause more good than a 1000 Men.

These collections (being of so much use to detect the scandalous lies and falsehoods of the factious, and to keep the strong-headed beast within the reigns of obedience) I thought fit to publish, that the world may see I have not been idle in the worst of times, but have done my endeavour (to the utmost of my talent) for the interest of the King and government; which that they may flourish in spighte of all his adversaries, is the hearty prayers [*sic*] of Your most Humble Servant., N. T.[12] **606/M8 606/M9**

1685b: J. Playford
A Third Collection of New Songs, never printed before. The words by Mr. D'Urfey. Set to music by the best masters in that science, viz. Dr. John Blow. Mr. Henry Purcell. Senior Baptist. Mr. Courtiville. Mr. William Turner. Mr. Thomas Farmer. Mr. John Lenton. Mr. Samuel Akeroyd. With thorow-basses for the theorbo, and bass-viol. London, printed by J.P. for Joseph Hindmarsh, at the Golden-Ball over against the Royal-Exchange in Cornhill, 1685. **589 463 509**

1685c: J. Playford
Catch that Catch Can: or the second part of the Musical Companion, being a collection of new catches, songs and glees, never printed before. Printed by J. P[ayford, Jr.] for John Playford, at his shop near the Temple Church, 1685.

To all lovers of music

Gentlemen, in my preface before the Fifth Book of Ayres and Songs lately published, I gave several reasons for my resolution of forbearing for the future to make any more collections of this nature, leaving it to my son and Mr. Carr's son; But having for some years past gathered into one book divers new catches, songs, and glees, much like those in my Musical Companion, which I did only to recreate myself with my musical friends, I am prevailed with at their request (and for the common benefit) to make them public; and because of their similitude, give them the title of the Second Part of the Musical Companion. The First Part contains about 100 rounds and catches, 6 dialogues, 33 ayres and songs for two voices, 60 choice ayres songs and glees for three voices, and 12 ayres and songs for four voices. This second part contains 70 new catches and songs for two, three, and four voices, many of them were printed from the authors' own copies, and the rest from the truest copies I could procure; however it is probable, that by often transcribing some errors may have crept in, which has occasion'd me to print a smaller number than usual, thereby to make way for a second and more correct impression, hoping such gentlemen as find any errors will be so kind as to rectifie them, by sending me some truer copies. Some faults there are in the words, which an intelligent musical reader will easily perceive, and mend with a pen. I am, gentlemen, your servant, J. Playford. **240 246 250 258 261 271 279 281 283 292 484 514 594 D1200 D102 S61 S68**

1685d: H. Playford
The Theater of Music: or, A Choice Collection of the Newest and best Songs sung at the Court and Public Theaters. The words composed by the most ingenious wits of the age, and

set to Music by the greatest masters in the science. With a
theorbo-bass to each song for the theorbo, or bass-viol.
Also, symphonies and ritornels in 3 parts to several of them
for the violins and flutes. The First Book. London, printed
by J. Playford, for Henry Playford and R[obert] C[arr] and
are to be sold near the Temple Church and at the Middle-
Temple Gate, 1685.

f.3 To Dr. John Blow, Master of the Children, and one of
the organists of His Majesty's Chappel-Royal. And, to Mr.
Henry Purcell, Composer in Ordinary to His Sacred
Majesty, and one of the Organists of His Chappel-Royal.
Gentlemen, this being the first essay of ours in this kind,
and being particularly obliged to you for your assistance
herein, (in perusing several of the songs of this book before
they went to the press, whose authors we could not so well
apply our selves to, and adding thorow-basses to such as
wanted them we presume farther on your generosity, and
beg the favour of you to patronize these our endeavours; and
also to give us leave to acknowledge ourselves, (as in
gratitude bound) Your obliged humble servants, R.C. / H.P.
To the authors in general of the following musical
compositions. Gentlemen. I hope the care we have taken, in
endeavouring to get the most correct copies of the following
songs, has rendered this collection as perfect as any of those
five books already printed: However, if some small errors
shall be found (tho' we hope the contrary), as we dare not
pretend to infallibility, so we hope you will not attribute
them to our neglect, but rather to our unhappiness in not
having an opportunity of communicating several of these
songs to the authors themselves before they were printed
off, as well as to the common infirmity of the press. For,
tho' most of these were printed from the authors' own
copies, yet several of them were only transcriptions, but

those, such as we thought likewise faithfully done. To prevent the hazard for the future of printing a song contrary to the author's own composition, we become petitioners to you (which we hope in justice to ourselves you will easily grant), that when you have made any new songs, you will be pleased to leave copies of them under your own hands, either at Mr. John Playford's shop in the Inner-Temple, or at Mr. John Carr's shop at the Middle-Temple Gate, and then we do faithfully promise forthwith to print them from such copies, whereby you may be assured to have them perfect and exact. This, as it will prevent such as daily abuse you, by publishing your songs lame and imperfect, and singing them about the streets like ordinary ballads; so it will particularly oblige Your Servants, R.C. / H.P.

1685e: H. Playford
The Theatre of Music: Or, A Choice Collection of the newest and best Songs. . . . The Second Book[13]*. . . 1685.* **289 367 378 398 409 422 437 510 520**

1686a: J. Playford
The Second Book of the Pleasant Musical Companion: Being a new collection of select catches, songs and glees for two and three voices. The second edition, corrected and much enlarged. London, printed for John Playford near the Temple Church or at his house over-against the Blue-Ball in Arundel-Street, 1686.[14]

f.2 Preface. Of this second volume of the Musical Companion a small impression was printed and published above two years since, of which I have a considerable number yet remaining, it being not so compleat and well done to my mind as I could have wish'd afterwards, and being not printed in a volume to joyn with the first book.

These reasons did hasten me sooner than I intended to a second edition, and to leave out several of those catches not suitable to the present mode, and to add many new ones; and also, in the last part of this book, I have joyned many new songs for two-voices, never before printed; and also some old reviv'd songs sometimes sung at the theaters: all which, I doubt not, but to many judicious lovers of musick will be very acceptable; having herein taken no small pains and care to have true copies from the composers, and truly printed, upon which account I also recommend my first volume, entitled, The Musical Companion tho' published ten years since, which is a very excellent magazine of vocal musick, containing four several varieties of musick in one compleat volume, viz. In the first part, 100 choice select catches; in the second part, 6 dialogues and 33 songs and ayres for two voices, cantus and bassus; the third part contains 60 songs and ayres for three voices, cantus, medius, and bassus; in the fourth and last part are 12 songs and ayres for four voices, cantus, medius, tenor and bassus: All which are contained in one volume, and the parts so printed, that the several persons may sing their parts out of that one book. These two volumes contain most of the choicest catches and songs, which have been composed by most of the eminent English masters for above this 30 years last past, wherefore I leave these as my *Ultimum Vale* of this kind of musick, and heartily wish, that they may prove useful and pleasant to all true companions and lovers of vocal musick. John Playford. **240 246   248 249 253 264 276 277 279 280 281 283 285 286 287 289 290 292 484 494 507 514 522 594 D100 D107 S54 S61 S68**

1686b: H. Playford
The Theater of Music . . . Book Three[15] (copy is the same

as that printed for the edition shown above). **438 481 483 498 512**

1686c: J. Playford
The Dancing-Master: Or, Directions for dancing country dances, with tunes to each dance for the treble-violin. The 7th edition, with addition of several new dances, never before printed. London, printed by J.P. and sold by John Playford, at his shop near the Temple Church, 1686. **S68**

1686d: J. Playford
The Delightful Companion or Choice New Lessons for the Recorder or Flute. To which is added several lessons for two and three flutes to play together. Also plaine and easie introductions for beginners and the several graces to this instrument. London: printed for John Playford, at his shop near the Temple Church; and for John Carr at his shop at the Middle-Temple-Gate, 1686. The second edition, corrected.[16] **T253 646 D100**

1686e: Benjamin Tooke
Poems and Songs by Thomas Flatman. The fourth edition, with many additions and amendments.

Me quoque vatem
Dicunt Pastores, sed non Ego credulus illis.

Virgil.

London, printed for Benjamin Tooke, at the Ship in St. Paul's Church-Yard. 1686.

To His Grace the Duke of Ormond, Lord Lieutenant of Ireland &c. in humble acknowledgement of his princely favours the poems are with all dutiful respect dedicated by His Grace's ever oblig'd, and most obedient servant, Thomas Flatman.

To the Reader. When I was prevail'd upon to make a

fourth publication of these poems with a great many additions, it was told me, that without a Preface the Book would be unfashionable; universal custom had made it a debt, and in this age the bill of fare was as necessary as the entertainment. To be civil therefore, and to comply with expectation, instead of an elaborate harangue in commendation of the art in general, or what, and what qualifications go to the making up of a poet in particular, and without such artificial imbellishments as use to be the ornament of prefaces, as sayings of philosophers, ends of verses, Greek, Latin, Hungarian, French, Welch, or Italian, be it known unto the reader, that in my poor opinion poetry has a very near resemblance to the modern experiment of the ambling-saddle; it's a good invention for smoothing the trott of prose; that's the mechanical use of it. But physically it gives present ease to the pains of the mind, contracted by violent surfeit of either good or bad usage in the world. To be serious, 'tis an innocent help to sham a man's time when it lies on his hands and his fancy can relish nothing else. I speak but my own experience; when any accident hath either pleas'd or vex'd me beyond my power of expressing either my satisfaction or indignation in downright prose, I find it seasonable for rhiming; and I believe from what follows it may be discern'd when 'twas fair weather, when changeable, and when the quicksilver fell down to storm and tempest. As to the measures observ'd by me, I always took a peculiar delight in the Pindarique strain, and that for two reasons, first, it gave me a liberty now and then to correct the saucy forwardness of a rhime, and to lay it aside till I had a mind to admit it; and secondly, if my sense fell at any time too short for my stanza, (and it will often happen in versifying) I had then opportunity to fill it up with a metaphor little to the purpose, and (upon occasion) to run that metaphor stark mad into an allegory, a practice very frequent and of admirable use amongst the moderns, especially the nobless of the faculty. But in good earnest, as to the subjects, which came in my way to write upon, I must declare that I have chosen only such as might be treated within the rules of decency, and without offence either to religion or good manners. The caution I receiv'd (by tradition) from the incomparable Mr. Cowley, and him I must ever acknowledge but to imitate, if any of the ensuing copies may deserve the name of good or indifferent. I have not vanity enough to prescribe how a Muse ought to be courted, and I want leisure to borrow from some treatises I have seen, which look like so many Academies of Complements for that purpose. I have known a man, who when he was about to write would screw his face into more disguises than Scaramuccio, or a Quaker at a meeting when his turn came to mount; his breast heav'd, his hair stood on end, his eyes star'd, and the whole man was disorder'd; and truly when he had done, anybody at first reading would conclude that at the time he made them he was possess'd with an evil spirit. Another that seem'd like Nostradamus (when the whim took him in the head to prophesie,) he sate upon his divining tripos, his elbow on his knee, his lamp by his side, all the avenues of light stopp'd, full of expectation when the little faint flames should steal in through a crevice of the shutters; This Gentleman indeed writ extreme melancholy madrigals. I have had the happiness to hear of a third too, whose whole life was poetical, he was a walking poem, and his way was this; finding that the fall of the leaf was already upon him, and prudently foreseeing that in the winter of his old age he might possibly want fodder, he carry'd always about him one of Raimund Lully's repositiories, a piece of mathematical paper, and in what company soever he came, the spoon was always ready for the civet-cat, nothing scap'd him that fell from a wit: At night his custom was to digest all that he had pirated that day, under proper heads; This was his arsenal, his inexhaustible magazine; so that upon occasion he had no more to do, than to give a snap, or two to his nails; a rub or two upon the features of his head, to turn over his Hint-book, and the matter was at hand, his business (after that piece of legerdemain) was only tacking, and tagging: I never saw but one of this author's compositions, and really it troubled me, because it put me in mind, how much time I had mispent in coffee-houses, for there was nothing in it, but what I could find a father for there; nay (with a little recollection,) a man might name most of the birds from whence he had pluckt his feathers. Some there are that beseech, others that hector their muses: some that diet their Pegasus, give him his heats and ayrings for the course; others that endeavour to stop up his broken wind with medicinal ale and bisquet; but these for the most part are men of industry. Rhiming is their proper business, they are fain to labour hard, and use much artifice for a poor livelihood, I wish 'em good trading. I profess I never had design to be incorporated into the society: my utmost end was merely for diversion of my self and a few friends whom I very well love: and if the question should be ask'd why these productions are expos'd, I may truly say, I could not help it; one unlucky copy, like a bellweather, stole from me into the common, and the rest of the flock took their opportunity to leave the enclosure. If I might be proud of any thing, it should be the first copy of the book, but therein I had the greatest advantage given me that any noble subject could afford. And so much for preface and poetry, till some very powerful star shall over-rule my present resolution. **326(mnp)**

1687a: J. Playford
An Introduction to the Skill of Musick, in Three Books. The

first contains the grounds and rules of musick, according to the Gam-ut, and other principles therof. The second, instructions and lessons both for the bass-viol and treble-violin. The third, the art of descant, or composing musick in parts: In a more plain and easie method than any heretofore published. By John Playford. In the Savoy, printed by E. Jones, for Henry Playford at his shop near the Temple Church. **109 D22**

1687b: H. Playford
A Pastoral Elegy on the Death of Mr. John Playford.[17] (Note, the notes with this mark * over them, are to be sung semiquavers.) The words by Mr. Tate. Set by Mr. Henry Purcell. "Gentle shepherds, you that know the charms of tuneful breath." London, printed for Henry Playford, 1687. **464**

1687c: John Carr, Sam. Scott
Comes Amoris; or the Companion of Love. Being a choice collection of the newest songs now in use. With a thorow bass to each song for the harpsichord, theorbo, or bass-viol. The First Book. London, printed by Nat. Thompson for John Carr and Sam. Scott, and are to be sold by John Carr at his shop at the Middle Temple Gate, Anno Domini, 1687.

To all true lovers of musick. The masters of the songs in the ensuing book, are of that real worth, and eminence in their faculty, that it would be a fulsome piece of disparagement in me to presume their commendation: my task therefore, (and the greatest thing I have to do, in publishing these, their excellent performances,) is to beg pardon for my self, and endeavour to stand fair in the opinion of musical souls; and the best way I can imagine to compass this my honest end, is to acknowledge this first attempt of mine a very bold one; a fault (I hope) will not be very hard to be absolv'd because none that are truly harmonious, can be ill-natur'd: And further, I do confess my self a very hearty well-wisher to this noble part of mathematicks, which I would not by any means should suffer any blemish by my neglect, and inadvertency. What mistakes may have happened in the printing, I shall not altogether be answerable for, having imploy'd my utmost care and vigilancy in the supervising of the press: I hope the world will as easily excuse mine, as they have formerly done the more unpardonable faults of old pretenders; and am steadfastly resolv'd (if this first essay may have the good fortune to find a kind reception in the world) to leave nothing unattempted that may promote the honour of musick by the most assidouous and most earnest diligence of your humblest servant, Samuel Scott. **282 406 430 487 505**

1687d: H. Playford
The Theater of Music: or A Choice Collection of the newest and best Songs sung at the Court and Public Theaters. The words composed by the most ingenious wits of the age, and set to music by the greatest masters in the science. With a theorbo-bass to each song for the theorbo, or bass-viol. Also symphonies and ritornels in 3 parts to several of them for the violins and flutes. The fourth and last book. London, printed by B. Motte, for Henry Playford . . . 1687.

In commendation of this book.
Oh for a muse divine, such sacred skill,
As does th'immortal seats with anthems fill!
That justly (Music) might thy praise rehearse,
Apollo's self must give those numbers force,
The god of music is the god of verse.
What charms, alas! can our dead rhimes impart,

Without th'inspiring great musician's art?
But when the vital air his genius gives,
The tuneful stanza from that moment lives.
Had never Orpheus music understood,
His rhimes had fail'd to charm the stupid wood:
The senseless stones had ne're obey'd his call,
Nor danc'd themselves into the Theban wall.

Then let our nobler bards this subject chuse,
The praise of music best deserves their muse.
Why should some vain cocquet employ your flame,
Or why some undeserving patron's name?
Expos'd in both attempts to this sure curse,
She jilts your passion, and he bilks your purse.
Mark but the upshot of your flatt'ring trade;
For after all the daubling you have laid,
They get no fame, but you are scandals made.
Not all your arts the world's just sense can null,
For that will still believe
Your miss a dowdy, and your patron dull.

                                    Nath. Tate. Licensed Rob.
                                    Midgley. October 23. 1686.

To all lovers and understanders of musick. Gentlemen,
this fourth and last book of the Theatre of Music, or, A New
and Choice Collection of Songs and Dialogues, will (doubt
not) be very acceptable to all the knowing gentlemen in the
skill of music, for several reasons I here mention: First, that
most of these songs and dialogues were composed by
eminent Dr. John Blow, and Mr. Henry Purcell, my ever
kind friends, and several other able masters, from whom I
received true copies, which were by them perused, before
they were put to the press. Secondly, that here is added two
excellent songs long since out of print, viz. Go perjur'd

man, set by Dr. Blow; and that dialogue, When Death shall part us from our kids, set by Mr. Matthew Lock; which two are here (with much care) exactly printed, by the diligent pains of my father Mr. John Playford, [of] whose known skill for printing of musick,[18] our nation is not ignorant. And lastly, this excellent book may be joyn'd and bound with the three former, will make a compleat volume: Notwithstanding all this care and pains, I must expect some of our new pretenders to publish and print music, will be disparaging this book, thereby to gain credit and custom to their own: But I pass them over in charity, with Go on and prosper; not doubting, but this (when it comes to the hands of judicious gentlemen, and understanders of music) they will find the difference; to whose judgements I submit, and shall always endeavour to express my self, gentlemen, Your most humble servant, Henry Playford. **355 362 406 430 432 487 492 495 497 505**

1687e: J. Playford
The Second Book of the Pleasant Musical Companion: Being a new collection of select catches, songs, and glees, for two and three voyces. The second edition corrected and much enlarged. (A new additional sheet to the catch-book) Printed for John Playford: London, 1686.[19] **240 246 248 249 253 264 276 277 279 280 281 283 285 286 287 288 289 290 292 485 494 509 514 522 594 D100 D107 S54 S61 S68**

1687f: Heptinstall
Vinculum Societatis, or The Tie of Good Company. Being a choice collection of the newest songs now in use. With thorow bass to each song for the harpsichord, theorbo, or

bass-viol. The first book of this character. London, printed by F. Clarke, T. Moore and J. Heptinstall, for John Carr, and R.C. and are to be sold by John Carr at the Middle Temple-Gate, and Sam. Scott at the Miter by Temple-Barr. Anno Domini, 1687.

To all true lovers of musick. Gentlemen, we well hope, our former diligent endeavours, (according to our capacity) to serve the musical souls of our nation, have been so hearty, that no very great aspersion can ly [*sic*] upon us for a total neglect of our duty: We also thankfully acknowledge the kind reception our labours have hitherto found from the ingenious, and the good natur'd; by which we have been so far encouraged as yet to add one (ornament at least) to our former attempts, and that is, this new character of the notes of the songs in this book, less troublesome to the eye, then those of the old way, which (if acceptable) will add fresh vigour to our future industry, and add much to the numerous obligations you have already heaped upon, Gentlemen, Yours, John Carr. R.C. Licensed June the 8th 1687. **287 391 417**

1687g: John Playford
Apollo's Banquet: Containing Instructions & Variety of New Tunes, Ayres, Jiggs, and several New Scotch Tunes for the Treble-Violin . . . John Playford. The 5th Edition . . . with new additions. London, 1687.

To all ingenious lovers and practitioners of musick. The treble violin is at this present the only instrument in fashion and the delight of most young practitioners in musick for its cheerful and sprightly sound, in setting forth the new airy tunes of these times. . . . **655 N774 MD100**

1688a: Jos. Knight and Fra. Saunders

A Fool's Preferment, or The Three Dukes of Dunstable. A Comedy. As it was acted at the Queens Theatre in Dorset-Garden, by their Majesties servants. Written by Mr. D'urfey. Together, with all the songs and notes to 'em, excellently compos'd by Mr. Henry Purcell. 1688. Licensed, May 21, 1688. R.P.[20]

Eupolis atq; Cratinus, Aristophanes que Poetae,
Atq; alii, quorum Comoedia prisca virorum est;
Si quis erat dignus describi, quod Malus, aut Fur,
Quod Maechus foret, aut Sicarius, aut alioqui
Famosus; multa cum libertate notabunt.
Hinc Omnis pendet Lucillius.

Horat. Stry. 4.

Printed for Jos. Knight, and Fra. Saunders at the Blue Anchor in the Lower Walk of the New Exchange in the Strand, 1688.

At the end of the play: New Songs Sung in The Fool's Preferment, or The Three Dukes of Dunstable. In the Savoy: Printed by E. Jones, for Jos. Knight and Fra. Saunders, at the Blue Anchor in the Lower-Walk of the New Exchange in the Strand, 1688. **571/1 to 4; 6 to 8**

1688b: J. Carr and S. Scott

Comes Amoris: or The Companion of Love. Being a choice collection of the newest songs now in use. With a thorow-bass to each song for the harpsichord, theorbo, or bass-viol. The second book. London, printed by Tho. Moore for John Carr at his Shop at the Middle Temple Gate, and Sam. Scott at his shop in Bell-Yard near Temple-Barr. 1688. **260 262 275 331/6(bass)**[21]

1688c: H. Playford

Harmonia Sacra; or The Divine Hymns and Dialogues: With
a thorow-bass for the theorbo-lute, bass-viol, harpsichord,
or organ. Composed by the best masters of the last and
present age. The words by several learned and pious
persons. Canon à 3 in the fifth and eighth below, rising a
note every time. [*"Laudate Dominum de Coelis, laudate eum
in excelsis."*] Imprimatur, Ex Aedib. Lamb. Nov. 7. 1687.
Guil. Needham RR, in Christo PacD. D. Wilhelmo Archiep.
Cant. a Sacr. Domest. In the Savoy. Printed by Edward
Jones, for Henry Playford, at his shop near the Temple
Church, MDCLXXXVIII.

To the Right Reverend Father in God, Thomas, Lord Bishop
of Bath and Wells: This collection of divine musick is (with
just veneration) most humbly dedicated by his Lordship's
devoted servant, Henry Playford.

To the Reader. The approbation which has been given by
those of the greatest skill in musick, and the encouragement I
have met with from a number of worthy subscribers do give
me just reason to hope, that this collection of divine songs
(tho' the first of this nature extant) will find a kind reception
with the best of men. The youthful and gay have already
been entertain'd with variety of rare compositions, where the
lighter sportings of wit have been tun'd by the most artful
hands, and made at once to gratify a delicate ear, and a
wanton curiosity. I now therefore address to others, who are
no less musical, though they are more devout. There are
many pious persons, who are not only just admirers, but
excellent judges too, both of musick and wit; to these a
singular regard is due, and their exquisite relish of the
former ought not to be pall'd by an unagreeable composition
of the later. Divine hymns are therefore the most proper

entertainment for them, which, as they make the sweetest, and indeed the only, melody to a religious ear, so are they in themselves the very glory and perfection of musick. For 'tis the meanest and most mechanical office of this noble science to play upon the ear and strike the fancy with a superficial delight; but when holy and spiritual things are its subject, it proves of a more subtile and refined nature, whilst darting it self through the organs of sense, it warms and actuates all the powers of the soul, and fills the mind with the brightest and most ravishing contemplations. Musick and poetry have in all ages been accounted divine and therefore they cannot be more naturally employed, than when they are conversant about heaven, that region of harmony, from whence they are derived. Now as to this present collection, I need say no more than that the words were penn'd by such persons, as are, and have been very eminent for learning and piety; and indeed, he that reads them as he ought, will soon find his affections warm'd, as with a coal from the altar, and feel the breathings of divine love from every line. As for the musical part, it was compos'd by the most skilful masters of this age; and though some of them are now dead, yet their composures have been review'd by Mr. Henry Purcell, whose tender regard for the reputation of those great men made him careful that nothing should be published, which, through the negligence of transcribers, might reflect upon their memory. Here, therefore the musical and devout cannot want matter both to exercise their skill, and heighten their devotion; to which excellent purposes that this book may be truly effectual is the hearty desire of your humble servant, Henry Playford.

[*Erratas to be amended with a pen*, followed by fourteen corrections printed in staff notation] **181 184 186 188 189 190 191 193 197 198 199 200 D22 S3**

1688d: H. Playford
The Banquet of Musick: or, A Collection of the newest and best Songs sung at Court, and at Public Theatres. With a thorow-bass for the theorbo-lute, bass-viol, harpsichord, or organ, composed by several of the best masters. The words by the ingenious wits of this age. The First Book. Licensed, Nov. 19, 1687. Rob. Midgley. In the Savoy: printed by E. Jones, for Henry Playford, at his shop near the Temple Church, 1688.

To the reader. Having already published a collection of this nature, entituled, The Theatre of Musick, containing many excellent songs, in four books, I am encouraged to proceed to this second volume, called, The Banquet of Musick, whereof you are here presented with the first book; hoping that both this and the following will receive the same favourable reception with the former, which will further encourage the endeavours of your humble servant, H. Playford. **262 275 423²² 491 493 543 S57**

1688e: H. Playford
The Banquet of Musick: or A Collection of the Newest and Best Songs sung at Court, and at Public Theatres. With a thorow-bass for the theorbo-lute, bass-viol, harpsichord, or organ. Composed by several of the best masters. The words by the ingenious wits of this age. The Second Book. Licensed, May 3, 1688 Rob. Midgley, In the Savoy: Printed by E. Jones, for Henry Playford, at his shop near the Temple Church, 1688. **353 395 408 420**

1688f: T. Moore and J. Heptinstall
Vinculum Societatis, or The Tie of Good Company. Being a Choice Collection of the Newest Songs now in Use. With thorow bass to each song for the harpsichord, theorbo, or

bass-viol. The second book; with small collection of flute tunes. London, printed by T. Moore, and J. Heptinstall, for John Carr, at his shop at the Middle-Temple-Gate, and Sam. Scott, at his shop in Bell-Yard within Temple-Bar, Anno Domini, MDCLXXXVIII. **267 351 353 420**

?1688: J. Conyer
The Modish London Life: or, The Merry Meeting. To an excellent new tune: or, My life and my death, or, Now, now the fight's done. Printed for J. Conyer. **606/5**

1689a: T. Moore and J. Heptinstall
Comes Amoris: or The Companion of Love. Being a choice collection of the newest songs now in use. With a thorow-bass to each song for the harpsichord, theorbo, or bass-viol. The Third Book. London, printed by T. Moore and J. Heptinstall for John Carr and Sam. Scott, at the Middle-Temple-Gate, Anno Domini 1689. **469 501 503**

1689b: H. Playford
The Banquet of Musick: or, A Collection of the newest and Best Songs sung at Court, and at the Publick Theatres. With a thorow-bass for the theorbo-lute, bass-viol, harpsichord, or organ. Composed by several of the best masters. The words by the ingenious wits of this age. The third book. Licensed, Dec. 1. Rob. Midgley. In the Savoy: printed by E. Jones, for Henry Playford, at his shop near the Temple Church, 1689. **255 517**

1689c: Henry Playford
The Second Part of Musick's Hand-maid: Containing the newest lessons, grounds, sarabands, minuets, and jiggs, set for the virginals, harpsichord, and spinet. London, printed

on copper-plates, for Henry Playford, at his shop near the Temple Church, 1689.

To the reader. Having already published the first part of Musick's Hand-maid, with necessary rules and directions for playing those lessons contained therein: Which book, for its great usefulness, having recommended itself to the world, I was encouraged and solicited by the lovers of musick to proceed in making this collection of new lessons for the practick part, the theorick having been (as I said) sufficiently directed in the former. I have accordingly with much care compleated this second part; consisting of the newest tunes and grounds, composed by our ablest masters, Dr. John Blow, Mr. Henry Purcell, &c. the impression being carefully revised and corrected by the said Mr. Henry Purcell. The first part having found so great success, I have so ordered it, that both parts may be bound together for such as are not furnished with the former, the two making a compleat book, and useful not only for beginners, but the more skilful in the art. I hope, what I have here published,will be kindly received from your humble servant, H.P. **337/5c 646 647 648 649 650 653 655 656 664 665 666/3 T683 T688 T689 T694 T695**

1689?: n.p.
An Opera Perform'd at Mr. Josias Priest's Boarding-School at Chelsey. By young gentlewomen. The words by Mr. Nat. Tate. The musick composed by Mr. Henry Purcell. **626(mnp)**

1690a: J. Tonson
Amphitryon: or, The Two Sosia's. A Comedy By Mr. Dryden.

Egregiam verò laudem, & spolia ampla refertis,
Una dolo Divûm si Fœmina victa duorum est.

Virg.

London. Printed for J. Tonson in the Strand. To the Honourable Sir William Levison Gower, Bart.- [The Epistle Dedicatory, after several pages of fulsome flattery, turns to the subject of music, and to Purcell:] . . . 'tis true, were this comedy wholly mine, I should call it a trifle, and perhaps not think it worth your patronage; but when the names of Plautus and Molière are join'd in it, that is, the two greatest names of ancient and modern comedy, I must not presume so far on their reputation, to think their best and most unquestion'd productions can be term'd little. I will not give you the trouble, of acquainting you what I have added, or alter'd in either of them, so much it may be for the worse; but only that the difference of our stage from the Roman and the French did so require it. But I am affraid, for my own interest, the world will too easily discover, that more than half of it is mine; and that the rest is rather a lame imitation of their excellencies, than a just translation. 'tis enough, that the reader know by you, that I neither deserve nor desire any applause from it: If I have perform'd any thing, 'tis the genius of my authors that inspir'd me; and if it has pleas'd in representation, let the actors share the praise amongst themselves. As for Plautus and Molière, they are dangerous people; and I am too weak a gamester to put my self into their form of play. But what has been wanting on my part, has been abundantly supplyed by the excellent composition of Mr. Purcell; in whose person we have at length found an Englishman, equal with the best abroad. At least my opinion of him has been such, since his happy and judicious performances in the late opera; and the experience I have had of him, in setting my three songs for this Amphitryon: To all which, and particularly to the composition of the Pastoral

Dialogue, the numerous quire of fair ladies gave so just an applause on the third day. I am only sorry, for my own sake, that there was one star wanting, as beautiful as any in our hemisphere; that young Berenice, who is misimploying all her charms on stupid country souls, that can never know the value of them; and losing the triumphs, which are ready prepar'd for her in the court and town. And yet I know not whether I am so much a loser by her absence; for I have reason to apprehend the sharpness of her judgement, if it were not allay'd with the sweeness of her nature; and, after all, I fear she may come time enough, to discover a thousand imperfections in my play, which might have pass'd on vulgar understandings. Be pleas'd to use the authority of a father over her, on my behalf; enjoin her to keep her own thoughts of *Amphitryon* to her self; or at least not to compare him too strictly with Molière's. 'tis true, I have an interest in this partiality of hers; but withal, I plead some sort of merit for it, in being so particularly as I am, Sir, Your most obedient, humble Servant, October. 24. 1690, John Dryden.

[subtitle] *The Songs in Amphitryon with the musick composed by Mr. Henry Purcell, London*: Printed by J. Heptinstall for Jacob Tonson, 1690. **572/9, 10ab, 11ab**

1690b: H. Playford
The Banquet of Music: or, A Collection of the newest and best Songs sung at Court, and at Publick Theatres. With a thorow-bass for the theorbo-lute, bass-viol, harpsichord, or organ. Composed by several of the best masters. The words by the ingenious wits of the age. The fourth and last book. This may be printed. Octob. 19, 1689. Rob. Midgley. In the

Savoy: printed by E. Jones, for Henry Playford, at his shop near the Temple Church, 1690. **256 469 501 503**

1690c: H. Playford
Apollo's Banquet: Containing instructions, and Variety of New Tunes, Ayres, Jiggs and several New Scotch Tunes for the Treble-violin. To which is added, the tunes of the newest French Dances, now used at Court and in Dancing-schools. The Sixth Edition, with new additions. In the Savoy: printed by E. Jones, for Henry Playford at his shop near the Temple Church, and at his house over-against the Blue-Ball in Arundel Street in the Strand, 1690.

To all ingenious lovers and practitioners of musick,
The treble violin is at this present the only instrument in fashion, and the delight of most young practitoners in musick for their chearful and sprightly sounds, in setting forth the new airy tunes of the times: This second book of the Banquet of Musick is replenished with variety of new and delightful tunes proper to these instruments, and also to the flageolet, being the newest tunes, ayres, jiggs, and minuets, now in use at publick theatres, and at Dancing-schools: Which book with the former will make a compleat volume, and fit to carry in the pocket being stitch'd together, both very useful and necessary for all that play to dancing either in the city or country; there being in the first book for the benefit of such learners as live remote from any professed teachers, some practical rules and instructions for the treble-violin, by which (with those instructions only) several persons have attained to play indifferently well.
This second book I question not but will be as kindly received by all ingenious lovers and practitioners of musick as the former which will further encourage the endeavours of

Your Friend, H.P. **T606/9 T629/12 646 649 655 656 T689 T695 S100(inc).**

1690d: J. Bullord and A. Roper
New Poems, consisting of Satyrs, Elegies and Odes . . .
London: Printed for J. Bullord and A. Roper, 1690.
626/Epilogue

1690e: J. Tonson
The Prophetesse; or The History of Dioclesian. Written by
F. Beaumont and J. Fletcher. With alterations and additions
after the manner of an opera [By Thomas Betterton] London,
for Jacob Tonson, 1690.

The Vocal and Instrumental Musick of the Prophetess, or the
History of Dioclesian. Composed by Henry Purcell, organist
of their Majesties Chappel, and of St. Peters Westminster.
London, printed by J. Heptinstall, for the author, and are to
be sold by John Carr, at his shop at the Middle-Temple Gate
near Temple-Barr. MDCXCI.
    To his Grace Charles, Duke of Somerset, Earl of
Hartford, Viscount Beauchamp of Hatch, Baron Seymour of
Trowbridge, Chancellor of the University of Cambridge,
Lord High Steward of Chichester, and Knight of the most
Noble Order of the Garter. Your Grace has been pleas'd so
particularly to favour the composition of the musick in
Dioclesian, that from thence I have been encourag'd to this
presumption of dedicating not only it, but also the unworthy
author of it to your protection. All arts and sciences have
receiv'd their first encouragement from great persons, and
owe their propagation and success to their esteem: like some
sort of fruit-trees, which being of a tender constitution, and
delicate in their nature, require the shadow of the cedar to

shield their infancy from blites and storms.

Musick and poetry have ever been acknowledg'd sisters, which walking hand in hand, support each other; as poetry is the harmony of words, so musick is that of notes: and as poetry is a rise above prose and oratory, so is musick the exaltation of poetry. Both of them may excel apart, but sure they are most excellent when they are joyn'd, because nothing is then wanting to either of their perfections: for thus they appear like wit and beauty in the same person. Poetry and painting have arrived to their perfection in our own country: Musick is yet but in its nonage, a forward child, which gives hope of what it may be hereafter in England, when the masters of it shall find more encouragement. 'tis now learning Italian, which is its best master, and studying a little of French air, to give it somewhat more of gayety and fashion.

Thus being farther from the sun, we are of later growth than our neighbour countries, and must be content to shake off our barbarity by degrees. The present age seems already dispos'd to be refin'd, and to distinguish betwixt wild fancy, and a just, numerous composition. So far the genius of your Grace has already prevail'd on us: many of the nobility and gentry have follow'd your illustrious example in the patronage of musick. Nay even our poets begin to grow asham'd of their harsh and broken numbers, and promise to file our uncouth language into smoother words.

Once more, therefore, I presume to offer my self and this composition with all humility to your Grace's protection, or at least till I can redeem so mean a present by one which may better deserve your acceptation. Be pleas'd to pardon my ambition, which had no other means to obtain the honor of being made known to you, but only this. The town, which has been so indulgent to my first endeavours in this kind, has encourag'd me to proceed in the same attempt; and your favour to this trifle will be a good omen not only [to] the success of the next, but also to all future performances of,

Your Grace's most obedient
and most obliged servant,
Henry Purcell.[23]

Advertisement. In order to the speedier publication of this book, I employed two several printers; but one of them falling into some trouble, and the volume swelling to a bulk beyond my expectation, have been occasions of this delay.

It has been objected that some of the songs are already common; but I presume that the subscribers, upon perusal of the work, will easily be convinc'd that they are not the essential parts of it. I have, according to my promise in the proposals, been very carefull in the examination of every sheet, and hope the whole will appear as correct as any yet extant.

My desire to make it as cheap as possibly I cou'd to the subscribers, prevail'd with me so far above the consideration of my own interest, that I find, too late, the subscription-money will scarcely amount to the expence of compleating this edition. **627**

?1690: John Clarke
Youth's Delight on the Flageolet the Second Part Containing the Newest Lessons with easier Directions than any heretofore; Being the 9th edition, with additions of ye best and newest tunes, Allso a scale of the Gamut the violin way. Sold by John Clarke at the Golden Violin, St. Paul's Church Yard. **30 629/17(ms addition)**

1691a: J. Tonson
Amphitryon; or The Two Sosia's. A comedy. As it is acted
at the Theatre Royal. [All data, including dedication, is the
same as entry for 1690a, except for printing information]
Printed for J. Tonson, at the Judges Head in Chancery-lane
near Fleet-street; and M. Tonson at Grays-Inn-Gate in
Gray's-Inn-Lane. 1691. **572/9, 10ab, 11ab**

1691b: H. Playford
*Apollo's Banquet: Containing Variety of the Newest Tunes,
Ayres, Jiggs, and Minuets, for the Treble-Violin, Now in
Use at Publick Theatres, and at the Dancing-Schools, being
most of them within the compass both of the Flute, and
Flagelet.* To which is added, some new songs and catches.
The second Book. In the Savoy: Printed by E. Jones, for
Henry Playford, and are to be sold at his shop near the
Temple Church, and at his house over-against the Blue-Ball
in Arundel-Street in the Strand, 1691.

To all lovers and practitioners of musick. The treble-violin
and flute are at present the only instruments in fashion, and
the delight of most young practitioners in musick (continues
as in 1690c, q.v.) **341/4b 403 572/2, 4, 5, 6, 7, 9,
10ab, N12, 597/2, 5, 7, 599, 607/2, 3, 4 T612/4
627/18, 33 628/10bc, 15a, T21, T27, 37, 38 655
D103**

1691c: T. Cross
Song from Dioclesian ["Sound fame, thy brazen trumpet"].
627/22

1691d: T. Cross
[*A Dialogue from Dioclesian*] Tell me why, my charming

fair, a dialogue in the Prophetess, London, T. Cross junr sculp. c. 1691

1691e: H. Playford

The Banquet of Musick: or a Collection of the newest and best Songs sung at Court, and at the Publick Theatres, being most of them within the Compass of the Flute. With a thorow-bass for the theorbo-lute, bass-viol, harpsichord, or organ. Composed by several of the best masters. The words by the ingenious wits of the age. The Fifth Book. This may be printed. December 2, 1690. Rob. Midgley. In the Savoy: printed by Edw. Jones; and sold by Henry Playford at his shop near the Temple Church, and by Sam. Scott at Mr. Carr's shop at the Middle-Temple-Gate, 1691. **291 502 525**

1691f: J. Heptinstall

The Vocal and Instrumental Musick of the Prophetess, or the History of Dioclesian. Composed by Henry Purcell, Organist of Their Majesties Chappel, and of St. Peters Westminster. London, printed by J. Heptinstall, for the author, and are to be sold by John Carr, at his shop at the Middle-Temple Gate near Temple-Barr. MDXCI. [The balance of the matter is identical to that reproduced under 1690e, q.v.]

1691g: J. Heptinstall

Vinculum Societatis, or The Tie of Good Company: Being a choice collection of the newest songs now in use. With thorow bass to each song for the harpsichord, theorbo, or bass-viol. The Third Book; with several new airs for the flute or violin. London, printed by T. Moore, and J. Heptinstall, for John Carr, at his shop at the Middle-Temple-

Gate, Anno Domini, MDCXCI. 588/3 599 608/3, 4(anon)

1691h: J. Tonson
King Arthur: or, The British Worthy. A Dramatick Opera.
By Mr. John Dryden.

Heîc alta Theatris
Fundamenta locant, Scænis decora alta futuris.

Virg. Æn.I.

Purpurea intexti tollunt aulæa Britanni.

Georg.3.10.

Tanton' placuit concurrere motu
Jupiter, æternâ Genteis in pace futuras?

Æneid. 12.

Et celebrare domestica facta.

Hor.

London: printed for J. Tonson in the Strand

To the Marquiss of Halifax.
My Lord,
This poem was the last piece of service, which I had the honour to do for my gracious master, King Charles the Second: and tho' he liv'd not to see the performance of it on the stage, yet the prologue to it, which was the opera of *Albion and Albanius,* was often practis'd before him at Whitehall, and encourag'd by his royal approbation. It was indeed a time, which was proper for triumph, when he had overcome all those difficulties which for some years had perplex'd his peaceful reign: But when he had just restor'd his people to their senses, and made the latter end of his government of a piece with the happy beginning of it, he

was on the sudden snatch'd away from the blessings and
acclamations of his subjects, who arriv'd so late to the
knowledge of him, that they had but just time enough to
desire him longer, before they were to part with him
forever... [there continues this panegyric on the reign of
King Charles the Second for several pages, before the
subject is turned to the circumstances under which *King
Arthur* was produced:]
    ... In the mean time, while the nation is secur'd from
foreign attempts, by so powerful a fleet, and we enjoy not
only the happiness but even the ornaments of peace, in the
divertisement of the town, I humbly offer you this trifle,
which if it succeed upon the stage, is like to be the chiefest
entertainment of our ladies and gentlement this summer.
When I wrote it, seven years ago, I employ'd some reading
about it, to inform my self out of *Beda, Bochartus,* and other
authors, concerning the rites and customs of the heathen
Saxons; as I also us'd the little skill I have in poetry to adorn
it. But not to offend the present times, nor a government
which has hitherto protected me, I have been oblig'd so
much to alter the first design, and take away so many
beauties from the writing, that it is now no more what it was
formerly, than the present ship of the Royal Sovereign, after
so often taking down, and altering, is the vessel it was at
first building. There is nothing better, than what I intended,
but the musick; which has since arriv'd to a greater
perfection in England, than ever formerly, especially passing
through the artful hands of Mr. Purcel, who has compos'd it
with so great a genius, that he has nothing to fear but an
ignorant, ill-judging audience. But the numbers of poetry
and vocal musick are sometimes so contrary, that in many
places I have been oblig'd to cramp my verses, and make
them rugged to the reader, that they may be harmonious to
the hearer: Of which I have no reason to repent me, because

these sorts of entertainment are principally design'd for the ear and eye; and therefore in reason my art should on this occasion, ought to be subservient to his. And besides, I flatter my self with an imagination, that a judicious audience will easily distinguish betwixt songs, wherein I have comply'd with him, and those in which I have follow'd the rules of poetry, in the sound and cadence of the words. Notwithstanding all these disadvantages, there is somewhat still remaining of the first spirit with which I wrote it: And tho' I can only speak by guess of what pleas'd my first and best patroness the Dutchess of Monmouth in the reading, yet I will venture my opinion, by the knowledge I have long had of her Grace's excellent judgement, and true taste of poetry, that parts of the airy and earthy spirits, and that fairy kind of writing, which depends only on the force of imagination, were the grounds of her liking the poem, and afterwards of her recommending it to the Queen. I have likewise had the satisfaction to hear, that her Majesty has graciously been pleas'd to peruse the manuscript of this opera, and given it her royal approbation. Poets, who subsist not but on the favour of sovereign princes and of great persons, may have leave to be a little vain, and boast of their patronage, who encourage the Genius that animates them. And therefore I will again presume to guess, that her Majesty was not displeas'd to find in this poem the praise of her native country, and the heroic actions of so famous a predecessor in the government of Great Britain, as King Arthur.

All this, my Lord, I must confess, looks with a kind of insinuation, that I present you with somewhat not unworthy your protection: But I may easily mistake the favour of her majesty for her judgement: I think I cannot be deceiv'd in thus addressing to your Lordship, whom I have had the honour to know, at that distance which becomes me, for so many years. 'tis true, that formerly I have shadow'd some part of your virtues under another name; but the character, tho' short and imperfect, was so true, that it broke through the fable, and was discover'd by its native light—What I pretend by this dedication, is an honour which I do my self to posterity, by acquainting them that I have been conversant with the first persons of the age in which I liv'd; and thereby perpetuate my prose, when my verses may possibly be forgotten, or obscur'd by the fame of future poets. Which ambition, amongst my other faults and imperfections, be pleased to pardon in, My Lord   Your Lordship's most obedient servant,

John Dryden.

1692: T. Cross
Philomela, or The Vocal Musitian: being a collection of the best and newest songs; especially those in the two operas, 'The Prophetess' and 'King Arthur,' written by Mr. Dryden: and set to musick by Mr. Henry Purcell. Printed on copper plates; and sold by T. Cross in Three Horse-show Court in Pye Corner; and J. Man at the Heart and Bible in Cornhill. T-C: Trinity 1692 (II.410] **627(inc) 628(inc)**

1692b1: J. Heptinstall
Some Select Songs as they are Sung in the Fairy Queen. Set to Musick, by Mr. Henry Purcell. London, printed by J. Heptinstall, for the author; and are to be sold by John Carr, at the Inner-Temple Gate near Temple-Bar, by Henry Playford at his shop in the Temple, and at the Theatre in Dorset-Garden. 1692. **629/10a, 12, 13, 17abc, 22b, 23, 25, 33b, 34b, 44bc**

1692b2: J. Tonson
The Fairy-Queen: an Opera. Represented at the Queen's Theatre by their Majestie's servants. London, printed for Jacob Tonson, at the Judge's Head, in Chancery-Lane. 1692. **1692(mnp)**

1692c: H. Playford
The Banquet of Musick: or, A Collection of the Newest and Best Songs Sung at Court and at Publick Theatres, being most of them within the Compass of the Flute. With a thorow-bass for the Theorbo-lute, bass-viol, harpsichord, or organ. Composed by several of the best masters. The words by the ingenious wits of the age. The sixth and last book. Licensed, February 17. 1691/2 Rob. Midgley. In the Savoy, printed by Edw. Jones; and sold by John Carr at his shop at the Middle-Temple Gate, and by Henry Playford at his shop near the Temple Church, 1692.

An advertisement to the reader. Having formerly printed five books, entituled, The Banquet of Musick, in which are many excellent songs set by the best masters, I have here ventured on this sixth and last book, which makes a compleat volume. **369 405 486 516 588/4 598/1 612/1, 3, 4**

1692d: See 1692b2, supra.

1692e-i: Baldwin
The Gentleman's Journal: or The Monthly Miscellany. By way of a letter to a gentleman in the country. Consisting of news, history, philosophy, poetry, musick, translations, &c. January-December, 1692. **365 379A 444 586 627/App. 3**

1692j: Song from King Arthur
Your hay it is mow'd. A new song in the dramatick opera.
Written by Mr. Dryden. London, c.1692. s.sh. fol. **628/37**

1692k: Song from Hail, bright Cecilia
The fife and all the harmony of war. A favourite song. 1692.
328/11b

?1692:
*A Scotch-song Sung by Mrs. Ayliffe at the Consort in York
Buildings.* Mr. Henry Purcell. Sawney is a bonny lad. **412**

ca. 1692: n.d., n.p.
The Dialogue in the last Opera, call'd The Fairy Queen. [In
British Library MS Mus. Add. 35043, f.1., an interleaved
single sheet folio] a book belonging to John Channing in
1694. **629/22b**

1693a: J. Heptinstall
Comes Amoris . . . The Fourth Book . . . London, printed
by J. Heptinstall for John Carr, and Samuell Scott, at the
Middle Temple Gate in Fleet-Street, 1693.

To Lionell Duckett, of Hartham, in the county of Wilts, Esq;
Sir, we hope it will be no offence in us to tell the world that
are pleased to be an encourager of the musical faculty, since
the patrons of that art have been observed to be the best sort
of men. They are persons whose minds and tempers seem to
be made up of an agreeable harmony. You are so great an
instance of this truth, that you your self are not more an
admirer of musick than mankind of you, as man as have the
happiness to know you.'tis your great felicity to be both a

lover of your country and beloved by your country. We confess 'tis above our station to pretend to panegyrick, yet the sense of our obligation to you will not permit us to be altogether silent. If this little volume prove acceptable to you, it will be as great a satisfaction to us as if it were approv'd by an Orpheus or Apollo. 'tis the utmost of our ambition to add, (as much as in us lies) to the diversion of gentlemen whose souls are refin'd enough to relish the charms of musick. We have therefore made bold to offer this endeavour to your patronage, depending upon that goodness and candour which are the natural result of your temper. Wherefore amongst the number of your admirers we beg leave to subscribe ourselves as we are in all respect and sincerity, Sir, your most devoted, humble servants,

John Carr, Samuell Scott.
263 331/6 379B 576 580/1 602/2 627/Appendix 3 629/50c

1693b: H. Playford
Harmonia Sacra: or, Divine Hymns and Dialogues. With a thorow-bass for the Theorbo-lute, bass-viol, harpsichord, or organ. Composed by the best masters. The words by several learned and pious persons. The second book.

Angels and men assisted by this art,
May sing together, though they dwell apart.
Mr. Waller of Divine Poesie.

Imprimatur, Juli I°. 1693. Guil. Lancaster. In the Savoy; printed by Edward Jones, for Henry Playford at his shop near the Temple Church, and at his house over-against the Blue-Ball in Arundel-Street in the Strand; Where also the First Book may be had. MDCXCIII.

To the Reverend Henry Aldrich, D.D. Dean of Christ-Church, and Vice-Chancellor of the University of Oxford.

Sir, This is the greatest thing that I can do, for the excellent musick, poetry, and piety of these papers; it has been my care indeed to save them from oblivion, but they are indebted to me now much more, for the defence and ornament of your name. In addresses of this kind, men are usually so far from suiting the subject of their treatises to the qualifications of the persons they apply to, that we may shortly expect to see musick dedicated to the deaf, as well as poetry to aldermen, and prayer-books to atheists; and though generally it is a difficult matter to find a worthy patron for any one of these excellencies, yet we happily find them all lodg'd in your self. It has indeed been very seldom known since the Royal Prophet's time, that any single man has been thus qualified, but they all meet so eminently in you, (not to mention those other great advantages, which distinguish you from the rest of the world,) that had it been possible for me to have been at a loss to whom I should have addressed myself, thousands would have named you in the same instant. To make this collection compleat, and that it might consist of some of the best foreign hands as well as our own, I have at the end inserted some of Gratiano's and Carissimi's compositions, which you, with the rest of the just judges of musick, so much esteem. Pardon me then, sir, if I presume to beg your protection for these papers, 'tis the utmost of my fidelity and love to my charge; and I shall now have the glory of providing better for other men's works, than ever the fondest author could do for his own. I am, Sir, Your most humble servant,

Henry Playford.

To Dr. Blow, and Mr. Henry Purcell, upon the First and Second Books of Harmonia Sacra.

> When sacred numbers, and immortal lays,
> Joyn'd to record the great almighty's praise

Indulgent heav'n the poet did inspire
With lofty song to fill the tuneful lyre.
Thus, when of old from Egypt's fruitful land
God brought forth Moses by a mighty hand,
His joyful tongue with untaught numbers flow'd,
Th'unusual harmony its author show'd.
The sea divided as he pass'd along,
Retreating back at his triumphant song.
When David's hand upon his harp was found,
Heav'n soon repenting, listen'd to the sound.
And struggling nature chang'd her wonted course,
Unable to resist his musick's sacred force.
His prince's rage this taught him to controul,
And tune the discords of his troubled soul.
Not fabled Orpheus, or Amphion's verse,
Can such amazing prodigies rehearse.
We here the mystic art may learn t'unfold,
And feel the wonders which we there are told.
No cloudy passions can our breasts invade,
When Sacred Harmony dispels the shade.
Here sprightly numbers raise our heighten'd zeal

The Church as yet could never boast but two
Of all the tuneful race from Jubal down to you.

To his unknown friend, Mr. Henry Purcell, upon his excellent compositions in the first and second books of Harmonia Sacra.

Long had dark ignorance our isle o'erspread,
Our musick and poetry lay dead.
But the dull malice of a barb'rous age
Fell most severe on David's sacred page;

To wound his sense, and quench his heav'n-born fire,
Three dull translators lewdly did conspire.
In holy dogg'rel and low-chiming prose,
The king and poet they at once depose.
Vainly he did th'unrighteous change bemoan,
And languished in vile numbers not his own:
Nor stop'd his usage here
For what escap'd in wisdom's ancient rhimes,
Was murder'd o'er and o'er by the composer's chimes.
What praises, Purcell, to thy skill are due;
Who hast to Judah's monarch been so true?
By thee he moves our hearts, by thee he reigns
By thee, shakes off his old inglorious chains
And sees new honours done to his immortal strains.
Not Italy, the mother of each art,
Did e'er a juster, happier son impart.
In thy performance we with wonder find
Bassani's genius to Corelli's joyned.
Sweetness combin'd with majesty, prepares
To raise devotion with inspiring airs.
Thus I unknown my gratitude express,
And conscious gratitude could pay no less.
This tribute from each British muse is due,
Our whole poetic tribe's oblig'd to you.
For where the author's scanty words have failed,
Your happier graces, Purcell, have prevail'd.
And surely none with equal ease
Could add to David and make D'urfey please.

T. Brown.

To my worthy friend Mr. Henry Playford, upon his
Harmonia Sacra.

      Musick and verse have been abus'd too long,
      Idly to furnish out some wanton song;

To varnish vice, to make loose folly shine,
And gild the vain delights of love, or wine:
Both heav'nly born, but constrain'd to fall
So far below their great original.
The erring world, not knowing how to trace
Through vile employments their celestial race,
Suppos'd their birth was, as their office, base.
Rescu'd by you, they have again put on
Those glorious rays with which at first they shone;
Assert their native honour; and excite,
With awful pleasure, rev'rence, and delight.
Here no loud rant, no wild ungovern'd strain
Invokes plump Bacchus, and his sordid train.
Here no fond couplet kindles am'rous fires,
No melting note gives birth to loose desires:
Each air, each line, which in this work appear,
Angels may fitly sing and saints may hear.
Go on, my friend; set sacred music free
From scandal, and more sacred poetry:
Publish'd by you, with double grace they shine,
Lovely and grave, harmonious and divine.

By an unknown hand.

134 182 183 192 196 D72 D77 S15

1693c: H. Playford

Joyful Cuckoldom, or the Love of Gentlemen and Gentlewomen. A collection of new songs with ye musick for ye lute, violin, flute, or harpsichord by Henry Purcell, Dr. John Blow, Mr. John Eccles, Mr. Morgan, Dr. John Reading, Mr. Baptist, &c.&c. Fairley engraven on copper plates. London, printed by J. Heptinstall for Henry Playford at his shop in ye Temple Change & for J. Church. Sold by Daniel Dring at ye Harrow and Crown at ye corner of Clifford's Inn Lane in Fleet Street. 1671(?)[24] **243 257**

259 331/6(BASS) 403 572/9, 10ab 574/10 576
580/1 582 587 595/1 601/1 602/1 607/10 612/1,
2, 3 627/9BC, M21, 31A, 33A, Appendix 1, 2
627/Appendix 1 628/10bc 629/10a, 12, M17, 23,
34b, 44b

1693d: H. Playford
The First Book of Apollo's Banquet: Containing
instructions, and variety of new tunes, ayres [etc. . . .] for
treble violin, to which is added the tunes of the newest
french dances . . . 7th edition corrected with new additions:
H. Playford . . . London, 1693. The Third Part of Apollo's
Banquet, containing several of the newest tunes of dances
for the treble-violin and flute, now in use at court, and in
dancing-schools. **420 T567 601/T1, T3 612/3 629/6,
T10, T12, T17, T23, 26, 44bc 655 656 T689
T695 N775 TD100(anon.)**

**1693e-j (Jan., Apr., June., Sept., Dec.): R.
Parker**
The Gentleman's Journal: or The Monthly Miscellany. In a
letter to a gentleman in the country. Consisting of news,
history, philosophy, poetry, music, translations &c. January
[etc]. 1692/3 Imprimatur, Charnock Heron. Vol. II.
London, printed, and sold by R. Parker at the Unicorn under
the piazza at the Royal Exchange in Cornhill; and R.
Baldwin, near the Oxford Arms in Warwick-lane, and at the
Black Lyon in Fleet-street, between the Two Temple-Gates.
1693. **321(mnp) 321/14ab 401 427 601/1, 3
627/Appendix 1, 2**

1693k: John Hudgebut
*Thesaurus Musicus: Being a Collection of the Newest Songs
performed at Their Majesties Theatres; and at the Consorts in
Viller-street in York-buildings, and in Charles-street Covent*

Garden. With a thorow-bass to each song for the harpsichord, theorbo, or bass-viol. To which is annexed a collection of aires, composed for two flutes, by several masters. The first book. London, printed by J. Heptinstall for John Hudgebut. And are to be sold by John Carr, at Middle-Temple Gate in Fleet-street, and by John Money, Stationer at the Miter in Miter Court in Fleet-street. And at most musick-shops in town. 1693.

To Thomas Drax, Esquire. Sir, By the advice and assistance of some eminent masters of musick, whom I have great reason to believe my very good friends, and by some care and industry of my own, I have collected this small volume, which I find wants nothing but your name to recommend it to the musical part of the world; the sence of this encourages me (but with all humility imaginable) to beg your protection of it , since none (especially who have had a gentleman-like-education) will be so unmannerly as to oppose what a person of your sense and merit has vouchsaf'd to patronise. I am not unsensible how ridiculous an attempt of panegyrick would appear in me, who am altogether as unfit for it, as to perform in a consort of musick, but this I must beg leave to affirm, that if persons of your rank and sphere, not only condescend to be patrons of the sons of Apollo, but to be performers also, we have all grounds imaginable to be assured, that our island will be as famous for excellent compositions and admirable performances in musick, as Rome, the long-acknowledg'd mistress of the world. Now sir I must beg if you should find any errors that you would not impute them to the want of skill in the masters, but either to mine or the printer's oversight, who do not pretend to infallibility. But this I need not have mention'd, since I know you are so generous as to connive at such faults, and I hope you will pardon this presumption of your already

infinitely oblig'd and most humble servant, John Hudgebutt.
247 333/7ab 601/1, 2 D136

1693l: J. Tonson
*The Fairy-Queen: An Opera . . . with Alterations, Additions
and several new songs . . .* Printed for Jacob Tonson . . .
London 1693. **629/21ab, 40ab**

1694a: R. Butt
*Richard Butt: A Collection, of One Hundred and Eighty
Loyal Songs All Written since 1678.* And intermixt with
several new love songs. To which is added, the notes set by
masters of musick. With a table to find every song. The
fourth edition with many additions. London, printed, and are
to be sold by Richard Butt, in Princess-Street in Covent
Garden. 1694. Price bound 2s. **606/M8, M9**

1694b: D. Warner
*A Collection of Some Verses out of the Psalms of David,
composed in two parts, cantus and bassus,* collected by
Daniel Warner . . . revised by Mr. Henry Purcell, etc.
Printed by E. Jones: London, 1694. 8º. [There is a second
engraved title page which states that 'most of the tunes are
collected out of Mr. John Playford's Whole Book of Psalms
in Three Parts.'] **None of Purcell's works included.**

1694c: H. Playford
An Introduction to the Skill of Musick, in Three Books. The
first contains the grounds and rules of musick, according to
the Gam-ut, and other principles thereof. The second,
instructions and lessons both for the bass viol and treble
violin. The third, the art of descant or composing musick in
parts: in a more plain and easie method than any heretofore
published. By John Playford. The Twelfth Edition.

Corrected and amended by Mr. Henry Purcell. In the Savoy, printed by E. Jones, for Henry Playford at his shop near the Temple Church. 1694

A Preface to all Lovers of Musick.

Musick in ancient times was held in as great estimation, reverence, and honour, by most noble and virtuous persons, as any of the liberal sciences whatsoever, for the manifold uses thereof, conducing to the life of man. Philosophers accounted it an invention of the gods, bestowing it on men to make them better condition'd than bare nature afforded, and conclude a special necessity thereof in the education of children; partly from its natural delight, and partly from the efficacy it hath in moving the affections to virtue; comprehending chiefly these three arts in the education of youth, grammar, musick, and gymnastic; this last is for the exercise of their limbs. Quintillian reports, in his time the same men taught both grammar and musick. Those then who intend the practice thereof, must allow musick to be the gift of god: yet (like other his graces and benefits) it is not given to the idle, but they must reach it with the hand of industry, by putting into practice the works and inventions of skilful artists; for merely to speak and sing are of nature, and this double use of the articulate voice the rudest swains of all nations do make; but to speak well and sing well are of art: Therefore when I had considered the great want of books, setting forth rules and grounds of this divine science of musick in our own language, it was a great motive with me to undertake this work, though I must confess, our nation is at this time plentifully stor'd with skilful men in this science, better able than my self to have undertaken this work; but their slowness and modesty (being, as I conceive, unwilling to appear in print about so small a matter,) has made me adventure on it, though with the danger of not being so well done as them might have perform'd it: And I was the rather induc'd thereunto, for that the prescription of rules of all arts and sciences ought to be deliver'd in plain and brief language, and not in flowers of eloquence; which maxim I have follow'd: For after the most brief, plain and easie method I could invent, I have here set down the grounds of music, omitting nothing in this art which I conceiv'd necessary for the practice of young beginners, both for vocal and instrumental musick. Also I have in a brief method set forth the art of composing two, three, and four parts musically, in such easie and plain rules as are most necessary to be understood by young practitioners. The work as it is, I must confess, is not all my own, some part thereof being collected out of other authors which have written on this subject, the which I hope will make it more approv'd. J. Playford. **109 870 871**

1694d: J. Carr
Comes Amoris . . . The Fifth Book . . . London, printed by J. Heptinstall for John Carr at his shop at the Middle-Temple-Gate in Fleet-street. 1694. **321/2, 5, 14a 381 429 518 573 596 629/4b**

1694e: s.sh.
Lads and lasses blithe and gay. A Scotch song in the second part of the play (by T. D'Urfey) call'd Don Quixote, sung by Mrs. Hudson and set to musick by Mr. Henry Purcell. London, 1694. **578/8**

1694f: T. Cross
Let the dreadful engines . . . T. Cross, London, 1694. **578/3**

1694g-l: R. Baldwin
The Gentleman's Journal . . . January-February, March,
April, May, July, October-November, 1694. **323/5a 358
364 412 578/3, 8 587 595/1**

1694m: H. Playford
Thesaurus Musicus . . . The second book . . . printed by J.
Heptinstall for Henry Playford . . . sold by Henry Playford
. . . and John Money . . . and at most musick-shops . . .
London, 1694. **412 579 582 592/10 627/Appendix 1,
Appendix 2 628/26 [1694n:**
Another issue: printed by J. Heptinstall for John
Hudgebutt, and sold by John Money . . .]

1694o: S. Briscoe
The Songs to the New Play of Don Quixote. As they are
sung at the Queen's Theatre in Dorset Garden. Part the First
. . . printed by J. Heptinstall for Samuel Briscoe . . .
London, 1694. **578/1 to 5**

1694p: S. Briscoe
The Songs to the New Play of Don Quixote. Part the first.
Set by the most eminent masters of the age. All written by
Mr. D'Urfey. *Decies repetita placebunt.* London, printed by
J. Heptinstall for Samuel Briscoe, at the corner of Charles-
street, Covent-Garden. 1694. Price Two Shillings.

To my much honoured and ingenious friends (Lovers of
musick). That frequent the Rose, Chocolate-house, Coffee-
houses, and other places of credit, in and about Covent-
Garden, and particularly, to the late worthy members of the
Witty Club. These two books of songs, sung in the first and
second part of Don Quixote, are with all veneration most

humbly dedicated, by, gentlemen, your much obliged and
most humble servant. T. D'Urfey. **578/1a, 2, 3a, 4a**

1694q: S. Briscoe
*The Songs to the New Play of Don Quixote as they are sung
at the Queen's Theatre in Dorset Garden* Part the second . . .
printed by J. Heptinstall for Samuel Briscoe . . . London,
1694. Price One Shilling Six Pence **578/6, 7**

1695a: H. Playford
*Deliciae Musicae: Being, a Collection of the Newest and
Best Songs Sung at Court and at the Publick Theatres, most
of them within the Compass of the Flute.* With a thorow-
bass, for the theorbo-lute, bass-viol, harpsichord, or organ.
Composed by several of the best masters. The First Book.
Licensed, April 23, 1695. D. Poplar. London, printed by J.
Heptinstall for Henry Playford near the Temple-Church; or
at his house over-against the Blew-Ball in Arundel-street;
where also the new catch-book may be had. 1695.

An Advertisement to the Reader. My design in this new
collection of musick is to give to the world the best
entertainment I can of that kind. What I publish is from Dr.
Blow's, Mr. Purcell's, and other eminent masters'
composition: the songs will commend themselves and my
undertaking will be justify'd by them. I shall continue to
make my collection, and publish it every term, so that
nothing will be old before it comes to your hands; and you
shall always have a new entertainment prepar'd, before you
have lost the relish of the former, by your servant. H.P.
396 410 414 441 601/2 610 613/1, 2

1695b: H. Playford
Deliciae Musicae . . . The second Book. **379c 521 600/3b
632/17**

1695c-i: single-sheet songs
486 570/10 573 603/10 629/17, 22bc 630/17h

1695j: H. Playford
*The New Treasury of Musick: or a collection of the choicest
and best song-books for these twenty years last past.* The
words composed by the most ingenious wits of this age, and
sett to musick by the greatest masters in that science. With a
thorow-bass to most songs, for the theorbo, lute or bass-
viol, harpsichord or spinnet. London, printed for Henry
Playford near the Temple-Church; or at his house over-
against the Blew-ball in Arundel-street: where also the new
catch-book may be had, 1695. [This volume consists of
Books I, II and IV of the 'Theatre of Music' (1685-7);
Books IV and V of 'Choice Ayres and Songs' (1683-4) with
the above new title page. See these entries for aggregate
contents.]

1695k: J. Hudgebutt
Thesaurus Musicus, Vol . III With new imprint: Sold by
John Young at ye Dolphin & Crown at the west end of St.
Paul's Church all kinds of musical instruments together with
everything appertaining to this science. As also all sorts of
cases made at reasonable rates. Licensed according to order,
London, printed by J. Heptinstall for John Hudgebut, and
are to be sold by John Carr, at his shop near the Middle-
Temple-Gate in Fleetstreet, where masters and shopkeepers
may have them and at most musick-shops in town. Price

One shilling six pence. 1695. **371 578/8 591 595/2a**

1695l: J. Hudgebutt
Thesaurus Musicus: Being a Collection of the Newest Songs Performed at his Majesties Theatres; and at the Consorts in Villier-street in York-buildings, and in Charles-street Covent-Garden. Most of the songs being within the compass of the flute. With a thorow-bass to each song, for the harpsichord, theorbo, or bass-viol. Composed by most of the ingenious masters of the town. The Fourth Book. London, printed by J. Heptinstall for John Hudgebutt, and are to be sold by John Carr, at his shop near the Middle-Temple-Gate in Fleetstreet, and Daniel Dring, at the Harrow and Crown at the corner of Cliffords-Inn-Lane in Fleetstreet, where masters and shopkeepers may have them. And at most musick-shops in town. Price One Shilling Sixpence. 1695 **410 570/10 628/29**

1695m: J. Heptinstall
The Songs in the Indian Queen: As it is now compos'd into an Opera. By Mr. Henry Purcell . . . printed by J. Heptinstall . . . sold by John May . . . and John Hudgebutt at Tho. Dring's . . . London, 1695. **630/4bdg, 4ehf(mnp), 7cf, 7abde(mnp), 13(mnp), 15(mnp), 17ah, 17bg(mnp), 19**

1695n: H. Playford
The Songs in the Tragedy of Bonduca. Set by Mr. Henry Purcell. Excellent musick-books lately printed for, and sold by Henry Playford . . . London, 1695(?) **574(inc)**

1695o: H. Playford
Three Elegies upon the Much Lamented Loss of our Late

Most Gracious Queen Mary. The words of the two first by Mr. Herbert. The latter out of the Oxford Verse; and sett to musick by Dr. Blow and Mr. Henry Purcell . . . London, printed by J. Heptinstall, for Henry Playford, near the Temple Church; or at his house over-against the Blew-Ball in Arundel-street, 1695. **383 504**

1695p: H. Playford
The Dancing Master: or, Directions for Dancing Country Dances, with tunes to each Dance for the Treble-Violin, The ninth edition corrected; with additions of several new dances and tunes never before printed . . . printed by E. Jones for H. Playford . . . 1695. **646 D136 S68**

1695q: T. Cross
A New Song the words by Mr. Congreve set to music by Mr. Henry Purcell and engraven exactly by Tho. Cross: 'Pious Celinda goes to pray'rs.' **410**

1695r:
Bonduca [see Term Catalogues, II, p. 590]. **574**

1695s: J. Walsh
The Complete Flute-Master, or The Whole Art of Playing on ye Recorder . . . London: Walsh, 1695 **570/3 611/2**

1695t:
Who can from joy refrain? A song perform'd at Windsor on the 24th of July, 1695. **342/2**

1696a: F. Purcell
A Choice Collection of Lessons for the Harpsichord or Spinnet, composed by ye late Mr. Henry Purcell, Organist of his Majesties Chappel Royal & of St. Peters Westminster.

London. Printed on copper plates for Mrs. Frances Purcell, Executrix of the author, and are to be sold by Henry Playford at his shop in the Temple Change, Fleet-street, 1696. **660 661 662 663 665/3, 4 666 667 668 669 T678 T680 T686 T687 T698**

1696b: T. Cross
A Collection of Songs Set to Musick by Mr. Henry Purcell. & Mr. John Eccles. Printed and sold by Tho. Cross at his house in Katherine Wheel Court on Snowhill near Holbourn Conduit and sold at the musick shops.[25] **328/4 500 598 604A**

1696c-e: single-sheet songs
609/10 613/2 631/10

1696f: H. Playford
Deliciae Musicae . . . The Third Book . . . printed by J. Heptinstall, for Henry Playford . . . The fourth book will be publish'd next term, which will make the first volume compleat. London. 1696. **574/10, 17 605/1, 3 609/10, 11, 12 628/35 631/10**

1696g: H. Playford
Deliciae Musicae: Being a Collection of the Newest and Best Songs Sung at Court and at the Publick Theatres, most of them within the Compass of the Flute. With a thorow-bass, for the theorbo-lute, bass-viol, harpsichord, or organ. Composed by several of the best masters. The Fourth Book. Printed by J. Heptinstall, for Henry Playford, and sold by him at his shop in the Temple-Change, Fleet-street. The four books, with 3 Elegies on our late gracious Queen Mary. Sett by Dr. Blow, and the late famous Mr. Henry Purcell, compleats the first volume. The first book of the second

volume will be published next term. 1696. Price One shilling. [The first book of the second volume appeared later in 1696 as: "*Deliciae Musicae:* being a collection of the newest and best songs with the additional musick to the Indian Queen, by Mr. Daniel Purcell, as it is now acted at His Majesties Theatre." The only relevant item in the entire volume is the copy of Daniel Purcell's 'What ungrateful devil makes you come?' listed in the Purcell catalogue as D144.]

1696h: H. Playford[26]
f.1 *Deliciae Musicae: Being A Collection of the Newest and Best Songs Sung at Court and at the Publick Theatres, most of them within the Compass of the Flute.* With a thorowbass, for the theorbo-lute, bass-viol, harpsichord, or organ. Composed by several of the best masters. The first volume compleat. London, printed by J. Heptinstall, for Henry Playford, and sold by him at his shop in the Temple-Change, Fleetstreet. The four books, with 3 elegies on our late gracious Queen Mary, sett by Dr. Blow, and the late famous Mr. Henry Purcell, Compleats the first volume. The first book of the second volume will be publish'd next term. 1696.

f.2 . . . *The First Book* . . . Licensed April 23, 1695. D. Poplar. Printed by J. Heptinstall, for Henry Playford near Temple-Church; or at his house over-against the Blew-Ball in Arundel-street: Where also the new catch-book may be had. 1695.

f.2' *A Table of the Songs contain'd in this Book.* Books now in the press and will be speedily published. Two elegys on our late gracious Queen Mary, one in English, set to musick by Dr. Blow, the other in Latin, set by Mr. Henry

Purcell.

Plain and Easy Directions to a young beginner, to learn the French Hautboy, with several outlandish Marches and other Tunes not only proper for that instrument, but also for the Violin and Flute; and the Queen's Farewell in 4 Parts by Mr. Peasible, and another by Mr. Tollet in 3 parts.

f.3 *An Advertisement to the Reader.* My design in this new collection of musick, is to give the world the best entertainment I can of that kind. What I publish is from Dr. Blow's, Mr. Purcell's and other eminent masters' composition; the songs will commend themselves, and my undertaking will be justify'd by them. I shall continue to make my collection, and publish it every term, so that nothing will be old before it comes to your hands; and you shall always have a new entertainment prepar'd before you have lost the relish of the former, by your servant, H. P. **396 410 414 441 601/2 610 613/1, 2**
The second book: **379C 521 600/3b 632/17**
The third book: **371 578/8 591 595/2 603/10**
The fourth book: **410 570/10 628/29**

1696i: S. Briscoe
New Songs in the Third Part of the Comical History of Don Quixote. Written by Mr. D'Urfey and sung at the Theatre Royal. With other new songs by Mr. D'Urfey. Being the last piece set to musick by the late famous Mr. Henry Purcell: and by Mr. Courteville, Mr. Akeroyd, and other eminent masters of the age. Engrav'd on copper-plates. London, printed for Samuel Briscoe, at the Corner-Shop of Charles-Street, in Russel-Street Covent-Garden, 1696. Price Three Shillings. Where are also to be had, the first and second parts of Mr. D'Urfey's songs, set to musick by Mr. Henry Purcell. **578/9**

1696n: J. Hudgebutt

Thesaurus Musicus: Being a Collection of the Newest Songs Performed at His Majesties Theatres; and at the Consort in Villier-street in York-buildings. Most of the songs being within the compass of the flute. With a thorow-bass to each song, for the harpsichord, theorbo, or bass-viol. To which is annexed a collection of airs, composed for two flutes, by several masters. The Fifth Book. London, printed by J. Heptinstall, for John Hudgebutt, and are to be sold by Samuel Scott, at his shop near the Middle-Temple-Gate in Fleetstreet, and Daniel Dring at the Harrow and Crown at the corner of Cliffords-Inn-Lane in Fleetstreet, where masters and shopkeepers may have them. And at most musick-shops in town. 1696. Price One Shilling Sixpence. **394 574/15, 16 D133 D140 D142 (ascribed to Daniel Purcell)**

1696r: H. Playford

The Second Part of the Dancing Master . . . All new dances, never before printed. Printed for Henry Playford, 1696. **605/T2, T3 609/2, T11 611/9**

1696s: J. Walsh

A Collection of New Songs, set by Mr. N. Matteis, made purposely for the use of his scholars, with a thorough bass to each song, for the Harpsichord, Theorboe or Bass Viol; to which is added some new airs for the violin and bass by the same author, as allso simphonies for two flutes by a person of quality; fairly engraved on copper-plates. The 1st Book. Price One shilling Six Pence. London. Printed for and sold by John Walsh, Musical Instrument maker in ordinary to his Majesty at the Harp and Ho-boy in Catherine Street nere [*sic*] Somerset House in the Strand, and likewise to be had at

Mr. Hare's shop in Freeman's Yard in Cornhill near the
Royal Exchange. 1696 **M517**

1697a: F. Purcell
*A Collection of Ayres, Compos'd for the Theatre, and upon
other Occasions.* By the late Mr. Henry Purcell. Violino
Primo [Violino Secondo, Tenore, Basso] London, printed
by J. Heptinstall, for Frances Purcell, Executrix of the
Author; and are to be sold by B. Aylmer at the Three
Pigeons against the Royal Exchange, W. Henchman in
Westminster Hall, and Henry Playford at his shop in the
Temple-Change, Fleetsreet, 1697.

To his Grace Charles, Duke of Somerset, Marquess and Earl
of Hertford, Viscount Beauchamp of Hatche, Baron
Seymour of Trowbridge, Chancellor of the University of
Cambridge, Lord High Steward of Chichester, and Knight
of the Most Noble Order of the Garter. May it please your
Grace, the favourable reception which the following
compositions have found in the theatre, has given me some
hopes that they will meet with a suitable encouragement from
the press and as I am sensible that the success of all
performances in this kind, as well as others, depends not
only upon their intrinsick worth, but upon the patronage of
illustrious and judicious persons, whose establish'd
reputation does often impute a value to the work they
vouchsafe to encourage; so in all that number I could not
find any one who has a better title either to that character or
to these pieces, which, though to my greater misfortune,
they are become fatherless, yet I cannot fear they will be
friendliness, whilst they are under the happy influence of
your Grace's protection.

The epistle dedicatory. 'Tis certain, that duty as well as interest leads me to so worthy a choice, your Grace having been pleas'd some time since to accept from my dear husband, the dedication of the musick in Dioclesian, part of which is contain'd, with some other compositions of his, in these sheets; so that the inscription of the whole collection is justly due your Grace, whose generous encouragement of his performances, as it has formerly laid the greatest obligations upon his person, so it will now continue them to his posterity, and at the same time do the highest honour to his memory, which I promise my self from your Grace's celebrated goodness, will in some measure be as acceptable to your Grace, as it is dear to your Grace's most oblig'd and most obedient servant, Frances Purcell. 570/1 to 9 572/1 to 8 574/1 to 9 577/1 to 7 592/1 to 9 597 603/1 to 9 607/1 to 9 611/1 to 8 627/1ab, 2b, 3ab, 4, 15, 19, 24, 25, 34 628/1a, 2, 3, 10a, 11, 15a, 17b, 18, 28, 31, 34, 40, App.3 629/1ab, 2ab, 3ab, 6, 10d, 15, 16, 17a, 18ab, 19, 26, 38, 41, 44a, 51, App 4. 630/1ab, 2ab, 3ab, 4a, 11, 17a, 18, 22

1697c: J. Heptinstall
Te Deum et Jubilate, for Voices and Instruments, perform'd before the Queen, Lords, and Commons, at the Cathedral-Church of St. Paul, On the Thanksgiving-day, for the Glorious Successes of Her Majesty's Army the last Campaign. Compos'd by the late famous Mr. Henry Purcell. The second edition. London. Sold by J. Walsh, servant to her Majesty, at the Harp and Hoboy in Katherine-Street, near Somerset-House in the Strand; J. Hare, Instrument-maker, at the Golden Viol and Flute in Cornhill, near the Royal Exchange; and P. Randall, Instrument-Seller, at the Violin and Lute by Paulgrave-Head Court, without Temple-

Bar, in the Strand.

Te Deum & Jubilate for Voices and Instruments made for St. Cecilia's Day, 1694. By the late Mr. Henry Purcell. London, printed by J. Heptinstall, for the author's widow, and are to be sold by Henry Playford, at his shop in the Temple-Change in Fleetstreet, 1697.

To the Right Reverend Father in God, Nathaniel, Lord Bishop of Durham. My Lord, The ambition I have to do the greatest honour I can to the memory of my dear husband, by inscribing some of his best compositions to the best patrons both of the science he profess'd, and of his performances in it, is the fairest apology I can make to your Lordship; as it was the main inducement to my self for placing your Lordship's name before this piece of musick. The pains he bestow'd in preparing it for so great and judicious an auditory, were highly rewarded by their kind reception of it when it was first perform'd, and more yet by their intention to have it repeated at their annual meeting; but will receive the last and highest honour by your Lordship's favourable reception of it from the press, to which I have committed it, that I might at once gratifie the desires of several gentlemen to see the score, and at the same time give my self an opportunity to acknowledge, in the most publick and grateful manner, the many favours your Lordhip has bestow'd on my deceased husband, and consequently on Your Lordship's most oblig'd, and most humble servant, F. Purcell. **232**

1697d: F. Purcell
Ten Sonatas in Four Parts. Compos'd by the late Mr. Henry Purcell. London, printed by J. Heptinstall, for Frances Purcel, executrix of the author; and are to be sold by B.

Aylmar at the Three Pigeons against the Royal Exchange, W. Henchman in Westminster-Hall, and Henry Playford at his shop in the Temple-Change, Fleetsreet. 1697.

To the Right Honourable The Lady Rhodia Cavendish. Madam, the following collection having already found many friends among the judicious part of mankind, I was desirous that it might not want the patronage of our sex, for whose honour as well as for the credit of this work, I have presum'd to place your ladyship's name before these sheets. And, certainly, madam, my ambition will be justify'd by all that have the happiness of knowing your excellent judgement, and the wonderful progress you have made (beyond most of either sex) in all ingenuous accomplishments, and particularly in this of musick, for which you have often been admir'd by the dear author of these compositions; whose skill in this science is best recommended to the world by telling it, that he had the honour to be your master: upon whose account, as well as on that of many personal obligations, I am prompted by gratitude no less than ambition to acknowlege my self in the most publick manner, Your Ladyship's most oblig'd and most obedient servant, Frances Purcell. **802 to 811**

1697e: J. Walsh

The Harpsichord Master. Containing plain and easy instructions for learners on the spinet or harpsicord; written by the late famous Mr. H. Purcell at the request of a particular friend, and taken from his own manuscript, never before publish'd, being the best extant, together with a choice collection of the newest aires and song-tunes, compos'd by the best masters, and fitted for the harpsicord, spinnet or harp, by those that compos'd them, all graven on copper plates. Price 1 shilling and 6 pence. Sold by J. Walsh

Musicall Instrument Maker in Ordinary to his Majesty, at the Golden Harp & Hoboy in Catherine Street near Summerset house in the Strand, and J. Hare Musickall Instrument seller at the Golden Viol in St. Paul's Church yard, & at his shop in Freeman's yard Cornhill.

There will nothing conduce more to the perfect attaining to play on the harpiscord or spinnet, then a serious application to the following rules. In order to which you must first learn the Gamut or scale of musick, getting the names of the notes by heart, & observing at the same time what line and space every note stands on, that you may know & distinguish them at first sight, in any of the following lessons, to which purpose I have placed a scheme of keys exactly as there are in the spinnet or harpsichord & on every key the first letter of the note directing to the names lines & spaces where the proper note stands.

A Scale of the Gamut. All lessons on the harpsicord or spinnet are prickt, on six lines and two staves, in score (or struck through both staves with strokes or bars joining them together) the first stave is the bass and consequently play'd with the left hand. In the foregoing example of the Gamut there are thirty black keyes, which is the number contain'd in the spinnet or harpsicord, but to some harpsicords they add to that number both above and below. Notes standing below the six lines, which have leger lines added to them are called double, as double CC fa-ut, or Double DD sol-re, so they are above on ye treble hand, but then are call'd in alt, as being the highest. There are likewise in the example twenty inward keyes which are white, they are the half notes or flats and sharps to the other keyes. A sharp is marked thus (*) and where it is placed before any note in a Lesson it must be play'd on the inner key or half note above, which will make it sound half a note higher. A flat is marked thus (b) and where it is placed to any note, it must be play'd on the inner key or half note below the proper note, and makes it sound half a note lower. As for example, the same inner key that makes A=re sharp does also make B=mi flat, so that the half notes throughout the scale are sharps to the plain keys below them and flats to the plain keys above them.

1697g: J. Hare

Youth's Delight on the Flagelet the third Part containing ye newest Lessons with easier Directions than any heretofore. Being the 11th edition wth additions of ye best & newest tunes. Printed for and . . . sold by John Hare . . . 1697. **430 T609/11**

1698: H. Playford

Orpheus Britannicus. A Collection of all the Choicest Songs for One, Two and Three Voices. Compos'd by Mr. Henry Purcell. Together, with such symphonies for violins or flutes, as were by him design'd for any of them: And a thorough-bass to each song; Figur'd for the organ, harpsichord, or theorbo-lute. All which are placed in their several keys according to the order of the Gamut. London, printed by J. Heptinstall, for Henry Playford, in the Temple-Change, in Fleet-street, MDCXCVIII.

To the honourable, the Lady Howard. Madam, were it in the power of musick to abate those strong impressions of grief which have continued upon me ever since the loss of my dear lamented husband, there are few (I believe) who are furnished with larger or better supplies of comfort from this science that he has left in his own compositions, and in the satisfaction I find that they are more valued by me (who must own my self fond to a partiality of all that was his) than those who are no less judges than patrons of his performances. I find, Madam, I have already said enough to justifie the presumption of this application to your Ladiship, who have added both these characters to the many excellent qualities which make you the admiration of all that know ˎyou. Your Ladiship's extraordinary skill in musick, beyond most of either sex, and your great goodness to that dear person, whom you have sometimes been pleased to honour with the title of your master, makes it hard for me to judge whether he contributed more to the vast improvements you have made in the science, or your Ladiship to the reputation he gain'd in the profession of it: For I have often heard him say, that as several of his best compositions were originally design'd for your Ladiship's entertainment, so the pains he bestowed in fitting them for your ear, were abundantly rewarded by the satisfaction he received from your approbation, and admirable performance of them, which has best recommended both them and their Author to all that had the happiness of hearing them from your Ladiship.

Another great advantage, to which my husband has often imputed the success of his labors, and which may best plead for your Ladiship's favourable acceptance of this collection, has been the great justness both of thought and numbers which he found in the poetry of our most refin'd writers, and among them, of that honourable gentleman, who has the the dearest and most deserved relation to your self, and whose excellent composition were the subject of his last and best performances in musick. Thus, Madam, your Ladiship has every way the justest title to the patronage of this book, the publication of which, under the auspicious influence of your name is the best (I had almost said the only) means I have left of testifying to the world, my desire to pay the last honours to its dear author, your Ladyship having generously prevented my intended performance of the duty I owe to his ashes, by erecting a fair monument over them and gracing it with an inscription which may perpetuate both the marble and his memory. Your generosity, which was too large to be confin'd either to his life or his person, has also extended itself to his posterity, on whom your Ladiship has been pleas'd to entail your favours, which must, with all gratitude, be acknowledged as the most valuable part of their inheritance, both by them, and your Ladyship's most oblig'd and most humble servant, Fr. Purcell.

The Bookseller to the reader. Whereas this excellent collection was design'd to have been publish'd some considerable time before now, the reason of its delay was to have it as compleat as possibly it could be made, both in regard to the memory of the great master, and the satisfaction of all that buy it. And to make amends to those gentlemen and ladies who subscrib'd early to this work, they will here find an addition of above thirty songs more than were at first propos'd, which (considering the extraordinary charge of paper, &c, at this time) is an additional expence to me, tho' I hope the compleatness of the work will recompence my care and trouble. The author's extraordinary talent in all sorts of musick is sufficiently known, but he was especially admir'd for the vocal, having a peculiar genius to express the energy of English words, whereby he mov'd the passions of all his auditors. And I question not, but the purchaser will be very well pleas'd in the choice of this collection, which will be a great satisfaction to your humble servant, Hen. Playford.
321/2a, 5, 14   323/5a   328/4   333/71b   335/5a
339/3ab   360   362   369   370   375   379C   380   387
394   396   406   413   422   423   428B   444   464
470   485   486   488   493   501   502 503   510   513
514   517   521   522   543   570/10   571/6   573

574/17   578/1, 3, 6, 9   579   580/1   584   585/1
586   589   592/10   596   598   601/2   602/1   603/10
604A   608   609/10   610   613   626/3a   627/35,
Appendix 1, Appendix 2   628/26, 29 35, 36, 38
629/4b,   22bc,   40b   630/13, 15, 17h 631/10
632/17 See also Term Catalogues III, 54

1699a: F. Purcell
A Choice Collection of Lessons for the Harpischord or Spinnet. Composed by ye late Mr. Henry Purcell Organist of his Majesties Chappel Royal & of St. Peters Westminster. The third edition with additions & instructions for beginners. Printed on copper plates for Mrs. Frances Purcell, executrix of the author, and are to be sold at her house in Great Dean's Yard. Westminster, 1699.   660   661   662   663   665/3, 4   666   667   668   669   T678   T680   T686   T687 T697   T698

1699b: H. Playford
Mercurius Musicus: or, The Monthly Collections of New Teaching Songs, compo'sd for the Theatres and other Occasions; with a thorow-bass for the harpsichord, or spinnett: The songs being transpos'd for the flute at the end of the book. For January, London: printed by William Pearson, next door to the Hare and Feathers, in Alders-gate-street; for Henry Playford, and sold by him at his shop in the Temple-Change, Fleet-street; and J. Hare at the Golden Viol in St. Paul's Church-Yard, and at his shop in Freeman's-Yard in Corn-Hill; and at all other musick shops in town. Price six pence. [London, 1699].

To all lovers of harmony. Gentlemen, These monthly

collections in miniature being so many favours, which the masters are pleased to oblige me with, make me fond to believe they have some kind reflections on the memory of my father; who, to the extent of his power has advanced musick in general, and that they intend to settle their good opinions in the right line. What I have to do, after my grateful acknowledgement, is to see their works perfectly printed from their originals, and so far to merit their esteem, as to be able to shew them, the vanity of some pedlars of musick, whose wares have often reach'd Rome it self, to the lessening of the characters the English masters so justly deserve. I shall take care, the songs shall be newest of the last month and I hope by the continuance of this and other collections; supported by their favours, that musick will grow more and more in esteem; and as it has been my utmost care to promote, so I hope these little collections being of small price, and continued new monthly, will prevent incouraging of these pedlars, who have so often impos'd on the world, which will lay greater obligations on Your humble servant, Henry Playford. **434 S74**

1699c: H. Playford
The Whole Volume of the Monthly Collections, intituled, Mercurius Musicus [for the year 1699] . . . Printed by William Pearson . . . for Henry Playford . . . and sold by him . . . and J. Hare . . . and J. Young . . . London, 1699. **434 D144**

c1700: F. Purcell
A Choice Collection of Lessons for the Harpsichord or Spinnett . . . Composed by ye late Mr. Henry Purcell, Organist of his Majesties Chappel Royal & or St. Peters, Westminster. The Third edition with additions and instructions for beginners. Printed on copper plates for Mrs.

Frances Purcell, Executrix of the Author, and are to be sold at her house in Great Dean's Yard, Westminster.

[Dedication] To Her Royal Highness, the Princess of Denmark. Your Highness's generous encouragement of my deceased husband's performancers in musick, together with the great honour your Highness has done that science in your choice of that instrument, for which the following compositions were made; will, I hope, justifie to the world or at least excuse to your goodness this presumption of laying both them and my self at your Highness's feet. This, Madam, is the highest honour I can pay his memory; for certainly, it cannot be more advantageously recommended either to the present or future age, than by your Highness's patronage which, as it was the greatest ambition of his life, so it will be the only comfort of his death to your Highness's most obedient servant, Frances Purcell.

Notes

1. This continuation of Hilton's *Catch that Catch Can* is the first edition of *The Musical Companion*. Its second part has a separate title page, but the pagination is continuous.
2. This is the third issue of this edition, containing the additional sheets of Lawe's composition, and eleven songs by Purcell, Jackson, and others. See Day and Murrie, p. 43, for full descriptions, of all issues.
3. The copy in British Library with pressmark K.7.i.20 bears the manuscript inscription, "25 Charles II," and has several notes written in the same hand.

4. According to Jeffrey Pulver, *A Biographical Dictionary of Old English Music*, p. 211 describes William Godbid as a "well-known printer who . . . printed for John Playford, senior, for twenty years, and was noted for his type-printing of music." After his death, ca. 1678, his widow, Anne Godbid inherited the business.

5. There are two issues, this being the first. The second contains additional works by composers of Pelham Humfrey's generation, reinforcing the emphasis of the original, which is dedicated to works of Marsh, Blackwell, Wm. Gregory, Robert Smith, John Bannister, James Hart, Stafford, etc.

6. A very significant figure in English music and Licenser of the Press during the reigns of Charles II and James II, L'Estrange was a staunch Tory and very active pamphleteer in the royalist cause. An amateur bass-violist, he had studied with John Jenkins and was a close friend of Christopher Simpson and Matthew Locke. He was also acquainted with John Hingeston, in whose house he performed chamber music before Oliver Cromwell during the Commonwealth. Pleading loyalty to the royalists he later explained that this had come about quite by chance.

7. L'Estrange's admirer remains anonymous, or at least is not to be identified in extant lists of those who were actively involved in music during the early years of Charles II's reign.

8. Widow of William Godbid, she managed his printing business after he died, ca. 1678, working with her husband's former apprentice, John Playford, nephew of John Playford, senior. Young Playford took over the business when she died.

9. John Birchenshaw, music teacher and writer during Commonwealth and Restoration periods. He taught Samuel Pepys, among others, and wrote a set of rules on composition which he reduced to one page. He also developed a theory of numbers relating to music.

10. See another issue for further information.

11. Note from British Library catalogue: "Imperfect, wanting the title-page and a leaf or leaves at the 'Directions.' The title has been supplied from the Term Catalogues. A title page supplied in MS from a 1675 edition gave the title erroneously as *The Pleasant Companion*. The blank verso of the thirteenth page bears two MS monograms of Samuel Pepys, in his autograph."

12. Nathaniel Thompson was a printer and bookseller active in Dublin and London from 1666 to 1688. (See Charles Humphries and William C. Smith, *Music Publishing in the British Isles*, p. 308.)

13. The textual matter for the second book is the same as that for the first except that "Signior Francesco's Gittar Book" is mentioned in the appended list of publications, and there is a full page—in small print—of other releases from the Playford press.

14. The front page bears the mansucript inscription: "The gift of Mr. John Playford to John Jackson—Oct. 8., 1685."

15. In the British Library copy, the collection is erroneously identified as the second volume in the printed title page. The error has been corrected by an anonymous hand, changing "2nd" to "3rd" book.

16. The copy in the British Library with pressmark K.4.b.16 bears John Gostling's signature on the title page.

17. Not the elder John Playford, but rather John Playford II, who died tragically and unexpectedly about this time.

18. Contrary to published opinion, John Playford was a printer, and not just a publisher, as this statement proves. It seems unlikely that Henry Playford would be mistaken about his own father. Further on this point, see F. B. Zimmerman, *Henry Purcell (1659-1695): His Life and Times* (Second revised edition, University of Pennsylvania Press, 1983), p. xxxiii.

19. The copy in the British Library was a presentation copy from John Playford, with his autograph, dated October 1685, on the title page to John Jackson, whose autograph is at the end of *The Cambridge Catch*.

20. These initials probably stand for Richard Parker, Bookseller at the Unicorn, under the Piazza of the Royal Exchange. (See Charles Humphries and William C. Smith, *Music Publishing in the British Isles* [London: Cassell, 1954], p. 252.)

21. The collection has only a few catches and one bass from Purcell's music, these appearing under the title, "A Small Collection of the Newest Catches for 3 Voices."

22. For the song "Anacreon's defeat" there is a marginal note as follows: "The notes with this mark * over them are to be sung Demiquavers."

23. As R. Ham discovered, most, if not all this dedication was ghost-written for Purcell by John Dryden, who may have penned at least parts

of it tongue in cheek. The advertisement which follows, as judged by style and content, would seem to have been written by Purcell himself. See R. Ham, "Dryden's dedication for the music of 'The Prophetesse,' 1691," P.M.L.A. (December 1935): 1065–1075.

24. The title page is in manuscript, obviously copied to replace the original printed title page, if, indeed, there ever was an original. The putative copyist got the date wrong.

25. There are no signatures among these 11 unpaginated leaves, which are engraved throughout. The copy in the Royal College of Music has a paper cover dated 1718, as written on the cover after the back had been badly mutilated.

26. This is the date and imprimatur of a title sheet printed especially for the collection, the whole being bound and redated in 1696, though many of the individual sheets were printed much earlier.

SELECTIVE LIST OF EDITIONS

This list of Purcell's edited music falls into two parts, the first being devoted to collections after 1700, and the second to individual pieces. Each part is presented in chronological order, and in the typographical style that governs all of the guide excepting that devoted to quasi-facsimile reproductions of forematter to Purcell's editions which appeared before 1700. For the user's convenience, work and section numbers appear with each entry. The list of Purcell's edited music is followed by an appendix devoted to published musical compositions inspired by his music.

I. COLLECTIONS (Listed in Chronological Order).

(NB: For collections published before 1700, see above, "Textual Matter from Editions of Purcell's Music, 1667-1700.")

The second book of the pleasant musical companion . . . The fourth edition, corrected and much enlarged. London, 1701. 240 241 242 243 244 245 248 249 252 253 254 255 256 257 259 260 262 263 264 265 266 267 268 269 270 272 273 274 275 276 277 280 281 282 283 284 285 286 287 288 289 290 291 292 351 574/10 594 599 D100 D102 S54 S56.

The dancing master . . . *11th edition corrected, with the*
   add'ns of new dance tunes, the whole printed in new
   character. London, 1701.   570/7, 8   605/T2, T3
   607/4   609/2, 3, 9, T11   611/9   646   D136   S125.

Apollo's banquet newly reviv'd: containing new and easie
   instructions for the treble-violin, with ayres, tunes,
   jiggs, minuets, sarabands, chacones and cybells, etc.
   (The eighth edition) entirely new London, 1701. 570/3
   574/2, 3   597/2   611/6   628/18   630/1b, 2b, 4a, 18
   D254.

Orpheus britannicus . . . The second book, which renders
   the first complete. London, 1702.   321/3, 7, 9a
   328/3b, 8ab   331/6(bass), 7a   333/3b, 4ab, 6b, 11b
   335, 2, 3   338/9a, 10a   342/2b, 2e, 3a, 4b, 6   352
   381   402   405   410   421   434   473   499   500   516
   518   520   525   546   572/11   574/12, 13b   578/7
   583/2   590   600/3b   607/11   627/22, 30, Appendix 3
   629/7b, 8, 21a, 29, 31, 34b, 35, 36a, 39b, 43, 45b,
   48b   630/4bdg, 7c, 17a, 19   632/10, 11a, 12, 13b, 14,
   16, 19.

Harmonia sacra. The first book. The 2d edition . . . enlarged
   and corrected; also four anthems of the late Mr. Henry
   Purcell, never before printed . . . London, 1703.   7
   19   31   33   181   184   186   188   189   190   191
   193   197   198   199   200   D22.

The dancing master . . . The whole work revised and much
   more correct than any former editions . . . London,
   1703. [Contents same as in 1701 ed.]

A choice collection of songs by severall masters. London,
   1704.   328/4   486   573   574/17   578/3   584   603/10
   604A   609/10   613/2   627/22   629/4b, 22bc   630/17h
   631/10.

The jovial companions, or merry club. . . catches . . . by the
   late Mr. Henry Purcell . . . London, n.d. [1704].   241

243 245 253 255 262 264 265 267 268 270 274 275 277 280 284 286 290 291 574/10 D100 D102 D103 D106 S54.

A choice collection of lessons . . . by . . . Dr. John Blow, and the late Mr. Henry Purcell . . . London, 1705. 646 647 648 649 650 653 655 656 T688 T689 T694.

A collection of the most celebrated songs and dialogues composed by the late famous Mr. Henry Purcell. London, ca. 1705. 321/21, 5, 14a 333/7ab 369 370 485 502 521 571/6 574/17 578/3, 6, 7, 9 608 609/10 627/22, 35 628/26 629/22bc 630/13 632/19.

Orpheus britannicus . . . The second edition with large additions . . . London, 1706. 321/2, 6b, 11, 12, 13ab 323/3, 5a 325/8a 328/4, 6, 9, 11b 333/7ab, 9, 10, 13a 335/5a 339/3ab 344/11a 360 365 369 370 379C 389 392 394 396 423 428B 465 470 485 486 488 489 496 501 502 503 513 514 517 521 522 523 570/10 571/6 573 574/15b, 16b, 17 578/1, 3, 4h, 6, 9 579 580/1 584 585/1 586 589 592/10 595/2 596 598 600/1b, 1d 601/2 602/1 603/10 604A 608 609/10 610 613 626/3a 627/6b, 13b, 35, Appendix 1, Appendix 2 628/9a, 12bc, 16b, 19, 20, 21, 22, 26ab, 29, 35, 36, 38 629/4b, 22bc, 40b 630/13, 15, 17h 631/10 632/17.

Wit & mirth, or pills to purge melancholy; being a choice collection . . . carefully corrected by Mr. J. Lenton. Vol. IV. London, 1706. 331/6(bass) 395 403 408 M574/6 576 582 587 588/4 601/1 605/1 607/11 609/12 M611/7 612/2, 3, 4 628/38 629/12, M17, 23, 34b D131.

The second book of the pleasant musical companion . . . The
fifth edition . . . London, 1707. 240 241 242 243
244 245 248 249 252 253 254 255 256 257
258 259 260 262 263 264 265 266 267 268
269 270 272 273 274 275 276 277 280 281
282 283 284 285 286 287 288 289 290 291
292 351 574/10 594 599 D100 D102 D103
D107 S54.

Wit and mirth . . . The third edition, Vols. I-IV. London,
1707 [copy in The British Library]. 371 379B 412
430 572/9, 10b 578/8 M578/8 591(mnp) 595/1
601/3 602/1 605/2, 3 606/8, 9 609/11(mnp)
627/9bc, 18, 31ab, 33a 628/10bc, 15bc, 37 629/10,
17 M630/20 M655 D1, 36 D142 S66 S68(mnp)
[copy in New York Public Library] 331/6 359 371
372 379B 384 395 403 408 412 519 572/9,
10b 574/M6, M17 576 578/2, M8 582 587
588/4 501(mnp) 601/1 602/1 605/1 606/8, 9
607/11 609/11(mnp), 12 M611/7 612/2, 3, 4
627/9bc, 18b, 33a 628/10bc, 15bc, 37, 38 629/12,
17, M17, 23, 34b M630/20 M655 D131 D136
D142.

The jovial companion . . . London, 1709. Contents same as
1704 edition.

Wit and mirth . . . *The second edition with additions.* Vol.
IV, London, 1709 [Copy in The British Library]. 395
M574/6 587 601/1 605/1 609/12 M611/7 646
[Copy in New York Public Library] 331/6(bass) 395
403 408 M574/6 576 582 587 588/4 601/1
607/11 609/12 M611/7 612/2, 3, 4 628/38
629/12, M17, 23, 34b D131.

*Catches for flutes; or a collection of the best catches
contriv'd and fitted for 1:2:3: or 4 flutes, to be
performed in the nature of catches, which makes a*

compleat consort of flutes, being the first of the kind yet publish'd . . . London, [1711]. 241 243 248 252 253 255 262 267 270 274 275 280 284 286 288 290 291 574/10 D100 D102 D103 D106.

Orpheus britannicus . . . *the second book* . . . *The second edition with additions*. London, 1711. The contents are the same as in the edition of 1702, with the following additions: 328/10b 515 578/4b 627/8 628/6c 629/50e 630/4h, 7b, 17bc D172 [Another issue in 1712].

A hundred & twenty country dances for the flute: Being a choice collection of the pleasant & most airy tunes out of all the dance books. London, 1711. 611/9 (in a minor) 646 653 D100 (anon.) D145 S72 S125.

Wit and mirth . . . *with several new songs by Mr. D'Urfey*. The third edition, Vol. III, London, 1712. 359 372 384 519 574/M6, M17 578/2.

The dancing master . . . Fifteenth edition . . . The whole work revised and done on the new-ty'd note. London, 1713. 570/8 605/T2, T3 609/2, 3, 9, T11 611/9 646 D100 D136 S125.

Harmonia sacra . . . Book II, the second edition, very much enlarged and corrected. London, 1714. 134 182 183 192 196 D72 D77 S15.

Wit and mirth . . . The fourth edition. Vols. I-V. London, 1714. Contents the same as the British Library copy of the edition of 1707, with the following additions: D135 D137 D145.

Songs compleat, pleasant and divertive. Vols. I and II. London, 1719. 291 320/2a(mnp) 333/2(mnp)7ab 405 M430 463 465(mnp) 481 509(mnp) 578/1(mnp), 2, 3(mnp), 6(mnp), 7, 9(mnp) 584(mnp) 589(mnp) 602/1(mnp), 2 608(mnp) M611/7 627/(mnp) M655 MT678 D137 D138(mnp).

Wit and mirth . . . Five vols. . . . London, 1719 [Copy in
The British Library]. 291 320/2a(mnp) 333/2, 7ab
359   371   372   379B   405   407   412   430   463
465(mnp)   481   489   509(mnp)   572/9, 10   M574
578/1(mnp), 2, 3(mnp), 6(mnp), 7, 8, M8, 9(mnp)
584(mnp)   589(mnp)   591(mnp) 601/3   602/1(mnp),
2   605/3   606/8, 9   608(mnp)   609/11   M611/7
627/9bc, 18b, 22(mnp), 31ab, 33a   628/10, 15bc, 37
629/10   M630/20   M646   M655   MT678   D135
D136   D138(mnp)   D142   S66   S68 [Copy in British
Museum]   290   320/2a(mnp)   333/2, 7ab   359   371
372   379B   384   405   407   412   430   M430   443
463   465(mnp)   481   489   509(mnp)   519   572/9,
10   574/M6, M17(mnp)   578/1(mnp), 2, 3(mnp),
6(mnp), 7, 8, M8, 9(mnp)   584(mnp)   589(mnp)
591(mnp)   595/1   601/3   602/1(mnp), 2   605/1, 2, 3
606/8, 9   608(mnp)   609/11   M611/7   627/9bc, 18b,
22(mnp), 33a   628/10, 37   629/10, 17   M630/20
M655   MT678   D135   D136   D137   D138(mnp)
D142   S68(mnp).

The pleasant music companion . . . The Sixth Edition . . .
London, 1720.   240   241   242   244   245   248
249   252   253   254   255   256   257   258   259
260   262   263   264   265   266   267   268   269
270   272   274   275   276   277   280   281   282
283   284   285   286   287   288   289   290   291   292
351   574/10   594   599   D100   D102   D196   D107
[Another issue, 1726].

Wit and mirth . . . .The sixth and last volume . . . London,
1720.   331/6(bass)   395   M403(mnp)   408   576
582   587(mnp)   588/4   601/1   M606/5(mnp)   607/11
609/12   612/2, 3, 4   628/M30bc(mnp)   629/12, M17,
23, 34b   D131   D144   D145, S72.

Orpheus britannicus . . . The third edition with large additions . . . Books I & II . . . London, 1721. 321/2a, 5, 6b, 11b, 12a, 13b, 14a 323/3, 5a 325/8a 328/3b, 4, 6, 8, 9, 11b 333/7, 9, 10, 13a 339/3ab 344/1a 360 365 369 370 379C 396 425 428A 465 469 485 486 488 489 503 513 514 515 517 521 522 523 571/6 573 574/15b, 16b, 17 578/1, 3, 4h, 6, 9 579 580/1 584 585/1 586 589 592/10 595/2 596 598 600/1bd 601/2 602/1 603/10 604/A 608 609/10 610 613 626/3a 627/6ab, 22bc, 40b 630/13, 15, 17h 631/10 632/17. Book II: The contents are the same as for the edition of 1702, omitting 472, and with the following additions: 328/10b 578/4b 627/8 628/6c 629/50e 630/4h, 7b, 17bc D172.

[*Orpheus britannicus*] *Mr. Hen^r. Purcel's favourite songs out of his most celebrated Orpheus britannicus and the rest of his works, the whole fairly engraven and carefully corrected.* London, ca. 1725. 321/2a, 5, 14a 333/7ab 369 370 379C 485 486 501 502 521 571/6 573 574/15b, 16b, 17 578/1, 3, 6, 7, 9 598 608 609/10 613/2 627/22, 35 628/26 629/4b, 22bc (Note: The British Library copy has contents as listed above, but imprint and title page are the same as for the edition of 1726).

Harmonia sacra . . . The first book, the third edition very much enlarg'd and corrected; also four excellent anthems of the late Mr. H. Purcell's, never before printed. London, 1726. 7 19 31 33 181 184 189 190 191 193 197 198 199 203.

Harmonia sacra . . . Book II. The 3d edition very much enlarg'd and corrected . . . London, 1726. 134 182 183 192 196 D72 D77.

[*Orpheus britannicus*] *Mr. Hen[r]. Purcell's favourite songs out of his most celebrated Orpheus brittanicus*[*sic*] *and the Rest of His Works, the whole fairly engraven and carefully corrected.* The second edition with additions . . . London, 1726. The contents are the same as in the 1725 edition, with the following omissions: 574/16b 578/6b 608/1 and the following additions: 335/5a 428A 444 584 602/1 628/38.

The catch club or merry companions, being a choice collection of the most diverting catches for three and four voices. Compos'd by the late Mr. Henry Purcell, Dr. Blow, (et altri) . . . London, ca. 1731. 240 241 242 243 244 245 248 249 252 253 254 256 257 259 260 262 263 264 265 266 267 268 269 270 272 274 275 276 277 280 282 283 284 285 286 288 290 291 292 351 574/10 599 D102 D106 D107 [another issue in 1733].

The musical entertainer, engrav'd by George Bickham, jun[r]. Vol. I. London, 1736. 379 578/9.

The musical entertainer, engrav'd by George Bickham, jun[r]. 2 vols. London, 1737. 370 574/15b, 16b 578/9 S61.

Thesaurus musicus. A collection of two, three, and four-part songs . . . To which are added some choice dialogues. Set to musick by . . . Dr. Blow, H. Purcell, Handel, Dr. Green, Dr. Purcell, Eccles . . . The whole revis'd by . . . [James Oswald]. Vol. I. London, [1744]. 333/7ab 335/5a 485 517 572/11ab 574/15b, 16b 578/1, 6 602/1 607/11 627/11 627/30.

Orpheus britannicus: A collection of choice songs for one, two and three voices with a through bass for the harpsichord. London, [ca. 1745]. 321/2 333/71b 335/5a 369 370 379C 394 423 428A 444 485 486 488 489 501 502 513 514 517 521

522   570/10   571/6   572/11ab   573   574/15b, 16b,
17   578/1, 3, 4h, 6, 7, 9   579   580/1   585   592/10
595/2   596   598   600/1b   601/2   602/1   604A   608
609/10   610   613/2   627/6ab, 13b, 22, 35, Appendix
627/2, 6, 29, 35, 36, 38   629/4b, 22bc   630/13, 15
631/10   632/17, 19   D171   S61   S68.

Thesaurus musicus, a collection of two, three and four part
songs, several of them never before printed. To which
are added some choice dialogues set to musick by the
most eminent masters, viz Dr. Blow, H. Purcell,
Handel, Dr. Green, Dr. Purcell, Eccles, Weldon,
Leveridge, Lampe, Carey   London,   1745.   323/3
333/7ab   335/5a   485   486   488   489   499   501
502   517   520   521   546   572/11   574/15b, 16b, 17
578/1, 3, 4h, 6, 7, 9   579   580/1   584   585   592/10
596   597   600/1b   601/2   602/1   604A   608   609/10
613/1, 2   627/ab, 13b, 22, 35, Appendix 1   628/26,
29, 35, 36   629/4b, 22bc   630/13, 15, 17bc   631/10
632/17, 19   D171   S61   S68.

Musarum brittanicarum thesaurus: or A choice collection of
English songs, dialogues and catches for two, three,
and four voices in score . . . Leicestershire, 1748.   245
275   333/6ab   486   574/10   628/35   629/22bc   S51
S61.

*A collection revival and refining (from the more gross &
obscene songs) of the old catch book together with a
variety of two, & three part songs* . . . by Abraham
Milner. London, ?1750.   241   262   269   270   274
275   281   284   286   287   333/6ab   419   486   500
502   517   520   521   525   546   574/10   585/2
628/26, 36   D100   D102   S61   S67.

*A collection of songs for two and three voices taken from the
Orpheus britannicus* . . . London, ?1755.   323/3
333/7ab   335/5a   485   486   488   489   499   501

502   503   517   520   521   N526   546   572/11ab
574/15b, 16b   578/6, 7   585/2   602/1   607/11   608
613/1   627/30   628/26, 29, 36   629/4b, 8b, 22bc
630/17bc   632/19   S53   S61.

Harmonia anglicana; or English harmony reviv'd. [London,
?1765].   335/5a   485   486   517   574/15b, 16b
578/1   602/1   613/1   628/26, 29, 30ef   632/17, 19.

The Essex harmony, being a choice collection of the most
celebrated songs and catches . . . by John Arnold, 3rd
ed. London, 1767.   274   287   574/10, 15b, 16b
585/2   S51.

Goodison's edition of Purcell's music. London, ?1790.   4
5   19   35   45   65   321   327   333   583   628   630
631   D241.

*A Collection of songs for two and three voices taken from
'Orpheus britannicus'* . . . London, n.d. [ca. 1790?].
333/6ab   335/2, 5a   485   486   489   499   501   502
503   517   520   521   N526   546   572/11ab
574/15b, 16b   578/1, 6, 7   585/2   602/1   607/11
608   613/1   627/30   628/16b, 30ef, 36, 38   D100.

Apollonian harmony: a collection of . . . glees, catches,
madrigals, canzonetts, rounds & canons . . . by
Aldrich, Arne . . . Purcell . . . and other . . . masters.
The words consistent with female delicacy. 6 Vols.
London, [ca. 1790].   230M/2f   262   267   274   275
419   495   523   574/10   578/1   605/3   609/11
626/7ab   628/16b, 30ef, 36, 38   D100.

The beauties of Purcell in two volumes . . . arranged with a
separate accompaniment for the Pianoforte . . . by Jos.
Corfe. London, 1805.   134   184   191   253   256
274   276   281   286   288   290   321/2a, 5, 14a
327/7   333/10   335/5a   355   370   405   485   498
499   501   502   503   517   521   522   546   571/6
574/12, 14, 15b, 16b, 17   578/1, 3, 6, 9   600/1bd

602/1   604A   609/10   613   626/7ab   627/5bc, 18b,
30, 32b, 35, 38, 19 to 27   628/10, 12, 13, 16b, 19,
20b, 21, 22, 23, 24, 25, 26, 29, 36   629/8bc, 29
630/13, 15, 17abch   631/2e, 5bcv, 6ab, 8, 10, 11a,
13a, 15b, 16b, 17ab   632/13b, 16   D102.

The beauties of Purcell . . . Selected, adapted and arranged
for pianoforte . . . by John Clarke. Vol. I. London,
1809.   321/2a   370   517   521   547/11b, 12, 14, 15b,
16b, 17   578/3, 9   604/A   613/1   628/10, 12, 13, 29,
328, 19b to 25a   630/13, 17h   631/2e, 3b, 5bc, 6ab,
11a, 12a, 13a, 14a, 14c.

*The musical antiquarian edition. The cathedral services,
anthems, hymns and other sacred pieces composed by
Henry Purcell.* Four volumes. Edited by Vincent
Novello. London, 1828, -32, -44.   2   3   4   5   6   7
8   9   11   13B   15   16   18   19   21   22   23   25   26
27   28   29   30   31   32   33   34 (Only mentioned in
preface, mnp)   35   36   37   38   39   40   41   42   43
44   45   47   48   49   50   51   52   54   55   56   57
58C   60   61   62   63   64   65   101   103ab   104   105
106   108   120   123   125   130   131   132   133   134
135   136   137   138   139   140   141   142   143   181
182   183   184   185   186   188   189   190   191   192
193   196   197   198   199   200   230   231   232   D8
D33   D70   D77   S1   S14   S15   S16. (N67 and N68
are mentioned in this preface as missing.)

40 songs, for voice and piano. (Realization by Sergius
Kagen), New York.

A choice collection of lessons for the harpsichord or spinnet,
London, 1696; and *Eight suites*; newly transcribed and
edited by Howard Ferguson from *A choice collection of
lessons for the harpsichord or spinnet (1696)* and the
manuscript sources. New York; see also *Suites, lessons
and pieces for the harpsichord, by Henry Purcell* . . . in

4 volumes, (ed. William Barclay Squire, 4 Vols. in 1; Chester Series no. 36-39), London, 1918; see also *Complete Harpsichord Music*, ed. Christopher Kite, London, 1983.

3 voluntaries [Voluntary for a double organ, D minor; Voluntary on The old hundredth, A major; Voluntary for cornet, C major]. (Gordon Phillips, ed.), New York, 1961. Kbd. score, 13 pp. The first is almost certainly by Henry Purcell, the second has been ascribed equally to Purcell and to Blow, while the third only appears under Purcell's name but probably is not his.

Hess, Albert G., ed. and arr. "Entrée d'Apollon, for soprano recorder or flute, oboe, violin, etc. and piano, virginal or harpsichord . . ." [Contains "Air de Monsieur Purcell," from a ms written about the year 1700 in possession of the author]. London, 1941. Score (8 p.) and recorder part.

Ayres for the Theatre (suite arr. by Leslie Bridgewater). London.

Fantasias and In nomines (ed. Thurston Dart), London, Novello; another edition (ed. Warlock-Mangeot) London, Curwen; another edition: *Fantasien für Streichinstrumente* (ed. Herbert Just), Hannover; another edition by Anthony Ford, Eulenburg.

Sonatas of Three Parts (ed. W. Gillies Whittaker, bowing revised by Mary G. Whittaker). Paris, L'Oiseau Lyre; another edition by Roger Fiske, London, Eulenburg, 1973; 2 vols., xxi, 40; xxi, 43. 790-801

Sonnatas of four parts [10 sonatas for 2 violins, violoncello, and basso continuo for harpsichord or organ], Compos'd by the late Mr. Henry Purcell. London, 1697. 802-811

II. EDITIONS OF SINGLE WORKS AND MOVEMENTS

ANTHEMS

1   Awake, put on thy strength, P. Soc. Ed. XIV, 41.

2   Behold, I bring you glad tidings *Zwei Sätze für kleines Streichorch aus dem Anthem 'Behold, I bring you glad tidings' (Eingerichtet von Hilmar Höckner)*, Wolfenbüttel.

2   Behold, I bring you glad tidings *Ehre sei Gott in her Höhe.*
    Other eds.: Herbert Just; P. Soc. Ed. XXVIII, 1 (ed. Nigel Fortune).

2.1   Overture to 'Behold, I bring you glad tidings.' (In 'Two Overtures from the Anthems,' ed. Robert Noble), London, O.U.P.

3   Behold, now praise the Lord, London, P. Soc. Ed. XIIIA, 49.

4   Be merciful unto me, London, P. Soc. Ed. XXVIII, 28.

5   Blessed are they that fear the Lord, London, P. Soc. Ed. XXVIII, 42.

6   Blessed be the Lord, my strength (ed. Whitford), New York; another edition, London, P. Soc. Ed. XXVIII, 60.

7   Blessed is he that considereth the poor, London, P. Soc. Ed. XXVIII, 71.

8   Blessed is he whose unrighteousness is forgiven, London, P. Soc. Ed., XIIIA, 71.

9   Blessed is the man that feareth the Lord, London, P. Soc. Ed., XXVIII, 83.

10   Blow up the trumpet in Zion, London, P. Soc. Ed. XXVIII, 96.

11   Bow down thine ear, O Lord, London, P. Soc. Ed., XIIIA, 103.

12   Give sentence with me, O God, London, P. Soc. Ed., XXXII, 117.

13A   Hear me, O Lord, and that soon, London, P. Soc. Ed. XIIIA, 87.

13B   Hear me, O Lord, and that soon, London, P. Soc. Ed. XIIIA, 90.

14   Hear my pray'r, O God, London, P. Soc. Ed. XXVIII, 125.

15   Hear my prayer, O Lord, New York, Belwyn; also published by Curwen, Broude, Novello, Presser, P. Soc. Ed. XXVIII, 135.

16   In Thee, O Lord, do I put my trust, London, P. Soc. Ed. XIV, 53.

17A   In the midst of life, London P. Soc. Ed. XIIIA, 1.

17B   In the midst of life, London, P. Soc. Ed. XXVIII, 215.

17   In the midst of life (ed. Paul Boepple), Presser, Philadelphia; also publ. by Carus.

[17C]   In the midst of life, London, P. Soc. Ed. XXIX, 41 (as part of the burial service, which begins with the first Funeral Sentence, 'Man that is born of a woman').

18   It is a good thing to give thanks, London, P. Soc. Ed. XIV, 1.

19   I was glad when they said unto me, London, P. Soc. Ed. XIV, 97.

20   I will give thanks unto thee, O Lord, London, P. Soc. Ed. XVII, 47.

21   I will give thanks unto the Lord, London, P. Soc. Ed. XXVIII, 139; also published by Lawson (ed. Shaw-Parker).

22   I will sing unto the Lord, London, P. Soc. Ed.
      XXVIII, 165.
23   Let God arise, London, P. Soc. Ed. XXVIII, 173.
24   Let mine eyes run down with tears, ed. A. Lewis,
      N. Fortune, London, Novello; also publ. by P.
      Soc. Ed. XXIX, 1.
25   Lord, how long wilt thou be angry? Philadelphia,
      Presser; also published by Moesler (with English
      and German texts), Novello, P. Soc. Ed. XXIX,
      19. [In *Das Chorwerk*, Heft 17, Fünf geistliche
      Chöre zu 4-6 stimmen].
26   Lord, who can tell how oft he offendeth? London,
      P. Soc. Ed. XXIX, 28.
27   Man that is born of a woman, London, Stainer; also
      published by Carus, Galaxy, P. Soc. Ed. XXIX,
      36, London, Novello.
28   My beloved spake, ed. E.J. Dent, London, P. Soc.
      Ed. XIIIA, 24, Novello; also published by
      Stainer, Carus.
29   My heart is fixed, O God, London, P. Soc. Ed.,
      XIV, 112.
30   My heart is inditing, London, P. Soc. Ed. XVII,
      69, Novello; also published by Schott.
31   My song shall be alway of the loving kindness of
      the Lord. [In R.J.S. Stevens, Sacred Music],
      London; see also Purc. Soc. Ed., XXIX, 51.
31   Overture to 'My song shall be alway,' London,
      O.U.P. (In 'Two Overtures from the Anthems,'
      ed. Robert Noble).
32   O consider my adversity, London, P. Soc. Ed.
      XXIX, 68.
33   O give thanks unto the Lord, London, P. Soc. Ed.
      XXIX, 88; also published by E.C. Schirmer.

34   O God, the King of glory (ed. Anthony Lewis and Nigel Fortune), London, P. Soc. Ed. XXIX, 108, Novello; also published by Lorenz.

35   O God, Thou art my God, London P. Soc. Ed. XXIX, 111.

36   O God, Thou hast cast us out, London, P. Soc. Ed. XXIX, 120.

37   O Lord God of hosts, London, P. Soc. Ed. XXIX, 130.

38   O Lord, grant the king a long life, London, P. Soc. Ed. XXIX, 141.

39   O Lord our governor, London, P. Soc. Ed. XXIX, 152.

40   O Lord, rebuke me not, London, P. Soc. Ed. XXIX, 168.

41   O Lord, Thou art my God, London, P. Soc. Ed. XXIX, 179.

42   O praise God in His holiness, London, P. Soc. Ed. XIV, 21.

43   O praise the Lord, all ye heathen, London, P. Soc. Ed. XXXII, 1.

44   O sing unto the Lord, London, P. Soc. Ed. XVII, 119, Novello; also publ. by Peters, Eulenberg, E.C. Schirmer, Hansen-Denm., & Galliard.

45   Out of the deep have I called, London, P. Soc. Ed. XXXII, 8, Novello; also published by Egtved, G. Schirmer.

46   Praise the Lord, O Jerusalem, London, Novello; also published by P. Soc. Ed. XVII, 146, London.

47   Praise the Lord, O my soul, and all that is within me, London, P. Soc. Ed. XIV, 131 Novello; also published by Belwin, Leslie.

48   Praise the Lord, O my soul, O Lord my God,
        London, P. Soc. Ed. XVII, 166.

49   Rejoice in the Lord alway, (Anthem never before
        published). [In *Cathedral* magazine, London, kbd.
        score, vol. 1, p. 136-145, Novello]; also
        published by Belwin, Bourne, CMSR,
        Concordia, C. Fischer, E.C. Schirmer, Stainer,
        P. Soc. Ed. XIV, 155, London.

50   Remember not, Lord, our offences, London, P.
        Soc. Ed. XXXII, 19, Novello; also published by
        Moseler, Peters, E.C. Schirmer, Walton.

51   Save me, O God, for Thy Name's sake, London, P.
        Soc. Ed. XIIIA, 64; also in *Das Chorwerk*, Heft
        17, Fünf geistliche Chöre zu 4-6 stimmen (ed.
        Friedrich Blume).

52   Sing unto God, O ye kingdoms of the earth,
        London P. Soc. Ed. XXXII, 23.

53   The Lord is King, be the people never so impatient,
        London, P. Soc. Ed. XXXII, 36.

54   The Lord is King, the earth may be glad, London,
        P. Soc. Ed. XXXII, 44.

55   The Lord is my light, London, P. Soc. Ed. XIV,
        78.

56   The way of God is an undefiled way, London, P.
        Soc. Ed. XXXII, 58.

57   They that go down to the sea in ships, London, P.
        Soc. Ed. XIIIA, 6; XXXII, 71.

58   Thou knowest, Lord, the secrets of our hearts [first
        setting, first version], London, P. Soc. Ed.
        XIIIA, 6.

58   Thou knowest, Lord, the secrets of our hearts
        [second setting 'Flatt trumpets'], London, P. Soc.
        Ed., XXXII, 88.

58   Thou knowest, Lord, the secrets of our hearts, London, P. Soc. Ed. XXII, 88, Novello; also published by Belwyn, Broude, Carus, Curwen, Fischer, Kjos, Schmitt, E.C. Schirmer, Shapiro, Spratt, Waterloo.

59   Thy righteousness, O God, is very high, London, P. Soc. Ed. XXXII, 124.

60   Thy way, O God, is holy, London, P. Soc. Ed. XXXII, 91.

61   Thy word is a lantern, London, P. Soc. Ed. XXXII, 101, Novello; also published by Belwyn.

62   Turn Thou us, O good Lord, London, P. Soc. Ed. XXXII, 111.

63   Unto Thee will I cry [In *Hortus Musicus*, 163] (ed. Herbert Just), Kassel; also in London, P. Soc. Ed. XVII, 20.

64   Who hath believed our report? London, P. Soc. Ed. XIIIA, 11.

65   Why do the heathen so furiously rage? London, P. Soc. Ed. XVII, 1.

N66   If the Lord himself, London, British Library, Add. MS 50860.

N67   I will love Thee, O Lord [In *Musical Quarterly*, ed. F. B. Zimmerman], New York, 1959 v. 45, no. 3, pp. 302-311; also publ. in P. Soc. Ed. XXVIII, 157, and in University of Pittsburgh Choral Series.

N68   Praise the Lord, ye servants (fragment), see Thematic Catalogue.

N69   The Lord is King, and hath put on glorious apparel, London, P. Soc. Ed. XXXII, 30.

CANONS

101 Alleluia ('Canon 4 in 2, *recte et retro*'), London, 1828-[44].
102 Domine non exaltatum est cor meum, London, P. Soc. Ed. XXXII, 172.
103 Gloria Patri et Filio, London, P. Soc. Ed., XXXII, 163.
104 Gloria Patri et Filio ('Canon 3 in 1'), London, P. Soc. Ed. XXXII, 159.
105 Gloria Patri et Filio ('Canon 4 in 1 *per arsin et thesin*'), London, P. Soc. Ed., XXXII, 161.
106 Glory be to the Father (*'Canon 4 in 1'*), London, Pur. Soc. Ed. XXXII, 168.
107 God is gone up (*'Canon 7 in 1 at the unison'*), London, Pur. Soc. Ed. XXXII, 170.
108 Laudate Dominum (*'Canon 3 in 1'*), London, P. Soc. Ed. XXXII, 170.
109 Miserere mei (*'Canon 4 in 2'*), London, P. Soc. Ed. XXXII, 171.
N110 Alleluia (*'Canon'*), Birmingham, ed. Michael Broome, ca. 1728.

CHANTS

120 Chant No. 1 in a minor, London, P. Soc. ed. XXXII, 174.
121 Chant No. 2 in G Major, London, P. Soc. ed. XXXII, 173.
122 Chant No. 3 in G Major, London, P. Soc. ed. XXXII, 174.
123 Chant No. 4 in d minor, London, C. & S. Thompson, 1767.

124   Chant No. 5 in G Major (authenticity not established).

125   Chant No. 6 in g minor, London, P. Soc. Ed. XXXII, 173.

126   Double Chant in a minor, York Minster MS 83, Score, 1757.

HYMNS, PSALMS, AND SACRED PART-SONGS

130   Ah! few and full of sorrows, London, P. Soc. Ed. XXX, 109.

131   Beati omnes qui timent (ed. Franklin B. Zimmerman), Delaware Water Gap, Pa.; also published by Novello; P. Soc. Ed. XXXII, 137.

132   Early, O Lord, my fainting soul, P. Soc. Ed. XXX, 117.

133   Hear me, O Lord, the great support, London, P. Soc. Ed. XXX, 127; also published separately by Novello.

134   In guilty night, 'Saul and the witch of Endor,' London, P. Soc. Ed. XXXII, 128; also available in Novello performing edition and in *Harmonia Sacra:* the figured bass realized by Benjamin Britten, the vocal parts edited by Peter Pears, ed. Benjamin Britten, London.

135   Jehovah quam multi, London, P. Soc. Ed. XXXII, 147; also published by Carus, Gray, E.C. Schirmer.

136   Lord, I can suffer thy rebukes, London, P. Soc. Ed. XXX, 136.

137   Lord, not to us, London, P. Soc. Ed., XXX, 146.

138   O all ye people clap your hands, London, P. Soc. Ed. XXX, 148; also published in performing edition by Novello, and by Egtved.

139 O happy man that fears the Lord, London, P. Soc. Ed. XXX, 157.

140 O, I'm sick of life, London, P. Soc. Ed. XXX, 160; also published by G. Schirmer.

141 O, Lord, our governor, London, P. Soc. Ed. XXX, 167.

142 Plung'd in the confines of despair, London, P. Soc. Ed. XXX, 180; also published by Shawnee Press.

143 Since God so tender a regard, London, P. Soc. Ed. XXX, 187.

144 When on my sickbed I langish, London, P. Soc. Ed. XXX, 194; also published by G. Schirmer.

SACRED SONGS AND DUETS

181 Awake and with attention hear, 'A morning hymn,' (ed. Vincent Novello), London, P. Soc. Ed. XXX, 109.

182 Awake, ye dead, London, P. Soc. Ed. XXX, 98.

183 Begin the song and strike the living lyre, London, P. Soc. Ed. XXX, 18.

184 Close thine eyes and sleep secure, 'Upon a quiet conscience,' (Words by Francis Quarles, London, P. Soc. Ed. XXX, 105; also ed. John Edmunds), Boston.

185 Full of wrath his threatening breath, London, P. Soc. Ed. XXX, 28.

186 Great God and just, London, P. Soc. Ed. XXX, 33.

187 Hosanna to the highest, London, P. Soc. Ed. XXX, 38.

188 How have I stray'd? London, P. Soc. Ed. XXX, 44.

189   How long, great God, London, P. Soc. Ed. XXX, 48.

190   In the black dismal dungeon of despair, London, P. Soc. Ed. XXX, 109; also in *Harmonia Sacra* (ed. Benjamin Britten), London, Boosey & Hawkes.

191   Let the night perish, 'Job's curse,' London, P. Soc. Ed. XXX, 57.

192   Lord, what is man? London, P. Soc. Ed. XXX, 62; also in *Harmonia Sacra, Three divine hymns* (ed. Benjamin Britten), London.

193   Now that the sun has veil'd his light, 'An evening hymn,' London, P. Soc. Ed. XXX, 70; also in *Harmonia Sacra* (ed. Michael Tippett and Walter G. Bergmann), London, Novello (adapted by H. A. Chambers); and in *Harmonica Sacra* (ed. Benjamin Britten).

194   O Lord, since I experienced have, London, P. Soc. Ed. XXX.

195   Sleep, Adam, sleep, 'Adam's sleep,' London, P. Soc. Ed. XXX, 75; also ed. John Edmunds, Boston.

196   Tell me, some pitying angel, 'The blessed virgin's expostulation,' London, P. Soc. Ed. XXX, 177; also arr. from the figured bass by Michael Tippett and Walter Bergmann; and available in *Harmonia Sacra* (the fig. bass realized by Benjamin Britten, the vocal parts edited by Peter Pears), London, Boosey & Hawkes.

197   The earth trembled, and heav'n closed, London, P. Soc. Ed. XXX, 85.

198   Thou wakeful shepherd, 'A morning hymn,' London, P. Soc. Ed. XXX, 88; also in *Harmonia Sacra,* Two divine hymns and an Alleluia (the

figured basses realized by B. Britten, the voc. pts.
ed. by P. Pears), London.

199   We sing to him, London, P. Soc. Ed. XXX, 91;
also ed. John Edmunds, Boston; and by Benjamin
Britten in *Harmonia Sacra.*

200   With sick and famish'd eyes, a song by Henry
Purcell, the words by George Herbert, London,
P. Soc. Ed. XXX, 94.

SERVICES

230   Service in B-flat Major, London, P. Soc. Ed.
XXIII, 1; see also Te Deum laudamus; Magnificat;
Nunc dimittis [In *Das Chorwerk*, Heft 17, Fünf
geistliche Chöre zu 4-6 stimmen] (ed. Friedrich
Blume), Wolfenbüttel; and also 'Hymn for the
holy communion, and other hymns,' [Musical
fragments in manuscript: Drexel 3326] bound in
with J. Gehot, Musical instructions for every
musical instrument; as also Nunc dimittis, *Der
Lobgesang Simeons*, Wolfenbüttel; as also
[Service in B-flat Major] Magnificat and Nunc
dimittis, mixed voices, organ, piano ad lib. (ed.
Walter Buszin), New York.

231   Evening service in g minor, London, P. Soc. Ed.
XXIII, 80; also ed. Maurice Bevan, London,
Novello; also published by Augsburg.

232   Te Deum, & jubilate, for voices and instruments,
made for St. Cecilia's Day, 1694, London, P.
Soc. Ed. XXIII, 90; also published by Eulenberg,
Kalmus, Novello, G. Schirmer, Schott.

CATCHES

240   A health to the nut-brown lass, London, P. Soc.
       Ed. XXII, 5.

241   An ape, a lion, a fox and an ass, London, P. Soc.
       Ed. XXII, 1.

242   As Roger last night, London, P. Soc. Ed. XXII, 1.

243   Bring the bowl and cool Nantz, London, P. Soc.
       Ed. XXII, 1.

244   Call for the reck'ning, London, P. Soc. Ed. XXII,
       2.

245   Come, let us drink, London, P. Soc. Ed. XXII, 2.

246   Come, my hearts, play your parts, London, P. Soc.
       Ed. XXII, 3.

247   Down with Bacchus, London, P. Soc. Ed. XXII,
       3.

248   Drink on, till night be spent, London, P. Soc. Ed.
       XXII, 4.

249   Full bags, a brisk bottle, London, P. Soc. Ed.
       XXII, 18.

250   God save our sov'reign Charles, London, P. Soc.
       Ed. XXII, 4.

251   Great Apollo and Bacchus, London, P. Soc. Ed.
       XXII, 4.

252   Here's a health, pray let it pass, London, P. Soc.
       Ed. XXII, 5.

253   Here's that will challenge all the fair, London, P.
       Soc. Ed. XXII, 5; also published by Schirmer,
       New York.

254   He that drinks is immortal, London, P. Soc. Ed.
       XXII, 4.

255   If all be true that I do think, London, P. Soc. Ed.
       XXII, 6.

256   I gave her cakes and I gave her ale, London, P. Soc. Ed. XXII, 6; also published by Schirmer, New York.

257   Is Charleroi's siege come too? London, P. Soc. Ed. XXII, 6.

258   Let the grave folks go preach, London, P. Soc. Ed. XXII, 7.

259   Let us drink to the blades, London, P. Soc. Ed. XXII, 7.

260   My lady's coachman, John, London, P. Soc. Ed. XXII, 8.

261   Now England's great council, London, P. Soc. Ed. XXII, 8.

262   Now we are met and humours agree, London, P. Soc. Ed. XXII, 9.

263   Of all the instruments that are, London, P. Soc. Ed. XXII, 9.

264   Once in our lives let us drink to our wives, London, P. Soc. Ed. XXII, 9.

265   Once, twice, thrice I Julia tried, London, P. Soc. Ed. XXII, 10; also published by Schirmer, New York.

266   One industrious insect, London, P. Soc. Ed. XXII, 10.

267   Pale faces, stand by, London, P. Soc. Ed. XXII, 10.

268   Pox on you for a fop, London, P. Soc. Ed. XXII, 11.

269   Prithee ben't so sad and serious, London, P. Soc. Ed. XXII, 11.

270   Room for th' express, London, P. Soc. Ed. XXII, 12.

271   Since the Duke is return'd, London, P. Soc. Ed. XXII, 12.

272   Since time so kind to us does prove, London, P. Soc. Ed. XXII, 12.

273   Sir Walter enjoying his damsel, London, P. Soc. Ed. XXII, 13.

274   Soldier, take off thy wine, London, P. Soc. Ed. XXII, 13.

275   Sum up all the delights, London, P. Soc. Ed. XXII, 13.

276   The Macedon youth left behind him this truth, London, P. Soc. Ed. XXII, 8.

277   The miller's daughter riding to the fair, London, P. Soc. Ed. XXII, 19.

278   The surrender of Lim'rick, London, P. Soc. Ed. XXII, 14.

279   'Tis easy to force, London, P. Soc. Ed. XXII, 14.

280   'Tis too late for a coach, London, P. Soc. Ed. XXII, 14.

281   'Tis women makes us love, London, P. Soc. Ed. XXII, 14.

282   To all lovers of music, London, P. Soc. Ed. XXII, 15.

283   To thee and to a maid, London, P. Soc. Ed. XXII, 15.

284   True Englishmen drink a good health to the Mitre, London, P. Soc. Ed. XXII, 15.

285   Under a green elm lies Luke Shepherd's helm, London, P. Soc. Ed. XXII, 16.

286   Under this stone lies Gabriel John, London, P. Soc. Ed. XXII, 16.

287   When V and I together meet, London, P. Soc. Ed. XXII, 16.

288   Who comes there? Stand! London, P. Soc. Ed. XXII, 16.

289   Wine in a morning makes us frolic, London, P. Soc. Ed. XXII, 17.

290   Would you know how we meet? London, P. Soc. Ed. XXII, 17.

291   Young Collin cleaving of a beam, London, P. Soc. Ed. XXII, 17.

292   Young John, the gard'ner, London, P. Soc. Ed. XXII, 18.

ODES, BIRTHDAY SONGS, WELCOME SONGS, AND OCCASIONAL VOCAL WORKS

320   Arise, my muse, 'Birthday song for Queen Mary,' 1690, London, P. Soc. Ed. XI, 36.

321   Celebrate this festival, 'Ode on the Queen's birthday,' 1693, London, P. Soc. Ed. XXIV, 36; also edited, O.U.P.

321.6   Let sullen discord smile, from 'Celebrate this festival,' [In *A suite of songs*] (Fig. basses realized by B. Britten, voc. pts. ed. by P. Pears); London, Boosey & Hawkes.

322   Celestial music did the Gods inspire, London, P. Soc. Ed. XXVII, 29.

323   Come, come ye sons of art, 'A birthday ode for Queen Mary,' 1694, London, P. Soc. Ed. XXIV, 87; also edited by Michael Tippett and Walter Bergmann, London, Schott; also published by Novello in performing edition.

323.3   Sound the trumpet, from 'Come ye sons of art away.' London, Alsbach & Doyer, Ashdown, Banks Music, Boosey, Elkan-Vogel, Harmonia, Presser, G. Schirmer, Schott, Southern.

323.5   Strike the viol, from 'Come ye sons of art away' (ed. John Edmunds), Boston.

324   Fly bold rebellion, 'The welcome song perform'd to his majesty in the year 1683,' London, P. Soc. Ed. XV, 116.

325   From hardy climes 'A song that was perform'd to Prince George upon his marriage with the Lady Ann,' 1683, London, P. Soc. Ed. XXVII, 1.

326   From those serene and rapturous joys 'On the king's return to White-hall, after his summer's progress, 1684,' London, P. Soc. Ed. XVIII, 1.

327   Great parent, hail 'Commemoration Ode performed at Christ Church, Dublin, January 9th, 1694,' London, P. Soc. Ed. XXVII, 59.

328   Hail, bright Cecilia, 'A Song for St. Cecilia's Day,' London, P. Soc. Ed. VIII, 1; also published by Schott.

328.5   Soul of the world, from 'Hail, bright Cecilia,' Philadelphia, Presser.

328.6   Thou tuns't this world, from 'Hail, bright Cecilia,' [In *A suite of songs*] (Fig. basses realized by B. Britten, voc. pts. ed. by P. Pears).

329   Laudate Ceciliam, 'A Latin song made upon St. Cecilia . . .' London, P. Soc. Ed. X, 44.

330   Light of the world, *Lost.*

331   Love's goddess sure was blind, 'Birthday song for Queen Mary,' 1692, London, P. Soc. Ed. XXIV, 1.

332   Now does the glorious day appear, 'Birthday song for Queen Mary,' ?1689, London, P. Soc. Ed. XI, 1.

333   Of old when heroes thought it base, 'The Yorkshire feast song,' London, P. Soc. Ed. I, 1.

333.4   The bashful Thames, for solo tenor and three recorders with accompaniment for harpsichord or piano, 'The Yorkshire feast song,' London, Novello; also publ, by E.C. Schirmer, Boston.

333.11 So when the glitt'ring Queen of Night, from 'Of old, when heroes thought it base,' [In *A suite of songs*] (Figured basses realized by Benjamin Britten, vocal parts ed. by Peter Pears), London.

334 Raise, raise the voice, 'A Song for St. Cecilia's Day,' London, P. Soc. Ed. X, 26.

335 Sound the trumpet, beat the drum, 'Birthday song for King James, 1687,' London, P. Soc. Ed. XVIII, 121.

336 Swifter, Isis, swifter flow, 'A Welcome Song in the Year 1681 For the King [Charles II],' London, P. Soc. Ed. XV, 24.

337 The summer's absence unconcerned we bear, 'A welcome song for his majesty at his return from New Market October the 21—1682,' London, P. Soc. Ed. XV, 83.

338 Welcome, glorious morn, 'Birthday song for Queen Mary' April 30th, 1691, London, P. Soc. Ed. XI, 72.

339 Welcome to all the pleasures 'Ode for St. Cecilia's day,' 1683, London, P. Soc. Ed. X, 1; also ed. by Walter Bergmann and Michael Tippett, London, Peters; also published by Cooper, Galliard, Novello.

340 Welcome, Vicegerent of the mighty King, 'Welcome song for Charles II' September 9th, 1680, London, P. Soc. Ed. XV, 1.

341 What shall be done in behalf of the man, 'A welcome song for his royall highness at his return from Scotland in the Year 1682,' London, P. Soc. Ed. XXII, 1.

342   Who can from joy refrain? 'A Birthday song for the
        Duke of Gloucester, July 24th, 1695,' London,
        P. Soc. Ed. XXII, 1.
342.1   Overture from 'Who can from joy refrain?' London,
        Novello.
343   Why are all the Muses mute? 'Welcome song for
        1685, being the first song performed to King
        James ye 2nd,' London, P. Soc. Ed. XVIII, 37.
344   Ye tuneful muses, raise your heads, 'Welcome song
        for King James II,' London, P. Soc. Ed. XVIII,
        80; also available in Novello's performing edition.

SOLO SONGS

351   Aaron thus propos'd to Moses: Not in Purcell
        Society Edition; see Commentary in *Henry
        Purcell, 1659-1695: An Analytical Catalogue of
        his music,* p. 178.
352   Ah! cruel nymph! you give despair, London, Pur.
        Soc. Ed. XXV, 1.
353   Ah how pleasant 'tis to love, London, Pur. Soc.
        Ed. XXV, 4; also available in an edition from
        Oxford University Press, London.
354   Ah! what pains, what racking thoughts, London,
        Pur. Soc. Ed. XXV, 4.
355   Amidst the shades and cool refreshing streams,
        London, Pur. Soc. Ed. XXV, 6.
356   Amintas, to my grief I see, London, Pur. Soc. Ed.
        XXV, 9.
357   Amintor, heedless of his flocks, London, Pur. Soc.
        Ed. XXV, 10.
358   Ask me to love no more, London, Pur. Soc. Ed.
        XXV, 11.

359 A thousand sev'ral ways I tried, London, Pur. Soc. Ed. XXV, 178.

360 Bacchus is a pow'r divine, London, Pur. Soc. Ed. XXV, 13.

361 Beware, poor shepherds! London, Pur. Soc. Ed. XXV, 18.

362 Cease, anxious world, your fruitless pain, London, Pur. Soc. Ed. XXV, 19.

363 Cease O my sad soul, London, Pur. Soc. Ed. XXV, 21; also available in an edition from Concord, St. Louis.

364 Celia's fond, too long I've lov'd her, London, Pur. Soc. Ed. XXV, 22.

365 Corinna is divinely fair, London, Pur. Soc. Ed. XXV, 24.

366 Corinna when you left the town, *Lost.*

367 Cupid, the slyest rogue alive, London, Pur. Soc. Ed. XXV, 26.

368 Farewell all joys! London, Pur. Soc. Ed. XXV, 32.

369 Fly swift, ye hours, London, Pur. Soc. Ed. XXV, 39.

370 From silent shades, 'Bess of Bedlam,' London, Pur. Soc. Ed. XXV, 45; Part for voice and figured bass, transcr. for flute at end, also [In 6 songs, *Orpheus britannicus,* the figured basses realized by Benjamin Britten, the vocal parts ed. Peter Pears].

371 Hears not my Phyllis? London, Pur. Soc. Ed. XXV, 45.

372 He himself courts his own ruin, London, Pur. Soc. Ed. XXV, 57.

373 How delightful's the life of an innocent swain, London, Pur. Soc. Ed. XXV, 45.

374   How I sigh when I think of the charms of my
        swain, London, Pur. Soc. Ed. XXV, 66.
375   I came, I saw, I was undone, London, Pur. Soc.
        Ed. XXV, 67.
376   I envy not a monarch's fate, London, Pur. Soc. Ed.
        XXV, 72.
377   I fain would be free, London, Pur. Soc. Ed. XXV,
        73.
378   If grief has any pow'r to kill, London, Pur. Soc.
        Ed. XXV, 82.
379A   If music be the food of love (First setting, version
        1), London, Pur. Soc. Ed. XXV, 83; also in 6
        songs, *Orpheus britannicus*, the figured basses
        realized by Benjamin Britten, vocal parts edited by
        P. Pears, London.
379B   If music be the food of love (First setting, original
        version), London, Pur. Soc. Ed. XXV, 84.
379C   If music be the food of love, (Second setting),
        London, Pur. Soc. Ed. XXV, 85; also available in
        an edition by Michael Tippett and Walter G.
        Bergmann, London; In Seven songs, *Orpheus
        britannicus*, the figured basses realized by
        Benjamin Britten, the vocal parts edited by Peter
        Pears, London, and in an edition by Robert Evett,
        Washington, D.C.
380   If pray'rs and tears, London, Pur. Soc. Ed. XXV,
        89.
381   I lov'd fair Ceilia, London, Pur. Soc. Ed. XXV,
        77.
382   I love and I must, London, Pur. Soc. Ed. XXV,
        74.
383   Incassum, Lesbia, 'The Queen's epicedium, elegy
        on the death of Queen Mary, 1695,' London, Pur.
        Soc. Ed. XXV, 87; also in an edition, the figured

bass realized by Benjamin Britten, the vocal parts edited by Peter Pears, New York, Boosey & Hawkes.

384 In Cloris all soft charms agree, London, Pur. Soc. Ed. XXV, 95.

385 In vain we dissemble, London, Pur. Soc. Ed. XXV, 96.

386 I resolve against cringing, London, Pur. Soc. Ed. XXV, 79.

387 I saw that you were grown so high, London, Pur. Soc. Ed. XXV, 80.

388 I take no pleasure, London, Pur. Soc. Ed. XXV, also available in an edition by John Edmunds, Boston, R. D. Row; and in 5 Songs for medium voice, the figured basses realized by Benjamin Britten, the vocal parts edited by Peter Pears, London.

389 Leave these useless arts in loving, London, Pur. Soc. Ed. XXV, 102.

390 Let each gallant heart, London, Pur. Soc. Ed. XXV, 103.

391 Let formal lovers still pursue, London, Pur. Soc. Ed. XXV, 105.

392 Love arms himself in Celia's eyes, London, Pur. Soc. Ed. XXV, 108.

393 Love is now become a trade, London, Pur. Soc. Ed. XXV, 111.

394 Lovely Albina's come ashore, London, Pur. Soc. Ed. XXV, 117.

395 Love's pow'r in my heart shall find no compliance, London, Pur. Soc. Ed. XXV, 117.

396 Love, thou cans't hear, tho' thou art blind, London, Pur. Soc. Ed. XXV, 112.

397   More love or more disdain, London, Pur. Soc. Ed.
      XXV, 120; also in an edition by Brodt.
398   Musing on cares of human fate, in *The Theatre of
      Music*, 1685, Book II, No. 4.
399   My heart, whenever you appear, London, Pur. Soc.
      Ed. XXV, 123.
400   Not all my torments can your pity move, London,
      Pur. Soc. Ed. XXV, 130; also in 6 songs,
      Orpheus britannicus, the figured basses realized
      by Benjamin Britten, the vocal parts edited by
      Peter Pears, London.
401   No watch, dear Celia, just is found, London, Pur.
      Soc. Ed. XXV, 128.
402   O! fair Cedaria, hide those eyes, London, Pur. Soc.
      Ed. XXV, 132.
403   O! how happy's he, who from bus'ness free,
      London, Pur. Soc. Ed. XXV, 136.
404   Olinda in the shades unseen, London, Pur. Soc. Ed.
      XXV, 141.
405   On the brow of Richmond hill, London, Pur. Soc.
      Ed. XXV, 142; also in Seven songs, *Orpheus
      britannicus*, the figured basses realized by
      Benjamin Britten, the vocal parts edited by Peter
      Pears, London, Boosey & Hawkes.
406   O solitude, my sweetest choice, London, Pur. Soc.
      Ed. XXV, 137.
407   Pastora's beauties when unblown, London, Pur.
      Soc. Ed. XXV, 144.
408   Phyllis, I can ne'er forgive it, London, Pur. Soc.
      Ed. XXV, 145.
409   Phyllis, talk no more of passion, London, Pur. Soc.
      Ed. XXV, 146.
410   Pious Celinda goes to pray'rs, London, Pur. Soc.
      Ed. XXV, 148; also in Seven songs, *Orpheus*

britannicus, the figured basses realized by Benjamin Britten, the vocal parts edited by Peter Pears, London, Boosey & Hawkes.

411 Rashly I swore I would disown, London, Pur. Soc. Ed. XXV, 150.

412 Sawney is a bonny lad, London, Pur. Soc. Ed. XXV, 151.

413 She loves and she confesses too, London, Pur. Soc. Ed. XXV, 156.

414 She that would gain a faithful lover, London, Pur. Soc. Ed. XXV, 159.

415 She who my poor heart possesses, London, Pur. Soc. Ed. XXV, 161.

416 Since one poor view has drawn my heart, London, Pur. Soc. Ed. XXV, 163.

417 Spite of the god-head, pow'rful Love, London, Pur. Soc. Ed. XXV, 166.

418 Sweet, be no longer sad, London, Pur. Soc. Ed. XXV, 169.

419 Vacant.

420 Sylvia, now your scorn give over, London, Pur. Soc. Ed. XXV, 162.

421 The fatal hour comes on apace, London, Pur. Soc. Ed. XXV, 36.

422 They say you're angry, London, Pur. Soc. Ed. XXV, 171.

423 This poet sings the Trojan wars, London, Pur. Soc. Ed. XXV, 174.

424 Through mournful shades and solitary groves, London, Pur. Soc. Ed. XXV, 179.

425 Turn, then thine eyes, London, Pur. Soc. Ed. XXV, 181; also in Seven songs, *Orpheus britannicus*, the figured basses realized by

Benjamin Britten, the vocal parts edited by Peter Pears, London.

426   Urge me no more, this airy mirth, London, Pur. Soc. Ed. XXV, 183.

427   We now, my Thyrsis, never find, London, Pur. Soc. Ed. XXV, 186.

428A What a sad fate is mine, London, Pur. Soc. Ed. XXV, 191.

428B What a sad fate is mine, London, Pur. Soc. Ed. XXV, 188. [NB: these two versions are shown in reverse order in the original Purcell Society Edition.]

429   What can we poor females do? London, Pur. Soc. Ed. XXV, 194.

430   When first Amintas sued for a kiss, London, Pur. Soc. Ed. XXV, 199; also edited by Michael Tippett and Walter Bergmann, London.

431   When first my shepherdess and I, London, Pur. Soc. Ed. XXV, 201.

432   When her languishing eyes said 'Love,' London, Pur. Soc. Ed. XXV, 202.

433   When I a lover pale do see, London, Pur. Soc. Ed. XXV, 203.

434   When my Acmelia smiles, London, Pur. Soc. Ed. XXV, 204.

435   When Strephon found his passion vain, London, Pur. Soc. Ed. XXV, 206.

436   When Thyrsis did the splendid eye, London, Pur. Soc. Ed. XXV, 207.

437   While Thyrsis, wrapt in downy sleep, London, Pur. Soc. Ed. XXV, 208.

438   Whilst Cynthia sang, London, Pur. Soc. Ed. XXV, 209.

439   Whither would my passion run? *Lost.*

440   Who but a slave, London, Pur. Soc. Ed. XXV, 211.

441   Who can behold Florella's charms? London, Pur. Soc. Ed. XXV, 212.

442   Why so serious, why so grave? London, Pur. Soc. Ed. XXV, 214.

443   Ye happy swains whose nymphs are kind, London, Pur. Soc. Ed. XXV, 215.

444   Stript of their green our groves appear, London, Pur. Soc. Ed. XXV, 167.

SOLO SONGS WITH CHORUS

461   Beneath a dark, a melancholy grove, London, Pur. Soc. Ed. XXV, 16.

462   Draw near, you lovers that complain, London, Pur. Soc. Ed. XXV, 29.

463   Farewell, ye rocks, ye seas, ye sands, London, Pur. Soc. Ed. XXV, 33.

464   Gentle shepherds, you that know the charms of tuneful breath, 'A pastoral elegy on the death of Mr. John Playford,' the words by Mr. Tate. Set by Mr. Henry Purcell, London, Pur. Soc. Ed. XXV, 49.

465   High on a throne of glitt'ring ore, London, Pur. Soc. Ed. XXV, 59.

466   Let us, kind Lesbia, give way in soft embraces, London, Pur. Soc. Ed. XXV, 106.

467   Musing on cares of human fate, London, Pur. Soc. Ed. XXV, 121.

468   No, to what purpose should I speak? London, Pur. Soc. Ed. XXV, 124.

469   Scarce had the rising sun appear'd, London, Pur. Soc. Ed. XXV, 152.

470   See, how the fading glories of the year, London, Pur. Soc. Ed. XXV, 153.

471   Since the pox or the plague, London, Pur. Soc. Ed. XXV, 164.

472   What hope for us remains now he is gone? London, Pur. Soc. Ed. XXV, 45.

473   Young Thyrsis' fate the hills and groves deplore, London, Pur. Soc. Ed. XXV, 216.

TWO-PART SONGS

480   Above the tumults of a busy state, London, Pur. Soc. Ed. XXII, 150.

481   A grasshopper and a fly, London, Pur. Soc. Ed. XXII, 54.

482   Alas, how barbarous are we, London, Pur. Soc. Ed. XXII, 153.

483   Come, dear companions of th' Arcadian fields, London, Pur. Soc. Ed. XXII, 40.

484   Come, lay by all care, London, Pur. Soc. Ed. XXII, 21.

485   Dulcibella, whene'er I sue for a kiss, London, Pur. Soc. Ed. XXII, 105.

486   Fair Cloe my breast so alarms, London, Pur. Soc. Ed. XXII, 97.

487   Fill the bowl with rosy wine, London, Pur. Soc. Ed. XXII, 55.

488   For love ev'ry creature is form'd, London, Pur. Soc. Ed. XXII, 118.

489   Go tell Amynta [Amintor], gentle swain, London, Pur. Soc. Ed. XXII, 133.

490   Haste, gentle Charon, London, Pur. Soc. Ed. XXII, 172.

491   Has yet your breast no pity learn'd? London, Pur. Soc. Ed. XXII, 66.

492   Hence, fond deceiver, London, Pur. Soc. Ed. XXII, 62.

493   Here, here's to thee, Dick, London, Pur. Soc. Ed. XXII, 69.

494   How great are the blessings, London, Pur. Soc. Ed. XXII, 43.

495   How sweet is the air and refreshing, London, Pur. Soc. Ed. XXII, 54.

496   In all our Cynthia's shining sphere, London, Pur. Soc. Ed. XXII, 125. [NB: The ascription to Henry Purcell is very doubtful, since the song is definitely ascribed to Daniel Purcell in the text of Elkanah Settle's *The World in the Moon*.]

497   In some kind dream, London, Pur. Soc. Ed. XXII, 159.

498   I saw fair Cloris all alone, London, Pur. Soc. Ed. XXII, 36.

499   I spy Celia, Celia eyes me, London, Pur. Soc. Ed. XXII, 141.

500   Julia, your unjust disdain, London, Pur. Soc. Ed. XXII, 139.

501   Let Hector, Achilles, and each brave commander, London, Pur. Soc. Ed. XXII, 82.

502   Lost is my quiet forever, London, Pur. Soc. Ed. XXII, 91; also available in a publication by E.C. Schirmer, Boston.

503   Nestor, who did to thrice man's age attain, London, Pur. Soc. Ed. XXII, 88.

504   O dive custos auricae domus [O guardian god of the house of Orange], 'Elegy upon the death of Queen Mary,' London, Pur. Soc. Ed. XXII, 112; also

available in an edition by Michael Tippett and Walter G. Bergmann, New York.

505   Oft am I by the women told, London, Pur. Soc. Ed. XXII, 52.

506   O! what a scene does entertain my sight, London, Pur. Soc. Ed. XXII, 166.

507   Saccharissa's grown old, London, Pur. Soc. Ed. XXII, 46.

508   See where she sits, London, Pur. Soc. Ed. XXII, 157.

509   Sit down, my dear Sylvia, London, Pur. Soc. Ed. XXII, 26.

510   Soft notes and gently rais'd accent, London, Pur. Soc. Ed. XXII, 32.

511   Sylvia, thou brighter eye of night, London, Pur. Soc. Ed. XXII, 155.

512   Sylvia, 'tis true you're fair, London, Pur. Soc. Ed. XXII, 38.

513   There ne'er was so wretched a lover, London, Pur. Soc. Ed. XXII, 20.

514   Though my mistress be fair, London, Pur. Soc. Ed. XXII, 23.

515   Trip it in a ring, London, Pur. Soc. Ed. XXII, 132.

516   Underneath this myrtle shade, London, Pur. Soc. Ed. XXII, 100.

517   Were I to choose the greatest bliss, London, Pur. Soc. Ed. XXII, 86.

518   What can we poor females do? London, Pur. Soc. Ed. XXII, 104.

519   When gay Philander left the plain, London, Pur. Soc. Ed. XXII, 20.

520   When, lovely Phyllis, thou art kind, London, Pur. Soc. Ed. XXII, 30.

521   When Myra sings, London, Pur. Soc. Ed. XXII,
        109.
522   When Teucer from his father fled, London, Pur.
        Soc. Ed. XXII, 48.
523   While bolts and bars my days control, London, Pur.
        Soc. Ed. XXII, 130.
524   While you for me alone had charms, London, Pur.
        Soc. Ed. XXII, 146.
525   Why, my Daphne, why complaining? London, Pur.
        Soc. Ed. XXII, 93.
N526   To this place we've now come, '94 Songs by Henry
        Purcell, D. Purcell, Blow, *et altri*' (undated
        edition).

THREE- AND FOUR-PART SONGS
AND LARGER VOCAL WORKS

541   Hark, Damon, hark, London, Pur. Soc. Ed.
        XXVII, 93.
542   Hark how the wild musicians, London, Pur. Soc.
        Ed. XXVII, 100.
543   How pleasant is this flowery plain, London, Pur.
        Soc. Ed. XXVII, 74. See also *Wie wonnig ist's
        auf Blumigem gefield* (ed. Herbert Just), Kassel.
544   If ever I more riches did desire, London, Pur. Soc.
        Ed. XXVII, 118.
545   In a deep vision's intellectual scene, London, Pur.
        Soc. Ed. XXVII, 140.
546   'Tis wine was made to rule the day, London, Pur.
        Soc. Ed. XXVII, 177.
547   We reap all the pleasures (fragmentary), London,
        Pur. Soc. Ed. XXVII, 156.
548   When the cock begins to crow, London, Pur. Soc.
        Ed. XXXII, 181.

INCIDENTAL MUSIC

570   Abdelazer, or the moor's revenge, London, Pur.
       Soc. Ed. XVI, 1; see also Abdelazer Suite (ed.
       Edward Fendler), New York, Music Press;
       [Abdelazer, selections] Hornpipe, air and minuet,
       (ed. Hilmar Höckner), Wolfenbüttel.

571   A fool's preferment, or The three dukes of
       Dunstable, London, Pur. Soc. Ed. XVI, 1.

571.6 I'll sail upon the dog star, London, Novello; also
       [In Seven songs, *Orph. brit.*, the fig. basses
       realized by B. Britten, voc. pts. ed. P. Pears,
       London.]

572   Amphitryon; or, The two Sosias. A comedy. As it is
       acted at the Theatre Royal. Written by Mr.
       Dryden, to which is added, the musick of the
       Songs, compos'd by Mr. Purcell, London, Pur.
       Soc. Ed. XVI, 21; also available in an edition by
       Novello, London.

573   Aureng-Zebe, or The great mogul, London, Pur.
       Soc. Ed. XVI, 42.

574   Bonduca, a tragedy, altered from Beaumont and
       Fletcher, the music composed A.D. 1695, by
       Henry Purcell, London, Pur. Soc. Ed. XVI, 42;
       also edited & preceded by an historical sketch of
       English dramatic music by Edward F. Rimbault,
       The Musical Antiquarian, London.

575   Circe, 'The sacrificial scene,' London, Pur. Soc.
       Ed. XVI, 95; also available in a separate
       performing edition, published by Novello.

576   Cleomenes, the Spartan Hero, London, Pur. Soc.
       Ed. XVI, 120.

577   Distressed Innocence, or the princess of Persia,
       London, Pur. Soc. Ed. XVI, 122; see also The

princess of Persia: incidental music composed for The princess of Persia and other plays (arr. by John Edmonds), Boston; and *Neue Stücke für kleinere Streichorchester, Zwei weitere Spielmusiken zum Trauerspiel, 'Distressed Innocence' und Lustspiel 'Amphitryon'* (ed. Hilmar Höckner), Kopenhagen.

577.8 Menuet from Distressed Innocence, In *Suite in 5 movements for orch.* (arr. by H.J. Wood), London.

578 Don Quixote [The Comical History of], London, Pur. Soc. Ed. XVI, 132.

578.3 Let the dreadful engines, London.

579 Epsom Wells, London, Pur. Soc. Ed. XVI, 132.

580 Henry the Second, King of England, London, Pur. Soc. Ed. XX, 38.

581 King Richard the Second, or the history of the Sicilian usurper, London, Pur. Soc. Ed. XX, 43.

582 Love triumphant, or Nature will prevail, London, Pur. Soc. Ed. XX, 70.

583 Oedipus, London, Pur. Soc. Ed. XXI, 1; see also *Festchor aus Purcell's Oper Oedipus Zuerst Bass solo mit Streich-instr. und Cembali, bei der Wiederholung 3st. Chor ohne Soprani; Alt und Tenor Oktave unter der 1 u. 2 Vne.* (arr. for piano, Steinitzer).

583.2 Music for a while [from *Oedipus*], (ed. Michael Tippett and Walter Bergmann), London; also *Arie zum Preise der Musik 1693 a.d. Oper Oedipus, gegeben in London.* (Arranged for piano in *Musikgeschichtlicher Atlas*, ed. M. Steinitzer), Freiburg; and, Music for a while [from *Oedipus*], Boston.

584 Oroonoko, London, Pur. Soc. Ed. XXI, 38.

585   Pausanias, the betrayer of his country, London, Pur. Soc. Ed. XXI, 44; another edition, London, Novello.

585.1   Sweeter than roses, from Pausanias (ed. Michael Tippett and Walter Bergmann), London; also in 6 songs, *Orph. brit.*, the figured basses realized by Benjamin Britten, the vocal parts edited by Peter Pears.

585.2   My dearest, my fairest, San Francisco, Foster & Hall; another edition, St. Louis, Harmonia.

586   Regulus, or the Faction of Carthage, London, Pur. Soc. Ed. XXI, 51.

587   Rule a Wife and Have a Wife, London, Pur. Soc. Ed. XXI, 85.

587.1   There's not a swain, in 6 songs, *Orpheus britannicus*, the figured basses realized by Benjamin Britten, the vocal parts edited by Peter Pears, London.

588   Sir Anthony Love, or the Rambling Lady, London, Pur. Soc. Ed. XXI, 87.

589   Sir Barnaby Whigg, or No wit like a woman's, London, Pur. Soc. Ed. XXI, 103.

590   Sophonisba, or Hannibal's overthrow, London, Pur. Soc. Ed. XXI, 109.

591   The Canterbury guests, or A bargain broken, London, Pur. Soc. Ed. XVI, 87.

592   The double dealer, London, Pur. Soc. Ed. XVI, 149; another edition, Paul Stassevitch, New York, Music Press.

593   The double marriage, London, Pur. Soc. Ed. XVI, 211.

594   The English Lawyer, London, Pur. Soc. Ed. XVI, 221.

595   The fatal marriage, or the Innocent adultery, London, Pur. Soc. Ed. XX, 1.

596   The female virtuosos, London, Pur. Soc. Ed. XX, 7.

597   The Gordian knot unty'd, London, Pur. Soc. Ed. XX, 23; another edition [The Gordian knot untied], *für zwei Violinen, Viola, Bassi; Cembalo ad lib.* (ed. Günter Kohr) Mainz.

598   The Indian emperor, or The conquest of Mexico, London, Pur. Soc. Ed. XX, 41.

599   The knight of Malta, London, Pur. Soc. Ed. XX, 44.

600   The libertine, or The libertine destroyed, London, Pur. Soc. Ed. XX, 45; another edition, London, Novello.

600.1a In these delightful, pleasant groves, London, Novello; also published by Allans, Banks, Boston, Bourne, Cramer, Ditson, Egtved, Leslie, Presser, E.C. Schirmer, Southern.

600.1b Nymphs and shepherds come away, London, Novello; also published by Allans, Ashdown, Banks, Cramer, Lawson, Leonard-Eng, Paterson and Warner.

601   The maid's last prayer, or Any rather than fail, London, Pur. Soc. Ed. XX, 72.

601.2a No, resistance is in vain, Philadelphia, Presser.

602   The marriage-hater match'd, London, Pur. Soc. Ed. XX, 84.

603   The married beau, or The curious impertinent, London, Pur. Soc. Ed. XX, 89.

604   The massacre of Paris, London, Pur. Soc. Ed. XX, 106.

605   The mock marriage, London, Pur. Soc. Ed. XX, 113; see also Novello's performance edition.

605.2   'Twas within a furlong of Edinborough town (ed.
         by Michael Tippett and Walter G. Bergmann),
         London.

605.3   Man is for a woman made, London, Boosey; also
         published by Elkan-Vogel; also in 6 songs,
         Orpheus britannicus, the figured basses realized
         by Benjamin Britten, vocal parts edited Peter
         Pears.

606   Theodosius, or The force of love, London, Pur.
         Soc. Ed. XX, 115.

607   The old bachelor, London, Pur. Soc. Ed. XXI, 19;
         another edition, *Ouvertürensuite aus der
         Bühnenmusik*, The old bachelor, Wolfenbüttel.

608   The Richmond heiress, or A woman once in the
         right, London, Pur. Soc. Ed. XXI, 53.

609   The rival sisters, or The violence of love, London,
         Pur. Soc. Ed. XXI, 63; another edition, suite for
         small orchestra, arranged from figured bass, for
         strings and ad. lib. wood-wind and percussion
         (ed. Imogen Holst), London.

609.11   Take not a woman's anger ill, in *5 Songs for
         medium voice* (fig. bass realized by B. Britten,
         voc. pts. ed. by P. Pears), London.

610   The Spanish friar, or The double discovery,
         London, Pur. Soc. Ed. XXI, 112.

611   The virtuous wife, or Good luck at last, London,
         Pur. Soc. Ed. XXI, 14.

612   The wives' excuse, or Cuckolds make themselves,
         London, Pur. Soc. Ed. XXI, 162.

613   Tyrannic love, or The royal martyr, London, Pur.
         Soc. Ed. XXI, 135.

OPERAS, SEMI-OPERAS ('AMBIGUES'), MASQUE

626   Dido and Aeneas, London, Pur. Soc. Ed. III, 1.

626   Dido & Æneas, an opera by Henry Purcell. Performed by members of the Purcell Operatic Society. May 1900 and March 1901, London. This programme designed and engraved by E.G. Craig, London.

626   Dido and Æneas, a tragic opera, in three acts, composed anno Domini 1675, by Henry Purcell; now first printed, for members of the Musical Antiquarian society (ed. G. Alex. McFarren) London, The Musical Antiquarian Society; also published by Novello.

626   Dido and Æneas, an opera (ed. William H. Cummings) New York, Gray.

626   Dido and Æneas (German translation by Dr. Anton Mayer, ed. Edward J. Dent).

626   Dido and Æneas: an opera by Henry Purcell (ed. Margaret Laurie and R. Thurston Dart), London.

626   Dido and Æneas; an opera composed by Henry Purcell (ed. William H. Cummings), London.

626   Dido and Æneas; libretto [by Nahum Tate] facsimile of the first edition, 1689, London.

626   Dido and Æneas; opera in three acts. Libretto by Nahum Tate; German translation by Ludwig Landgraf (ed. Benjamin Britten and Imogen Holst), London.

626   Dido and Æneas; tragic opera in 3 acts by Nahum Tate, after the score of the Musical Antiquarian Society (vocal score by Gustav Blasser, Deutscher text von R. St. Hoffman, ed. and orchestrated by Artur Bodanzky), Wien.

626   The loves of Dido and Æneas [libretto] an opera;
         written by Nahum Tate and set to music by Mr.
         Henry Purcell. Performed, with several other
         pieces, by the Academy of Ancient Music, on
         Thur., April 21, 1774, London.

626.8   When I am laid in earth, Dido's recitative and aria
         (ed. and arr. by Edward J. Dent, Deutsche
         übersetzung von Dr. Anton Mayer, London.

627   The Prophetess, or The history of Dioclesian,
         London, Pur. Soc. Ed. IX, 1.

627   The vocal and instrumental music of The
         prophetess; or, The history of Dioclesian
         composed by H.P., London, for the author,
         1691. Full score, NYPL copy has memoranda by
         Vincent Novello on the lining paper and
         elsewhere.

627.18   Prelude from Act 3 Dioclesian, in Suite in 5
         movements for orch. (arr. by H. J. Wood),
         London.

627.26   The masque in Dioclesian. New York, Gray.

627   Tunes and dances from Dioclesian, arr. for string
         orchestra (ed. Philip Weston), New York.

627.16   *Chaconne aus der Oper Dioclesian, für 3
         Blockflöten oder andere Melodieinstrumente,*
         Wolfenbüttel.

627.16   *Chaconne aus der Oper Dioclesian; (im
         altitalienische Triosatz für 2 Altblockflöten und
         basso continuo, ed. Willi Hillemann),* Locarno.

627.16   Chaconne from Dioclesian, for two treble recorders
         and keyboard (ed. Walter G. Bergmann),
         London.

627.18   What shall I do? from 'Dioclesian' London.

627.22 Sound, Fame, thy brazen trumpet, in A suite of songs (fig. basses realized by B. Britten, voc. pts. ed. by P. Pears), London.

628 King Arthur, or the British worthy, London, Pur. Soc. Ed. XXVI, 1.

628 King Arthur (abridged edition by W.H. Cummings), London.

628 King Arthur, his magical history. Based on an opera by John Dryden, new version, set to music by Henry Purcell (realized by Philip Ledger, ed. & adapted by Colin Graham), London, Libretto.

628 King Arthur, an opera in five acts, written by John Dryden, composed by Henry Purcell, and now first printed for members of the Musical Antiquarian Society (ed. Edward Taylor), London.

628 The music in Dryden's King Arthur, composed by Henry Purcell, (ed. by J.A. Fuller Maitland for the Birmingham Festival), London.

628 [King Arthur selections] Suite for strings, from the opera King Arthur (arr. Julian Herbage), London.

628.1 Come if you dare, 'Aria and Chorus from King Arthur,' London.

628.15 How blest are shepherds from 'King Arthur,' in 5 Songs for medium voice, (fig. bass realized by B. Britten, voc. pts. ed. by P. Pears), London.

628.29 Two daughters of this aged stream, from 'King Arthur,' New York, Cramer.

628.35 You say 'tis Love from 'King Arthur,' Boston, E.C. Schirmer.

628.38 Fairest isle, in Seven songs, *Orpheus britannicus*, the figured basses realized by Benjamin Britten, voc. pts. ed. P. Pears London.

629 The fairy queen, London, Pur. Soc. Ed. XII, 1.

629   *Die Nacht, Gesänge für eine hohe Stimme und Streichinstrumente*, condensed score and 4 parts. [1. Die Nacht, The fairy queen; 2. Die Mondfinsternisse, Yorkshire feast song; 3. Dido's Abschied, Dido & Aneas] (ed. by Herbert Just), Kassel.

629   The fairy queen (ed. Anthony Lewis), London.

629   The fairy queen; an opera . . . as performed at the New Theatre, Cambridge, 10-14 Feb. 1931, with the dialogue taken from Shakespeare's A midsummer night's dream in place of the alterations of 1692. Cambridge, 1931.

629   The fairy queen; for 2 sopranos, mezzo-soprano, 2 countertenors, two tenors and two basses, chorus and orchestra . . . a shortened version for concert performance (ed. Benjamin Britten and Imogen Holst) London, 1970.

629   The music in the fairy queen; 'English Opera (1692).' The drama adapted from A midsummernight's dream, by Shakespeare (ed. Anthony Lewis), London, 1966.

629   [The fairy queen] <Spielmusik zum Sommernachtstraum, für vier Streich- oder Blasinstrumente und Basso continuo> (ed. Hilmar Höckner), Kassel, 1961.

629.5   Trip it in a ring, from 'The fairy queen' (ed. John Edmunds), Boston.

629.7   [The fairy queen], Come all ye songsters of the sky (ed. John Edmunds), Boston.

629.14 [The fairy queen] Hush no more, New York, Foster.

629.17 [The fairy queen] If love's a sweet passion, London, Novello.

629.27 Symphony from The fairy queen (in Three
   Overtures for Trumpets, Drums and Strings).
   London, Novello.

629.39 [The fairy queen]: 'An epithalamium, or wedding
   song' (ed. Michael Tippett and Walter G.
   Bergmann), London, 1950.

629.47 [The fairy queen] Hark how all things in one sound
   rejoice, ed. John Edmunds, Boston.

629.48 Hark! the ech'ing air, 'The Fairy Queen,' in *5
   Songs for medium voice* (fig. bass realized by B.
   Britten, voc. pts. ed. by P. Pears), London.

629.50 [The fairy queen] Turn then thine eyes, ed. John
   Edmunds, Boston.

630 The Indian queen, London, Pur. Soc. Ed. XIX, 1.

630 The songs in the Indian queen, as it is now
   compos'd into an opera, London, 1695.

630.4 Why should men quarrel, from 'The Indian queen,'
   in A suite of songs (fig. basses realized by B.
   Britten, voc. pts. ed. by P. Pears) London.

630.16 Trumpet overture from 'The Indian queen,'
   London, Novello.

630.17 I attempt from love's sickness, in *5 Songs for
   medium voice* (fig. bass realized by B. Britten,
   voc. pts. ed. by P. Pears), London.

630.17 [The Indian queen] I attempt from love's sickness to
   fly, London, Novello.

630.2 When Sylvia in bathing, 'A song on a lady's going
   into the bath,' (made by Mr. Tho. Durfey to a tune
   of Mr. Henry Purcell's & exactly engrav'd by
   Tho: Cross. London).

631 The tempest, or The enchanted isle, London, Pur.
   Soc. Ed. XIX, 111.

631.6 Full fathom five, from 'The tempest,' London,
   Novello.

632   Timon of Athens, the man-hater, London, Pur. Soc.
           Ed. II, 1.
632.10   Prelude to 'Hark, how the songsters,' from Timon,
           in *Suite in 5 movements for orch.* (arr. by H. J.
           Wood), London.

KEYBOARD WORKS: HARPSICHORD

641   Air in G major.
642   Almand and Corant in a minor, London, ed. Paer.
643   Almand (with division) in G major, London, Pur.
           Soc. Ed. VI, 47.
644   Corant in G major, London, Pur. Soc. Ed. VI, 48.
645   Ground in gamut, London, Pur. Soc. Ed. VI, 33.
646   Lilliburlero. A new Irish tune, London, Pur. Soc.
           Ed. VI, 31.
647   March in C major, London, Pur. Soc. Ed. VI, 28.
648   March in C major, London, Pur. Soc. Ed. VI, 28.
649   Minuet in a minor, London, Pur. Soc. Ed. VI, 29.
650   Minuet in G major, London, Pur. Soc. Ed. VI, 48.
651   Minuet in G major, London, Pur. Soc. Ed. VI, 48.
652   Prelude in a minor, London, Pur. Soc. Ed. VI, 40.
653   Rigadoon in C major, London, Pur. Soc. Ed. VI,
           48; see also <Rigaudoon für Clavier aus Musickes
           Hand-maid> by Playford, 1689, in Steinitzer, H.,
           ed. Musikgeschichtlicher Atlas, Freiburg.
654   Saraband with division in a minor, London, Pur.
           Soc. Ed. VI, 35.
655   Scotch Tune (A new Scotch tune) in G major,
           London, Pur. Soc. Ed. VI, 30.
656   Sefauchi's farewell, London, Pur. Soc. Ed. VI, 32.

SUITES

642   Purcell's ground, with variations for the harpsichord or piano forte, London.

642   Purcell's ground, A favorite lesson with variations for the harpsichord, London.

660   Suite in G major [Prelude, almand, corant and saraband], London, Pur. Soc. Ed. VI, 1.

661   Suite in g minor [Prelude, almand, corant and saraband], London, Pur. Soc. Ed. VI, 2.

662   Suite in G major [Prelude, almand, corant], London, Pur. Soc. Ed. VI, 6.

663   Suite in a minor [Prelude, almand, corant, saraband], London, Pur. Soc. Ed. VI, 1.

664   Suite in B-flat major [Alman, corant, saraband], Paer, 156-7.

665   Suite in C major [Prelude, almand, corant, saraband and jigg] Dart, *Musick's Handmaid*, 21-2.

666   Suite in C major [Prelude, almand and corant], London, Pur. Soc. Ed. VI, 13.

667   Suite in D major [Prelude, almand, hornpipe], London, Pur. Soc. Ed. VI, 16.

668   Suite in d minor [Almand (Bell Barr), corant, hornpipe], London, Pur. Soc. Ed. VI, 18.

669   Suite in F major [Prelude, almand, corant and minuet], London, Pur. Soc. Ed. VI, 20.

670   The queen's dolour, Wm. Barclay Squire, No. 22 [Now Doubtful].

671   Prelude for ye fingering (Howard Ferguson).

T675   Air in d minor, London, Pur. Soc. Ed. VI, 37.

T676   Air in d minor, London, Pur. Soc. Ed. VI, 41.

T677   Canary in B-flat major, New York, MS Drexel 5609.

T678   [Cibell] Trumpet tune, called the Cibell, London, Pur. Soc. Ed. VI, 27.

T679   Chacone (with canon) in a minor, London, Pur. Soc. Ed. VI, 6.

T680   Chacone in g minor, London, Pur. Soc. Ed. VI, 24.

T681   Ground in c minor, London, Pur. Soc. Ed. VI, 39.

T681A   Ground in d minor, London, MS Egerton 2959.

T682   A new ground in e minor, London, Pur. Soc. Ed. VI, 30.

T683   Hornpipe in B-flat major, London, MS Additional 22099.

T684   Hornpipe in d minor, London, Pur. Soc. Ed. VI, 38.

T685   Hornpipe in e minor, London, Pur. Soc. Ed. VI, 47.

T686   Jig in g minor, London, Pur. Soc. Ed. VI, 26.

T687   March in C major, London, Pur. Soc. Ed. VI, 23.

T688   Minuet in d minor, London, Pur. Soc. Ed. VI, 32.

T689   New Minuet in d minor, London, Pur. Soc. Ed. VI, 29.

T690   Overture in c minor, Pauer, 160.

T691   Overture in D major, Pauer, 164.

T692   Overture in D major, Pauer, 162.

T693   Overture, air and jig in gamut-flat, London, Pur. Soc. Ed. VI, 56.

T694   Song tune in C major, London, Pur. Soc. Ed. VI, 28.

T695   Song tune in C major, Dart, *Musick's Handmaid*, 4.

T696?   Suite in d minor [Air, air (minuet)], London, *The Lady's Banquet*, 1706.

T697   Trumpet Tune in C major, London, Pur. Soc. Ed. VI, 27.

T698   Trumpet Tune in C major, London, Pur. Soc. Ed. VI, 24.

ORGAN

716   A verse in F major, London, Pur. Soc. Ed. VI, 36.

717   Voluntary in C major, London, Pur. Soc. Ed. VI, 35.

718   Voluntary in d minor, London, Pur. Soc. Ed. VI, 61.

719   Voluntary for double organ, London, Pur. Soc. Ed. VI, 64.

720   Voluntary in G major, London, Pur. Soc. Ed. VI, 53.

721   Voluntary on the 100th Psalm in A major, London, Pur. Soc. Ed. VI, 59; also in *Masterpieces of organ music,* no. 10 (ed. Norman Hennefield), New York, 1944.

MUSIC FOR STRINGS: FANTASIAS AND RELATED FORMS

730   Chacony à 4 in g minor, London, Pur. Soc. Ed. XXXI, 61; see also an edition by Benjamin Britten, London, an edition by Hannah Bryant, London, and an arrangement for recorder, quartet or cello and violin or viols by Richard Coles, London.

731   Fantasia '3 parts upon a ground,' London, Pur. Soc. Ed. XXXI, 52; see also an edition by Denis Stevens and R. Thurston Dart, New York.

732   Fantasia à 3 in d minor, London, Pur. Soc. Ed. XXXI, 1.

733   Fantasia à 3 in F major, London, Pur. Soc. Ed. XXXI, 3.

734   Fantasia à 3 in g minor, London, Pur. Soc. Ed. XXXI, 5.

735   Fantasia à 4 in g minor, London, Pur. Soc. Ed. XXXI, 7.

736   Fantasia à 4 in B-flat major, London, Pur. Soc. Ed. XXXI, 10; another edition in *The Sackbut*, v. 1 no. 2, London.

737   Fantasia à 4 in F major, London, Pur. Soc. Ed. XXXI, 13.

738   Fantasia à 4 in c minor, London, Pur. Soc. Ed. XXXI, 16.

739   Fantasia à 4 in d minor, London, Pur. Soc. Ed. XXXI, 19.

740   Fantasia à 4 in a minor, London, Pur. Soc. Ed. XXXI, 22; also in an edition transcribed for 4 horns by Irving Rosenthal, Los Angeles.

741   Fantasia à 4 in e minor, London, Pur. Soc. Ed. XXXI, 25.

742   Fantasia à 4 in G major, London, Pur. Soc. Ed. XXXI, 28.

743   Fantasia à 4 in d minor, London, Pur. Soc. Ed. XXXI, 31.

744   Fantasia à 4 in a minor, London, Pur. Soc. Ed. XXXI, 94.

745   Fantasia upon one note à 5 in F major, London, Pur. Soc. Ed. XXXI, 34.

746   In nomine à 6 in g minor, London, Pur. Soc. Ed. XXXI, 37.

747   In nomine à 7 in g minor, London, Pur. Soc. Ed. XXXI, 39.

748   Pavan à 3 in A major, London, Pur. Soc. Ed. XXXI, 46.

749   Pavan à 3 in A-re-flat, London, Pur. Soc. Ed. XXXI, 44.

750   Pavan à 3 in B-flat, London, Pur. Soc. Ed. XXXI, 49.

751 Pavan à 3 in Gamut, London, Pur. Soc. Ed. XXXI, 42.

752 Pavan à 4 in g minor, London, Pur. Soc. Ed. XXXI, 49; also, edited by André Mangeot, London, Curwen.

SONATAS AND RELATED FORMS

770 Overture and suite fragment in G major, London, Pur. Soc. Ed. XXXI, 68; also edited by W. Gillies Wittaker, London, O.U.P.

771 Overture in d minor [Grave, canzona, adagio], London. Pur. Soc. Ed. XXXI, 76.

772 Overture à 5 in g minor, London, Pur. Soc. Ed. XXXI, 82.

N773 Prelude for solo violin in g minor, London. Pur. Soc. Ed. XXXI, 93.

N774 'Mr. Purcell's jigg', London, *Apollo's Banquet*, 1687.

N775 The Staircase overture 'The noise of foreign wars,' Oxford, Bodleian, The Tatton Park Collection, vol. 3.

N756 Pavan à 4 in g minor, Yale Music MS Osborn 515.

N757 Pavan à 4 in f minor, Yale Music MS Osborn 515.

780 Sonata in g minor, London, Pur. Soc. Ed. XXXI, 95; another edition by R. Thurston Dart, London; other editions: (ed. Alfred Moffat) London, Lengnick; also *Sonate g-moll, für Violine, Cembalo (Klavier) und Violoncell ad lib.* (hrsg. von Felix Schroeder) Wiesbaden.

790 Sonata I in g minor, London, Pur. Soc. Ed. V, 1; another edition: *Zwei Trio-Sonaten, I. G moll, II. B dur, für zwei Violinen und Bass mit Generalbass*, Mainz; another edition, for two

pianos, four hands (edited by Celius Dougherty), New York.

791 Sonata II in B-flat major, London, Pur. Soc. Ed. V, 9.

792 Sonata III in d minor, London, Pur. Soc. Ed. V, 18.

792.2 Vivace, from 'Sonata No. 3 in A minor,' in *Suite in 5 movements for orch.* (arr. by H. J. Wood), London.

793 Sonata IV in F major, London, Pur. Soc. Ed. V, 27.

794 Sonata V in a minor, London, Pur. Soc. Ed. V, 35.

795 Sonata VI in C major, London, Pur. Soc. Ed. V, 42.

796 Sonata VII in e minor, London, Pur. Soc. Ed. V, 51.

797 Sonata VIII in G major, London, Pur. Soc. Ed. V, 61.

798 Sonata IX in c minor, London, Pur. Soc. Ed. V, 71.

799 Sonata X in A major, London, Pur. Soc. Ed. V, 82; another version 'newly edited by Thurston Dart,' London.

800 Sonata XI, f minor, London, Pur. Soc. Ed. V, 88.

801 Sonata XII in D major, London, Pur. Soc. Ed. V, 88.

SONATAS OF FOUR PARTS

802 Sonata I in b minor, London, Pur. Soc. Ed. VII, 1.

803 Sonata II in E-flat major, London, Pur. Soc. Ed. VII, 13; see also Sonata No. 2 in E-flat major, in Trio Sonatas . . . (ed. W. Woehl), London, Peters.

804   Sonata III in a minor, London, Pur. Soc. Ed. VII, 23.

805   Sonata IV in d minor, London, Pur. Soc. Ed. VII, 1; see also Sonata No. 4 in d minor, in Trio Sonatas . . . (ed. W. Woehl), London, Peters.

806   Sonata V in g minor, London, Pur. Soc. Ed. VII, 46; see also:

806.2 Largo, from Sonata No. 5, in g minor, in Suite in 5 movements for orch. (arr. by H.J. Wood), London.

807   Sonata VI in g minor, London, Pur. Soc. Ed. VII, 57.

808   Sonata VII in C major, London, Pur. Soc. Ed. VII, 70.

809   Sonata VIII in g minor, London, Pur. Soc. Ed. VII, 82.

810   Sonata IX ('The Golden') in F major, London, Pur. Soc. Ed. VII, 93; see also The golden sonata (ed. Benjamin Britten), London; another edition in Trio Sonatas . . . (ed. W. Woehl), London, Peters.

811   Sonata X in D major, London, Pur. Soc. Ed. VII, 106; see also Sonata No. 10 in D major, in Trio Sonatas . . . (ed. W. Woehl), London, Peters.

TRUMPET AND STRINGS

850   Sonata in D major, London, Pur. Soc. Ed. XXXII, 86; see also Sonata for trumpet and organ (ed. by Corliss R. Arnold), St. Louis; another edition, Robert King, North Easton, Mass.; another edition by E.H. Tarr, London.

WIND CONSORT

860   March and Canzona, London, Pur. Soc. Ed.
XXXI, 92; another edition 'Funeral music for
Queen Mary,' Wakefield, Mass.; another edition:
March and canzona for the funeral of Queen Mary
(1695) [for two trumpets and two trombones with
optional timpany (ed. R. Thurston Dart)],
London; another edition: Music for the funeral of
Mary II, [with compositions now printed for the
first time, in Sammelbände der Internationale
Musik-Gesellschaft] (ed. W. Barclay Squire)],
Leipzig.

APPENDIX

LIST OF WORKS MODELLED AFTER
PURCELL'S COMPOSITIONS

*   Arne, Thomas Augustine. The Songs, Airs, Duets and Chorusses in the Masque of King Arthur, . . . compos'd by Henry Purcell and Dr. Arne. Score. London, n.d.

*   Arnold, Samuel. The Music in Bonduca (an arrangement). London, n.d.

*   Babin, Victor. *Twelve variations on a theme by Purcell for violoncello and piano.* New York, 1946. Score (32 pp.) and violoncello part.

*   Bauer, Harold. Variations and finale on a theme, Siciliano, by Henry Purcell. New York, 1944. Score, 10 pp.

*   Britten, Benjamin. *The young person's guide to the orchestra, variations and fugue on a theme of Purcell.* Op. 34, London, 1947, Full score, and spoken commentary by Eric Crozier.

*   Carter, Elliot. *A fantasia about Purcell's Fantasia on One Note,* for brass quartet. New York, Associated Publishers, ca. 1977.

*   Davies, Peter Maxwell. *Fantasia and two pavannes after Henry Purcell,* for instrumental ensemble, full score.

*   Jacobs, Gordon. *Variations for strings on an air by Purcell*. London, 1930.

*   Lambert, Constant. *Comus* (ballet).

*   Maler, William. *Streichquartett in G für zwei Violinen, Bratsche und Violincello*. [The second movement is a set of variations on Purcell's A new Scotch tune.] Mainz, 1936, Score, 28 pp.

*   Moeschinger, Albert. *Variations und Finale über ein Thema von Henry Purcell für Streichorchestra, Pauken und kleine Trommel*, Op. 32, Mainz, 1935, score, 49 pp.

*   ———. *Variations & Fugue on a Theme by Purcell*, for organ.

*   Müller-Hartmann, Robert. *Variations on a Theme by Purcell*, for pianoforte.

*   Pierné, Gabriel. *Prélude de concert pour basson sur un thème de Purcell*. Op. 53, Conservatoire national de musique de Paris, morceau de concours (1933), Paris, 1933, piano score and bassoon part.

BIBLIOGRAPHY

SHORT TITLES,
CLASSIFIED BY SUBJECT MATTER

A. Sources Providing Contemporary
Background Material

Ashbee, Andrew. *Lists of payments to the King's Musick*
Ashbee, Andrew. *Records of the English court* (vol. I)
Ashbee, Andrew. *Records of the English court* (vol. II)
Avery, E. A. *The London stage*
Cibber, Colley. *An apology*
Day, Cyrus Lawrence, and Eleanore Boswell Murrie.
    English song-books
Downes, John. *Roscius Anglicanus*
Elkin, Robert. *The old concert rooms of London*
Evelyn, John. *Diary*
Guy, Henry. *Moneys received*
Halfpenny, Eric. "Musicians at James II's coronation"
Highfill, Phillip H., *et al. A biographical dictionary*
Jensen, H. James. "English Restoration attitudes toward
    music"
Klakowich, Robert. "Harpsichord music by Purcell and
    Clarke in Los Angeles"
LaFontaine, Henry Cart de. *The King's Musick*
Langbaine, Gerard. *An account of the English dramatick
    poets*

Lawrence, W. J. "Foreign singers and musicians at the
    court of Charles II"
Noble, Jeremy. "Purcell and the Chapel Royal"
North, Roger. *An essay of musical ayre*
North, Roger [ed. John Wilson]. *Roger North on music*
Playford, John. *An introduction to the skill of musick*
Rimbault, E.F. *The old cheque-book*
Tilmouth, Michael. "A calendar of references to music in
    newspapers published in London and the provinces
    (1660-1719)"
Tilmouth, Michael. "Index to 'A calendar of references to
    music in newspapers published in London and the
    provinces (1660-1719)'"
Westrup, Jack. "Royal music under the Stewarts"
Wood, Anthony à. *Life and times of Anthony Wood*

B. Biographical Material

1. General Views

Anonymous. "Memoirs of the life and writing of Henry
    Purcell"
Arundell, Dennis Drew. *Henry Purcell*
Bingley, William. *Musical biography*
Bridge, J. Frederick. *Twelve good musicians*
Burney, Charles. *A general history*
Busby, Thomas. *A general history*
Colles, H.C. "Musical London"
Cummings, W.H. *Purcell*
Demarquez, Susanne. *Purcell*
Dupré, Henri. *Purcell*
Dupré, Henri. *Purcell,* English version
Hawkins, Sir John. *A general history*
Hawkins, Sir John. *Musical biography*
Highfill, Phillip H., *et al. A biographical dictionary*
Holland, A.K. *Henry Purcell*
Holst, Imogen. *Henry Purcell*

Hutchings, A. *Purcell.*
Legàny, Dezsö. *Purcell*
Luckett, Richard. "Or rather our musical Shakespeare"
Ravenzwaij, G. van. *Purcell*
Runciman, John F. *Purcell*
Sietz, Reinhold. *Henry Purcell*
Tilmouth, Michael. "Henry Purcell, assistant lexicographer"
Westrup, Jack Allen. *Purcell*
Westrup, Jack Allen. "Fact and fiction about Henry Purcell"
Young, Percy M. *Henry Purcell*
Young, Percy M. *A history of British music*
Zimmerman, Franklin B. "Purcell and the Dean of
    Westminster"
Zimmerman, Franklin B. *Henry Purcell, 1659-1695*

2. Chronology, Commemorative Events, and Compositions

Cooper, Gerald M. "The chronology of Purcell's music"

3. Finances

Ashbee, Andrew. *Lists of payments to the King's Musicke*
Ashbee, Andrew. *Records of the English court*
Guy, Henry. *Moneys received*
LaFontaine, Henry Cart de. *The King's Musick*

4. Genealogy

Flood, W.H. Grattan. "Irish ancestry"
Westrup, J. "Purcell's parentage"
Zimmerman, F.B. "Purcell's family circle"

5. Historical and Social Backgrounds

Harley, John. *Music in Purcell's London*
Jensen, H. James. "English Restoration attitudes toward
    music"

Price, Curtis. "Political allegory in late-seventeenth-century
    English opera"
Zimmerman, Franklin B. "The social and political functions
    of the Restoration anthem"
Zimmerman, Franklin B. *Henry Purcell, 1659-1695: his life
    and times,* first edition
Zimmerman, Franklin B. *Henry Purcell, 1659-1695: his life
    and times,* second revised edition

6. Handwriting and Autographs

Fortune, Nigel and Franklin B. Zimmerman. "Purcell's
    autographs"
Hughes-Hughes, A. "Henry Purcell's handwriting"
Squire, William Barclay. "An unknown autograph"
Walker, F.H. "Purcell's handwriting"
Wood, B. "A newly identified Purcell autograph"
Zimmerman, Franklin B. "Purcell's handwriting"

7. Memoirs, Diaries, Letters, etc.

Anonymous. "Memoirs of the life and writing of Henry
    Purcell"
Evelyn, John. *Diary*
North, Roger. *Memoires of musick*
Pepys, Samuel. *Diary*

8. Personality

Antcliffe, Herbert. "The naïveté of Purcell"

9. Poetry

Bridges, Robert Seymour. "Purcell ode"
Scholes, Percy A. "Purcell in praise of princes"
Zimmerman, Franklin B. "Poets in praise of Purcell"

10. Portraits

Shaw, William A. "Three unpublished portraits of Henry Purcell"
Zimmerman, Franklin B. "Purcell portraiture"

11. Poetry and Music Composed in Honor of Purcell

Blow, John. *Ode on the death of Mr. Henry Purcell*
Bridges, Robert Seymour. "Purcell ode and other poems"
Clarke, Jeremiah. *Music on Henry Purcell's death*
Squire, William Barclay. "An elegy on Henry Purcell"
Zimmerman, Franklin B. "Poets in praise of Purcell"

C. The Music

1. General Views

Arundell, Dennis Drew. *Henry Purcell*
Bliss, Arthur. "Henry Purcell"
Colles, H.C. "Music in four countries"
Harley, John. *Music in Purcell's London*
Hollander, John. *The untuning of the sky*
Meffen, J. "A question of temperament: Purcell and Croft"
Ravenzwaij, G. van. "Henry Purcell's muzikale synthese"
Westrup, Jack Allen. *Purcell*

2. Chamber Music

Bridge, Sir J. Frederick. "Purcell's fantazias and sonatas"
Bucht, Gunnar. *Purcell och den engelske fancyn*
Chazanoff, Daniel. *Early English chamber music*
Dart, Thurston. "Purcell's chamber music"
Favre-Lingorow, Stella. *Der Instrumentalstil von Purcell*
Hogwood, Christopher. *The trio sonata*
Holman, Peter. "The trumpet sonata in England"

Illing, Robert. *Henry Purcell's Sonata in g minor for violin and continuo: an account of its survival from both the historical and technical points of view*

Klenz, William. *The church sonatas of Henry Purcell*

Koeltzsch, Hans. "Purcells Gambenfantasien"

Mangeot, André. "The Purcell fantasias"

Meyer, E.H. *English chamber music*

Nelson, Everett E. *An introductory study of the English three-part string fancy*

Shaw, Watkins. "Purcell sonatas"

Stevens, Denis. "Purcell's art of fantasia"

Tilmouth, Michael. *English chamber music*

Tilmouth, Michael. "The techniques and forms of Purcell's sonatas"

Wailes, Marylin. "Four short fantasias by Henry Purcell"

Warlock, Peter. "Purcell's fantasias for strings"

Wesley-Kropik, H. "Henry Purcell als Instrumental-komponist"

3.   Concerts

Elkin, Robert. *The old concert rooms of London*

4.   Discography

Greenhalgh, Michael J. *The music of Henry Purcell*

Mayer, George L. "The vocal works"

Price, Curtis A. "Purcell's theatre music on record"

Stevens, Denis. "Purcell on the gramophone"

5.   Editions

Beechy, Gwillen. "Henry Playford's Harmonia Sacra"

Ford, Robert. "Purcell as his own editor: the funeral sentences"

King, A. Hyatt. "Benjamin Goodison and the first 'Complete Edition' "

King, A. Hyatt. "The first complete edition of Purcell"

6. Facsimiles

Playford, John (F.B. Zimmerman, ed.). *An introduction to the skill of musick, in three books*
Zimmerman, Franklin B., ed. *The Gostling manuscript*

7. Incidental Music

King, A. Hyatt. *Henry Purcell and the London stage*
King, A. Hyatt. *Music in the Restoration theatre*
Wesley-Kropik, H. "Henry Purcell als Instrumental-komponist"

8. Influence

Anonymous. "Purcell and Italian music"
Ayres, J. C. *The influence of French composers*
Bridge, J. Frederick. "Purcell and Nicola Matteis"
Colles, H. C. "Lully and Purcell"
Dart, Thurston. "Purcell and Bull"
Fuller-Maitland, J. A. "Foreign influences on Henry Purcell"
Lawrence, W. J. "Foreign singers and musicians"
Statham, Heathcote D. "The influence of the Elizabethan composers"
Westrup, Jack Allen. "Das Englische in Henry Purcells Musik"
Westrup, Jack Allen. "Foreign musicians in Stuart England"
Zimmerman, Franklin B. "Handel's Purcellian borrowings"
Zimmerman, Franklin B. "Musical borrowings in the English Baroque"
Zimmerman, Franklin B. "Purcell and Monteverdi"
Zimmerman, Franklin B. "Purcellian passages in the compositions of G. F. Handel"

9. Instrumentation

Burkhart, R. E. *The trumpet in England*

Bergmann, W. "Henry Purcell's use of the recorder"
Conley, Philip R. "The use of the trumpet"
Smithers, Don. *The music and history of the Baroque
    trumpet*

10. Keyboard Music

Cooper, Barry. "Did Purcell write a trumpet voluntary?"
Cudworth, Charles. "Some new facts about the trumpet
    voluntary"
Dart, Thurston. "The Cibell"
Dart, Thurston. "Purcell's harpsichord music"
Downes, Ralph. "An organist's view"
Ferguson, Howard. "Purcell's harpsichord music"
Ferguson, Howard. "Two Purcell discoveries"
Klakowich, Robert. "Harpsichord music by Purcell and
    Clarke in Los Angeles"
Siedentopf, H. "Eine Komposition Purcells im
    Klavierbuch"

11. Odes and Other Occasional Music

Baldwin, Olive, and Thelma Wilson. "Who can from joy
    refraine?"
Gordon, Lewis W. "The odes of Henry Purcell"
Halfpenny, Eric. "Musicians at James II's coronation"
Husk, William Henry. *An account of the musical
    celebrations on St. Cecilia's day*
Leininger, George. *The odes of Henry Purcell*
McGuinness, Rosamond. *English court odes*
Scholes, Percy A. "Purcell in praise of princes"
Squire, William Barclay. "Purcell's music for the funeral of
    Mary II"

12. Opera

Arundell, Dennis. *The critic at the opera*
Buttrey, John. "Dating Purcell's Dido and Aeneas"
Buttrey, John. "The evolution of English opera"

Charleton, D. "King Arthur: a dramatick opera"
Cummings, W.H. "Purcell and Dr. Arne"
Dent, Edward J. *Purcell's The Fairy Queen*
Dent, Edward J. The foundations of English opera
Flood, W.H. Grattan. "Purcell's Dido and Æneas"
Fuller-Maitland, J.A. "Purcell's 'King Arthur'"
Gray, Alan. "Purcell's dramatic music"
Ham, Roswell G. "Dryden's dedication for the music of
     'The Prophetess'"
Holst, Imogen. "Purcell's librettist, Nahum Tate"
Langbaine, Gerard. *An account of the English dramatick
     poets*
Lewis, Anthony. "Notes and reflections on a new edition of
     Purcell's 'The Fairy Queen'"
Lewis, Anthony. "Purcell and Blow's 'Venus and Adonis'"
Marco, Guy. "The variety in Purcell's word-painting"
Moore, Robert E. "The music to Macbeth"
Moore, Robert E. *Henry Purcell & the Restoration theatre*
Prendergast, Arthur H.D. *Masques and early operas*
Price, Curtis A. *Henry Purcell and the London stage*
Price, Curtis A. *Music in the Restoration theatre*
Price, Curtis. "Political allegory in late-seventeenth-century
     English opera"
Price, Curtis, and Irena Cholij. "Dido's bass sorceress"
Savage, R. "The Shakespeare-Purcell Fairy Queen"
Squire, William Barclay. "Purcell's dramatic music"
Squire, William Barclay. "Purcell's 'Fairy Queen'"
Tiggers, Piet. "'King Arthur' van Henry Purcell"
White, Eric Walter. "Early theatrical performances of
     Purcell's operas"
White, Eric Walter. "New Light on 'Dido and Aeneas'"
White, Eric Walter. *The rise of English opera*

13. Orchestral Music

Browning, Alan. "Purcell's 'Stairre Case Overture'"
Favre-Lingorow, Stella. *Der Instrumentalstil von Purcell*
Wesley-Kropik, H. "Henry Purcell als Instrumental-
     komponist"

14. Performance Practices and Performers

Baldwin, Olive, and Thelma Wilson. "Purcell's sopranos"
Bergmann, W. "Henry Purcell's use of the recorder"
Bicknell, Joan Colleen. "On performing Purcell's vocal
    music"
Britten, Benjamin. "On realizing the continuo in Purcell's
    songs"
Donington, Robert. "Further seventeenth-and eighteenth-
    century evidence"
Donington, Robert. "Performing Purcell's music today"
Noble, Jeremy. "Purcell and the Chapel Royal"
Pears, Peter. "Homage to a British Orpheus"
Shaw, Watkins. "Purcell's 'Bell' anthem and its
    performance"

15. Purcell's Influence

Arkwright, G.E. "A note on Purcell's music"
Bliss, Arthur. "Henry Purcell"
Chissel, Joan. "St. Cecilia—Purcell and Britten"
Colles, H.C. "Purcell restored"
Cummings, W.H. "Purcell and Dr. Arne"
Griffiths, David. "The music in York Minster"
Luckett, Richard. "Or rather our musical Shakespeare"
Meffen, J. "A question of temperament: Purcell and Croft"
Rendall, E.D. "The influence of Henry Purcell on Handel"
Shaw, Watkins. "Eight concerts of Henry Purcell's Music"
Westrup, Jack Allen. "Purcell and Handel"
Zimmerman, Franklin B. "Musical borrowings in the
    English Baroque"

16. Purcell's Style

Arkwright, G.E. "A note on Purcell's music"
Favre-Lingorow, Stella. *Der Instrumentalstil von Purcell*
Lewis, Anthony. *The language of Purcell*
Quervain, Fritz de. *Der Chorstil Henry Purcells*

Whittaker, William Gillies. "Some observations on
  Purcell's harmony"
Zimmerman, Franklin B. "Purcell and Monteverdi"

17. Relation of Music and Text

Arundell, Dennis. "Purcell and natural speech"
Bicknell, Joan Colleen. *Interdependence of word and tone*
Duckles, Vincent Harris. "English song"
Gooch, Bryan Niel Shirley. *Poetry and music in England*
Hollander, John. *The untuning of the sky*
Marco, Guy. "The variety in Purcell's word-painting"
McGuinness, Rosamond. "The ground-bass in the English
  court ode"
Moore, Robert Etheridge. *Henry Purcell & the Restoration
  theatre*
Rohrer, Katherine Tinely. *The energy of English words*
Scholes, Percy A. "Purcell in praise of princes"
Zimmerman, Franklin B. "Sound and sense in Purcell's
  single songs"

18. Sacred Music

Anderson, William W. *The stylistic development of Henry
  Purcell as revealed by his sacred verse anthems*
Arkwright, G.E.P. "Purcell's church music"
Beechy, Gwillen. "Henry Playford's Harmonia Sacra"
Bumpus, John S. *A history of English cathedral music*
Dennison, P. "The stylistic origins of the early church
  music"
Ford, Anthony D. "A Purcell service"
Ford, Robert. "A sacred song not by Purcell"
Ford, Robert. "Purcell as his own editor: the funeral
  sentences"
Fortune, Nigel. "The domestic sacred music"
Foster, Myles Birkit. *Anthems and anthem composers*
Griffiths, David. "The music in York Minster"
Howard, Michael. "An anthem by Henry Purcell"
Long, Kenneth R. *The music of the English church*

Noble, Jeremy. "Purcell and the Chapel Royal"

Quervain, Fritz de. *Der Chorstil Henry Purcells*

Shaw, Watkins. "Purcell's 'Bell' anthem and its
    performance"

Statham, Heathcote D. "Purcell's church music"

Theile, Eugen. "Die Kirchenmusik Henry Purcells"

Van Tassel, E. "Two Purcell discoveries—1: Purcell's
    Give Sentence"

Westrup, Jack Allen. "Church music at the Restoration"

Wienandt, Elwyn A. and Robert Young. *The anthem*

Wood, Bruce. "Two Purcell discoveries; 2. A coronation
    anthem"

Zimmerman, Franklin B. "A newly-discovered anthem by
    Purcell"

Zimmerman, Franklin B. "Anthems of Purcell"

Zimmerman, Franklin B. "Musical styles and practices in
    Purcell's anthems"

Zimmerman, Franklin B. "Purcell's Service Anthem"

Zimmerman, Franklin B. "Purcell's concerted anthems"

Zimmerman, Franklin B. "Purcell's polyphonic anthems"

Zimmerman, Franklin B. "The anthems of Henry Purcell"

Zimmerman, Franklin B. "Thematic unity in Purcell's
    concertato anthems" Pt. I

Zimmerman, Franklin B. "Thematic unity in Purcell's
    concertato anthems" Pt. II

Zimmerman, Franklin B. "A newly-discovered anthem by
    Purcell"

Zimmerman, Franklin B., ed. *The Gostling manuscript*

19. Songs

Bicknell, Joan Colleen. "On performing Purcell's vocal
    music"

Colles, H.C. *Voice and verse*

Cutts, John P. "An unpublished Purcell setting"

Duckles, Vincent Harris. "English song"

Duncan, Edmonstoune. "The songs of Henry Purcell"

Lamson, Roy. "Henry Purcell's dramatic songs"

Laurie, Margaret. "Purcell's extended solo songs"

Squire, William Barclay. "An unknown autograph"

20. Sources

Boito, Diane. "Manuscript music in the James Marshall and Marie-Louise Osborn collection"

Charteris, Richard. "Some manuscript discoveries"

Dart, Thurston. "Purcell and Bull"

Fortune, Nigel. *A new Purcell source*

Griffiths, David "The music in York Minster"

Holst, Imogen. "A note on the Nanki Collection of Purcell's works"

Krummel, D.W. *English music printing, 1553-1700*

McLean, Hugh. "Blow and Purcell in Japan"

Rose, Gloria. "A new Purcell source"

Shaw, Watkins. "A collection of musical manuscripts"

Squire, William Barclay. "An unknown autograph of Henry Purcell"

Wood, Bruce. "A newly identified Purcell autograph"

Zimmerman, Franklin B. "Anthems of Purcell"

Zimmerman, Franklin B. "Purcell and Monteverdi"

Zimmerman, Franklin B. "Restoration music manuscripts at Lincoln cathedral"

Zimmerman, Franklin B., ed. *The Gostling manuscript*

21. Stage Music

Browning, Alan. "Purcell's 'Stairre Case Overture'"

Covell, R. "Seventeenth-century music for The Tempest"

Cutts, John. "Music and the supernatural in 'The Tempest'"

Espinós, Víctor. "Las realizaciones musicales del Quijote"

Gray, Alan. "Purcell's dramatic music"

Laurie, Margaret. "Did Purcell set The Tempest?"

Laurie, Margaret. *Purcell's stage works*

Manifold, J.S. "Music in Purcell's theatre"

McManaway, J.G. "Songs and Masques in *The Tempest* "

Mellers, Wilfred. "Purcell and the Restoration theatre"

Moore, Robert Etheridge. *Henry Purcell & the Restoration theatre*

Price, Curtis A. *Music in the Restoration theatre*
Price, Curtis A. "Restoration theatre music restored"
Rendall, E.D. "Some notes on Purcell's dramatic music"
Rumery, L.R. "Choral music in Purcell's dramatic works"
Squire, William Barclay. "Purcell's dramatic music"
Swalin, Benjamin F. "Purcell's masque in Timon of
      Athens"
Westrup, Jack Allen. "Purcell's music for 'Timon of
      Athens'"

22. Techniques and Formal Procedures

McGuinness, Rosamond. "The ground-bass in the English
      court ode"
Miller, Hugh M. "Henry Purcell and the ground bass"
Nelson, Everett. *An introductory study of the English three-
      part string fancy*
Quervain, Fritz de. *Der Chorstil Henry Purcells*
Rohrer, Katherine Tinely. *The energy of English words*
Schjelderup-Ebbe, Dag. *Purcell's cadences*
Whittaker, William Gillies. "Some observations on
      Purcell's harmony"

23. Thematic Catalogs, Lists, and Indexes

Anonymous. "Index to the songs and allusions in The
      Gentleman's Journal, 1692-94"
Holman, Peter. "The trumpet sonata in England"
Smith, Alan. *An index of the works of Henry Purcell*
Thiemann, Susan. *The works of Henry Purcell*
Zimmerman, Franklin B. *Henry Purcell, 1659-1695: an
      analytical catalogue of his music*
Zimmerman, Franklin B. *Henry Purcell: 1659-1695:
      melodic and intervallic indexes to his complete works*

24. Theory and Instruction

Colles, H.C. "Some musical instruction books"
North, Roger. *An essay of musical ayre*

Playford, John. *An introduction to the skill of musick*
Squire, William Barclay. "Purcell as theorist"
Zimmerman, Franklin B. "Air, a catch-word"
Zimmerman, Franklin B., ed. "John Playford's
    Introduction to the skill of music, 12th edition"

25. Attributions

Browning, Alan. "Purcell's 'Stairre Case Overture'"
Bunten, Alice C. "God save the king"
Cooper, Barry. "Did Purcell write a trumpet voluntary?"
Covell, R. "Seventeenth-century music for The Tempest"
Cudworth, Charles. "Some new facts about the trumpet
    voluntary"
Cutts, John P. "An unpublished Purcell setting"
Fiske, Roger. "The Macbeth music"
Ford, Robert. "A Sacred Song not by Purcell"
Laurie, Margaret. "Did Purcell set The Tempest?"
McLean, Hugh. "Blow and Purcell in Japan"
Moore, Robert E. "The music to Macbeth"
Petre, R. "A new piece by Henry Purcell"
Rose, Gloria. "Purcell, Michelangelo Rossi, and J.S. Bach"
Zimmerman, Franklin B. "A newly-discovered anthem by
    Purcell"
Zimmerman, Franklin B. "Jeremiah Clarke's trumpet
    voluntary"

26. Bibliographical Reference Works, Indexes, and Guides

Anonymous. "Index to the songs and musical allusions in
    The Gentleman's Journal, 1692-94"
Day, Cyrus Lawrence and Eleanore Boswell Murrie.
    English song-books
Greenhalgh, Michael J. *The music of Henry Purcell*
King, A. Hyatt. "Benjamin Goodison"
King, A. Hyatt. "The first complete edition of Purcell"

FULL CITATIONS,
ALPHABETICAL BY AUTHOR,
WITH SELECTIVE COMMENTARY

Anderson, William W. *The stylistic development of Henry Purcell as revealed by his sacred verse anthems.* D.M.A. Dissertation, University of Kansas (1986). 1779 pp. Musical examples, notes, appendix, including graphic chart for each anthem discussed, chronological listing, and classified bibliography.

>   An interesting study, in which some of the analytical discussions might have led to new conclusions, except that borrowed opinions from secondary sources seemed to stand in the way.

Anonymous. "Memoirs of the life and writing of Henry Purcell, the celebrated English composer, illustrated with his portrait, finely engraved." *Universal Magazine*, vol. 61 (1777): 281-86.

>   A rather cursory, uncritical approach to Purcell's life and works, which, however, is among the earliest complete treatments of this subject matter.

Anonymous. "Index to the songs and musical allusions in The Gentleman's Journal, 1692-94." *Musical Antiquary* (1911): 225-34.

>   This little article provides a very useful study of the popular image of Purcell and musical contemporaries just before the time of his death.

Anonymous. "Purcell and Italian Music." *Musical Times,* vol. 58 (1917): 157.

This is a short, but valuable discussion of Italian influence on Purcell, mentioning chiefly that of Lelio Colista, whose sonatas Purcell cited in his edition of the third part of Playford's *Introduction to the skill of music*.

Antcliffe, Herbert. "The naïveté of Purcell." *Chesterian,* no. 17 (1921): 13-15.

Without defining the term, the author posits naïveté as one of Purcell's primary characteristics, inventing evidence where needed to support his thesis.

Arkwright, G.E.P. "Purcell's church music." *Musical Antiquary,* vol. 1 (1910): 63-72, 234-48.

An excellent early study of this genre, though somewhat brief and inconclusive so far as Purcell's musical style is concerned.

Arkwright, G.E.P. "A note on Purcell's music." *Music and Letters,* vol. 2 (1921): 149-62.

Quoting Burney (q.v.) on Purcell's fading fame, the author says that his negative prophecy has been fulfilled in modern times. He cites Purcell for jejune illustrations, harmonic transgressions, and a style generally passé. These criticisms are not well taken.

Arundell, Dennis Drew. "Purcell and natural speech." *Musical Times,* vol. 1100 (1959): 323-24.

Though brief, this article brings refreshing insights into the analysis of Purcell's vocal music, and will be of value to singers and others interested in Purcellian performance practices. According to Arundell, Purcell's subtlest skill was that of setting the English language to music, a skill for which he had a virtually infallible ear.

Arundell, Dennis Drew. *The critic at the opera.* London: Ernest Benn, 1957. xiii, 424 pp. Foreword, bibliography, index, illustrations; list of composers and conductors.

Chapter 12, "Purcell and opera" (pp. 144-54), is an excellent summary of Purcell's stage musical activities, with perceptive appraisals of several of the operatic works. Inexplicably, he omits *The Indian queen* and gives only passing reference to *The fairy queen.*

Arundell, Dennis Drew. *Henry Purcell.* London: Oxford University Press, 1927. 136 pp. Frontispiece, illustrations (including facsimiles, music, portrait), genealogy, bibliographical footnotes, history, analysis, criticism, biography.

Perhaps the most succinct and informative of all studies of Purcell's life and works, this book is rendered all the more pleasant by an attractive style. Summarizing stylistic developments in each Purcellian genre, Arundell displays fine musical understanding. This is a valuable general study.

Ashbee, Andrew, transcr. & ed. *Lists of payments to the King's Musick in the reign of Charles II* (1660-1685). Snodland, Kent: A. Ashbee, 1981. xiv, 129 pp.

Concise information on actual payments to musicians, including amount of annual payment, name of payee, reason for payment, period represented, date of payment, and amount paid. As compared to other compilations of this sort, accuracy is exemplary. Interestingly enough, Henry Purcell II is constantly referred to among "the violins."

Ashbee, Andrew, transcr. & ed. *Records of the English court, vol. I (1660-1685)*. Snodland, Kent: A. Ashbee, 1986. xviii, 317 pp. Indexes of places and persons.

An extensive revision, completion and thorough remodelling of LaFontaine's *The King's Musick*, this is the first of a series of four or more volumes that will be appearing in the near future. Mr. Ashbee has inventoried a great many new source documents.

Ashbee, Andrew, calendarer & ed. *Records of the English court, vol. II (1685-1714)*, Snodland, Kent: A. Ashbee, 1987. xvi, 246 pp. Indexes of places and persons.

See above.

Avery, Emmet L., ed. *The London stage 1660-1800: A calendar of plays, entertainments, and afterpieces together with casts, box-receipts and contemporary comment.* Part I, edited by William van Lennep. Carbondale: Southern Illinois University Press, 1960. ccxci, 532 pp. Index.

This monumental study, pioneered by van Lennep, and completed after his death, appears in five parts, the first of which he nearly finished. Although dedicated mainly to theatrical affairs, as the title indicates, the compilation includes all manner of commentary on music, musicians, concert life, incidental music for the stage, opera, semi-opera and other lyrical forms and the development of all these, both within and outside the realm of the theatre. The chief value of this work to Purcell research is to be found in commentary on stage pieces for which he provided music. But there is much useful information on other aspects of his life and works. In sum, this is an indispensable reference work for Purcell study.

Ayres, J. C. *The influence of French composers on the work of Purcell.* London, 1964.

Baldwin, Olive, and Thelma Wilson. "Purcell's sopranos." *Musical Times,* vol. 123 (1982): 602-09.

This article first discusses the careers of two singers, Arabella Hunt and Charlotte Butler, whose names are frequently associated with Purcell's music. While the former seems to have sung mainly for Queen Mary or at private houses, the latter became Purcell's leading soprano and a favorite dancer on the stage. Other singers also are discussed, including Mrs. Ayliffe, Mrs. Dyer, Catherine Shore, Miss Cross, and Mrs. Bracegirdle, for whom Purcell wrote no songs, however. An excellent article, this brings together a great deal of interesting information on Purcell's female vocalists, with mention also of a few male singers.

Baldwin, Olive, and Thelma Wilson. "Who can from joy refraine?" *Musical Times,* vol. 122 (1981): 596-99.

Fortified with quotations from contemporary newspapers and from Narcissus Luttrell's *Historical relations of state affairs,* this article provides a very informative account of the genesis of Purcell's last ode for the Stuart dynasty, and of its interesting political background. The authors also have provided an excellent guide to the text and useful hints on modern performance of the work.

Beechy, Gwillen. "Henry Playford's Harmonia Sacra." *The Consort*, vol. 42 (1986): 14.

This article presents a brief introduction to the life and career of Henry Playford, followed by eleven examples in facsimile of pages from the first edition of *Harmonia Sacra*, vol. I. The reproductions are excellent.

Bergmann, W. "Henry Purcell's use of the recorder." *Recorder and Music,* vol. 7 (1983): 310-13.

A fairly thorough account of the recorder in Purcell's music, this study dwells mainly on practical applications rather than on dramatic significance of the use of the instrument.

Bicknell, Joan Colleen. *Interdependence of word and tone in the dramatic music of Henry Purcell.* Ph.D. dissertation, Stanford University, 1960. xi, 256 pp. Appendix, bibliography.

Stronger in analysis than in criticism, this study nevertheless provides an interesting account of this essential aspect of Purcell's creative genius. Compared to Rohrer's study listed below, this is more limited both in approach and in conclusions reached.

Bicknell, Joan Colleen. "On performing Purcell's vocal music: some neglected evidence." *Music Review,* vol. 25 (1964): 27-34.

Citing passages from Thomas Morley, Girolamo
Frescobaldi, Christopher Simpson, Thomas Mace and
Roger North, Dr. Bicknell draws together evidence
from across a century. Her suggestions are well-taken
and tasteful, for the most part, but do not bear the stamp
of authenticity they might have had if based on sources
chronologically closer to Purcell. Her study is more
helpful, however, than that listed below for Peter Pears.

Bingley, William. *Musical biography; memoirs of the lives
and writings of the most eminent musical composers
and writers who have flourished in the different
countries of Europe during the last three centuries.*
Reprint of 1834 ed., New York: Da Capo, 1971. 2
vols., 405 and 395 pp. Explanatory index.

These essays include brief biographical notices on
Christopher Gibbons, Albertus Brynne, William Child,
John Banister, Matthew Locke, Pelham Humfrey,
Michael Wise, John Abell, John Playford, Nicholas
Staggins, John Blow. These are mere digests of
Burney's accounts of the same figures. Bingley's
account of Purcell is taken word for word from Burney,
with some digesting of longer passages.

Bliss, Arthur, "Henry Purcell." *Chesterian,* new series no.
17 (1921): 13-15.

As an important composer in the development of the
English musical renaissance of the twentieth century,
Bliss writes effectively on the impact of Henry Purcell
on modern English musical life.

Blow, John. "Ode on the death of Mr. Henry Purcell; for
two countertenors, two treble recorders, and
harpsichord . . . with violoncello *ad lib.* Edited by

Walter Bergmann." London: Schott; New York: Associated Music Publishers, 1962. Score, 24 pp. and 4 parts.

Boito, Diane. "Manuscript Music in the James Marshall and Marie-Louise Osborn Collection." *Notes,* vol. 27 (December 1970): 237-44.

This is an inventory of the entire collection, including the following Purcell-bearing items: (1) Autograph MS of works by Henry Purcell, Pelham Humfrey; (2) "Elizabeth Segar, Her Booke" in which she identifies only the dialog between Corydon and Mopsa. Quite evidently, she missed a lot.

Bridge, J. Frederick. *Twelve good musicians; from John Bull to Henry Purcell.* London: Kegan Paul, Trench and Trubner, 1920. vii, 144 pp. Note on Henry Purcell, brief index, biographical sketches.

The relevant essays on Matthew Locke, Pelham Humphrey, John Blow provide excellent background information on the period.
That on Henry Purcell (pp. 108-41, plus note) is one of the better early summaries of Purcell's life and works, with an interesting hint that the Purcell family may have originated near Chirk, in Shropshire.

Bridge, J. Frederick. "Purcell and Nicola Matteis." *Sammelbände der Internationale Musik-Gesellschaft,* jahrg. 1 (1900): 623-26.

Purcell's trio sonatas marked new departure, influenced by the Italian band of Maria of Modena. As tradition had it, Purcell knew works of Carissimi, Cesti, Colonna, Gratiani, Bassani, and Stradella; to this group, H. Davy added Frescobaldi, H. Parry added Vitali, and F. Bridge added Matteis, with special emphasis as provided in this article. This is a useful work for appraisal of the history of the study of Italian influence on Henry Purcell, but less useful than studies of the same subject by Dart, Favre-Lingorow, Hogwood, Klenz, Tilmouth and Wessley-Kropik.

Bridge, J. Frederick. "Purcell's Fantazias and Sonatas." *Proceedings of the Musical Association,* session 42 (1915-16): 1-13; discussion, pp. 11-13.

After describing the physical attributes of the autograph (now British Library MS Add. 30930), Bridge analyzes the fourth fantasia (in c-minor) with phrase-by-phrase commentary on its technical make-up. No hint of the delightful mystery of this work, or other fantasias, found its way into his prose. He then turned to the *Sonatas of 1683*, identifying Nicola Matteis as the principal, indeed, the only, Italian who influenced Purcell's trio sonata compositions. He ends by correcting a few of Purcell's "harmonic mistakes," and by offering general, though vague, remarks about Sonatas Nos. Four and Six of the first set, promising to return to the Sonatas of 1697 at a future date. This study also is less helpful than those of later authors, as mentioned in the item immediately above.

Bridges, Robert Seymour. "Purcell ode and other poems." In *Collected Works*. Chicago, 1896. xxiv, pp. 30-54.

Britten, Benjamin. "On realizing the continuo in Purcell's songs." *Henry Purcell (1659-1695): essays on his music,* edited by Imogen Holst. London: Oxford University Press, 1959. Pp. 7-13.

Apt commentary on the art of songwriting as practiced by Purcell and expert commentary on realizing the bass line. Some stylistic ambiguity arises from the author's shifting from harpischord to piano as the basic instrument Writing from a composer's point of view, Britten gives advice that is less useful than that of Donington's general article on performance practice listed below.

Browning, Alan. "Purcell's 'Stairre Case Overture.'" *Musical Times,* vol. 121 (1980): 768-69.

Mr. Browning in this article writes of the new overture by Purcell, which he discovered in MS 515 of the Osborne Collection, housed in the Beinecke Rare Book Library at Yale Univeristy. The version given is almost identical with that discovered by Nigel Fortune in the Tatton Park MSS (see below). According to Browning the MS contains specimens of Purcell's early handwriting style.

Bucht, Gunnar. "Purcell och den engelske fancyn. Till 300-åraminnet av tonsättarens fodelse." *Musikrevy,* lg.13 nr. 7 (1958): 233-35, 245.

Bumpus, John S. *A history of English cathedral music 1549-1889.* 2 vols. London: T. Werner Laurie, 1908. 267 and 313 pp. Plates, including music facsimiles.

Lucid commentary on Purcell's sacred music, with much useful information on the works of his English contemporaries, predecessors and followers. The account is occasionally marred by misinformation or omissions, but generally reliable nonetheless. The modern reader will find less that is valuable than in studies by Dennison, Fortune, Foster, Long and Wienandt/Young, as listed below.

Bunten, Alice C. *"God save the king."* *6 facsimiles of the earliest prints of our national anthem.* London: Schott, 1902. P. 13. With annotations by A.C. Bunten.

The music is variously attributed to Henry Carey, John Bull, James Oswald, and Purcell. While not a definitive answer to the question of ultimate authorship, this compilation provides a great deal of interesting data.

Burkhart, R.E. *The trumpet in England in the seventeenth century with emphasis on its treatment in the works of Henry Purcell and a biography of the Shore family of trumpeters.* D.M.A. dissertation, University of Wisconsin, 1972. 142 pp. UM 72-9111.

Chief interest of this dissertation centers in Chapter II: 'The trumpet in Purcell's works from 1690-1695,' but the entire study is very useful for its excellent presentation of the backgrounds and sequelae to Purcell's trumpet usage. (One might wish for an adequate discussion of the trumpet tune *per se,* but that is another matter.) Chapter II is a very closely worked analysis of all Purcell's writing for trumpet, with excellent commentary on the contemporary scene, and fine suggestions on performance practices and interpretive problems. Chapter III deals with the period before 1690 and is very useful for an understanding of Purcell's usage, even though none of his works is discussed. For other excellent studies on the same subject, see Conley and Smithers, below.

Burney, Charles. *A general history of music; from the earliest ages to the present period.* London, 1789. 4

vols., 622 pp. Copious music examples, notes and indexes to each of four volumes.

Essays on all the major composers of the period, written with Burney's fine musical insights and understanding. Despite some evidence of prejudice against certain stylistic characteristics of post-Restoration music, Burney's account of the period still must be considered among the best available.

Busby, Thomas. *A general history of music from earliest times to the present; comprising the lives of eminent composers and musical writers.* 2 vols. London: G. and W.B. Whittaker and Simpkin and Marshall, 1819. 552, 523 pp.

The whole accompanied with notes and observations, musical examples, no index. Busby has paraphrased biographical portions from Burney's history, leaving out a great deal of important information. He differs from Burney in musical judgement and analysis, however, and advances other examples to illustrate some of his points.

Buttrey, John. "The evolution of English opera between 1656 and 1695: a reinvestigation." Dissertation, Cambridge University, 1967. 280 pp.

A very careful analysis of all the data then available, including new information presented by Avery, van Lennep, and their colleagues. The study is full of youthful enthusiasm for concepts and ideas already developed by Denis Arundell and Eric Walter White *et al.*

Buttrey, John.   "Dating Purcell's Dido and Aeneas."
Proceedings of the Royal Musical Association, vol. 94
(1967-68): 51-62.

    A detailed study of the evidence, which, however,
produces no new conclusions beyond those already
provided by Denis Arundell and Eric Walter White.

Charleton, D.   "King Arthur: A dramatick opera." *Music
and Letters,* vol. 64 (1983): 183-92.

    To "stress the integrity of King Arthur, with special
reference to its music," the author analyzes in detail the
text and music of King Arthur. He points out that
Dryden had modelled this dynastic legend after *Orlando
furioso,* providing for a curious and unexpected link
with Handel's *Alcina.* This is an interesting and
informative study, achieving rare success in tracing the
intricate network of relationships between music and
text. Charleton's summing up makes clear the political
purpose of the opera: "For *King Arthur* is the story not
primarily of the events of St. George's Day, nor even of
the eleventh decisive defeat of the Saxons, but a series
of trials that display the worthiness of two persons to
make a dynastic marriage." This penetrating study lays
bare permanent values of *King Arthur*—values which
hitherto have lain hidden.

Charteris, Richard.   "Some manuscript discoveries of
    Henry Purcell and his contemporaries in the Newberry
    Library, Chicago." *Notes,* vol. 37 (1980-81): 7-13.

    This article is devoted to MS additions to four
printed books in the Newberry Library. These are (1)
Case 6A143, Christopher Simpson, *The Division Viol*
(2nd edition, 1667); (2) Case VM3.1P985, Henry
Purcell, *A Collection of Ayres Compos'd for the*

Theatre, 1697, which has 1st and 2nd treble parts of G. B. Bassani's *Sonatas of 1683* (Amsterdam) with unique pieces by John Eccles, Gottfried Finger, Solomon Eccles, Thomas Pickmore, the *Trumpet Sonata* by Henry Purcell, and various miscellaneous pieces; (3) Case VMT 252 P72.1 John Playford, *Musick's Handmaid* (1678) including twenty-four pieces in MS copy, among them a keyboard transcription of Purcell's "Ah! cruel, bloody fate,"(Z606/9); and Case MS VM 2.3E58r, MS Volume entitled "Eliz. Roper, Her Booke, 1691." Purcellian contents include 630/1A, "Almand," 630/2B; a Prelude, possibly by Purcell, 570/6 & 7; and finally, a new and unique piece, "Mr. Purcell's Ground." This is a new and important addition to known Purcell resources.

Chazanoff, Daniel. *Early English chamber music from William Byrd to Henry Purcell.* Columbia University, 1964. 274 pp. Musical examples, bibliography, appendix listing modern editions.

The author has restricted bibliographical references entirely to secondary sources, thus severely limiting the range and scope of his study and at the same time opening his work to misinformation. Commentary on Purcell's music is amateurish, devoted mainly to surface characteristics.

Chissel, Joan. "St. Cecilia—Purcell and Britten." *Monthly Musical Record,* vol. 73 (1943): 123-27.

Comparing Purcell's first St. Cecilia Ode ('Welcome to all the pleasures') to Benjamin Britten's *Hymn to St. Cecilia,* the author recounts the legend of the musical saint before discussing two of Purcell's other St. Cecilia compositions—'Hail bright Cecilia'

and *Te Deum & Jubilate in D Major*. The article ends
with a brief analysis of Britten's work.

Cibber, Colley. *An Apology for the Life of Colley Cibber,
Comedian, and Late Patentee of the Theatre-Royal,
With an Historical View of the Stage during his own
time. Written by Himself.* The Second Edition,
London, 1740. 488 pp.

A detailed discussion of the principal figures
involved in the post-Restoration development of the
London stage, with enlightening commentary on its
early history. Direct reference to Purcell occurs only in
Anthony Aston's *A Brief Supplement to Colley Cibber,
Esq.,* a modern edition of which appeared in 1889,
edited by Lowe. But Cibber's journal nevertheless
provides a valuable background to the history of the
stage in the Purcellian era.

Clarke, Jeremiah. *Music on Henry Purcell's death.* Edited
by Walter Bergmann. London, 1961. 36 pp.

Colles, H.C. *Voice and verse; a study in English song.*
London: Oxford University Press, 1928. xii, 167 pp.
A series of lectures at Glasgow University, 1927.
Musical illustrations, notes.

Commentary on Purcell occurs mainly in the fifth
and sixth lectures, and presents fully informed
opinions, showing an excellent grasp of Purcell's
significant achievments. The fourth lecture, "Towards
English Opera," sheds significant light on the
development of this institution, which was very
important in Purcell's career.

Colles, H.C. "Lully and Purcell." *Essays and lectures.* London: Oxford University Press, 1945. Pp. 50-51.

Comparing Purcell most favorably to his French contemporary, the author demonstrates a close musical understanding of both composers.

Colles, H.C. "Musical London from the Restoration to Handel." *Essays and lectures.* London: Oxford University Press, 1945. Pp. 8-46.

A brief general survey which emphasizes Purcell's importance in the development of music in England through the time of Handel.

Colles, H.C. "Purcell restored." *Essays and lectures.* London: Oxford University Press, 1945. Pp. 47-49.

This comment on new interest in Purcell among twentieth-century audiences is refreshing, by contrast to the usual jeremiads on neglect.

Colles, H.C. "Some musical instruction books of the seventeenth century." *Proceedings of the Musical Association,* vol. 55 (1928): 31-49.

Discussing Purcell's share in Playford's *Introduction,* Colles sketches backgrounds. He suggests that the high marks W. Barclay Squire gave Purcell as theorist were perhaps too high.

Colles, H.C. "Music in four countries at the end of the seventeenth century; III: England." *The growth of music, vol. I.* London: Oxford University Press, 1956. Pp. 73-84.

This study shows Purcell's paramount position in English and continental music history up to the end of the seventeenth century.

Conley, Philip R. "The use of the trumpet in the music of Purcell." *The Brass Quarterly,* vol. 3 (1959): 2-11.

This is an excellent summary of Purcell's use of the trumpet revealing an intimate understanding of the Baroque trumpet and its repertory. It compares favorably with the studies of Purcell's use of trumpet by Burkhart and Smithers.

Cooper, Barry. "Did Purcell write a trumpet voluntary?— I." *Musical Times*, vol. 119 (1978): 791-93.

According to Mr. Cooper, the answer to the question is "yes." In this, the first of two articles on the subject, he indicates that Purcell is represented by one, or at least a part of one of the *"Ten Select Voluntaries for the Organ Composed by Orlando Gibbons, Blow, Purcell, Doctr. Green, Doctr. Boyce, Mr. James Martin Smith, Organist at Gloucester, and J. Stafford Smith, Book IIId"* (London: Longman & Broderip, ca. 1780).

Cooper, Barry. "Did Purcell write a trumpet voluntary?— II." *Musical Times,* vol. 119 (1978): 1073-75.

In this second article Mr. Cooper arrives by labyrinthine processes of elimination at no. 9, in the collection mentioned at the end of part one of this article. In his opinion, this sonata was the joint work of Purcell and Blow: "It cannot be proved that Purcell and Blow were the authors of these two movements. But with the evidence as it stands it seems extremely likely that they were. If so, the first movement is closer to

Blow than Purcell and the second movement is more typical of Purcell—the theme is even reminiscent of the Amen from his Jubilate in D." On this shaky ground the author leaves us waiting for solider evidence to support his hypothetical identification of this voluntary as the work of Henry Purcell. The fact that Purcell is mentioned on the title page, however, warrants inclusion of the piece among Purcell's *opera dubia*.

Cooper, Gerald M. "The chronology of Purcell's music." *Musical Times,* vol. 84 (1943): July, 203-04; August, 236-38; September, 270; October, 299-301; November, 331-32; December, 363-65.

This is a valuable study, superseded only after two decades.

Covell, R. "Seventeenth-century music for The Tempest." *Studies in Music (SMA),* vol. 2 (1968): 43-63.

Commencing with Shakespeare's play, and its rich musical opportunities, Professor Covell traces in painstaking detail the works of various composers who wrote music for the play. Coming to Purcell's contributions and supposed contributions towards the end of the study, he discusses these very fairly and sensibly. In view of the doubts that have been cast on Purcell's authorship of many of these items, this is a useful study even though all questions on the authenticity of Purcell's music have not, indeed may never be, fully answered.

Cudworth, Charles. "Some new facts about the trumpet voluntary." *Musical Times,* vol. 94, no. 4 (1953): 401-03.

Reviewing the original edition of the "Trumpet Voluntary," published by Mr. William Sparks, Mr. Cudworth points out that it was brought out as Purcell's even though there was no ascription to him in any source. He then proceeded to identify the actual composer, Jeremiah Clarke, as proved in British Library MSS Add. 30839 and 39565-7.

Cummings, W.H. "Purcell." *The great musicians*, edited by Frances Hueffer. London: S. Low, Marston, Searle, and Rivington, 1881; rev. ed., London and New York: Haskell House, 1937. viii, 124 pp.

A pioneer work, weakened by an uncritical approach to factual evidence, and an amateurish evaluation of Purcell's music.

Cummings, W.H. "Purcell and Dr. Arne." *Musical Times,* vol. 36 (1896): 15-16.

An interesting discussion of Arne's revision and alteration of Purcell's *King Arthur,* with commentary on Arne's character.

Cutts, John P. "An unpublished Purcell setting." *Music and Letters*, vol. 38 (1957): 1-13.

The new Purcell work Dr. Cutts discovered was already well known at the time his article was published. However, he did discover a new version of the song, "The earth trembled [Z197]." At the same time he has provided a useful inventory and description of a new manuscript source.

Dart, Thurston. "Purcell and Bull." *Musical Times,* vol. 104 (1963): 30-31.

Description, inventory and discussion of a new Purcell autograph manuscript, given to Professor Dart by Boris Ord. The MS includes an eight-part canon on *Miserere* by John Bull, gatherings containing fancies by Orlando Gibbons and Giovanni Coperario, and a gathering of miscellaneous transcriptions and copy including passages from Monteverdi's *Cruda amarilli, Troppo ben può,* and *T'amo mia vita,* all from his *Fifth Book of Madrigals,* an anonymous dialogue, "As Celia," and Nicholas Lanier's "Shepherd, in faith I cannot stay." This is a very useful article on Purcell's musical heritage and an impressive addition to his list of autograph manuscripts.

Dart, Thurston. "Purcell's chamber music." *Proceedings of the Royal Musical Association,* vol. 85 (1958-59): 81-93.

Probably the best study to date on the entire body of Purcell's chamber music, this article is based on Professor Dart's preparation of volume XXXI of the Purcell Society Edition. He discusses the four components of Purcell's chamber music, evaluates their sources, establishes a new chronology, and provides useful suggestions with regard to performance and ornamentation. It is an excellent and a very useful article in a great number of areas.

Dart, Thurston. "The Cibell." *La Revue Belge de Musicologie,* vol. 6 (1952): 24-30.

The author identifies Purcell's *Cibell* as the first English tune in imitation of the Lullian cibell, as presented in *Atys.* This exists in a version for harpsichord in Purcell's *Choice Collection of Lessons for the Harpsichord or Spinnet,* and in a five-part version for trumpet and strings in the Magdalene College, Cambridge, part-books now on loan to Fitzwilliam Museum Library.

Dart, Thurston.   "Purcell's harpsichord music." *Musical Times,* vol. 100 (1959): 324.

A penetrating study, approached both from the point of view of the performing artist and skilled musicologist. Though viewed by Westrup as relatively unimportant, Purcell's keyboard works, according to Dart, deserve far more attention than they get. In this short article he provided a succinct inventory and evaluation which served useful purpose until the appearance of Howard Ferguson's lengthier, more detailed article on the same subject. (See below.)

Day, Cyrus Lawrence, and Eleanore Boswell Murrie. *English song-books, 1, 1651-1702; a bibliography with a first-line index of songs.* London: Oxford University Press, 1940. xxi, 439 pp. Plates and illustrations, with indexes of composers, authors, sources, song-books, and a general index.

This is the standard reference work on the subject, presenting such accuracy and completeness of information as to be unique. It is an indispensable research tool for Purcell's vocal music.

Demarquez, Susanne. *Purcell.* (Collection Euterpe.) Paris: Colombe, 1951. 181 pp. Musical examples, bibliography, discography.

Beginning with a potted history of 'the epoch,' Demarquez rehashes information from other biographical sources but brings nothing new to light.

Dennison, P. "The stylistic origins of the early church music." *Essays on opera and English music,* edited by F.W. Sternfeld, Nigel Fortune and Edward Olleson. Oxford: Blackwell, 1975. Pp. 44-61.

First analyzing the contents of Purcell's autograph score-book, Fitzwilliam Museum MS 88, the author evaluates the influence on Purcell of his two teachers, Pelham Humfrey and John Blow, with passing reference also to Matthew Locke. After discussing the anthem styles of these composers at some length, the author classifies all of Purcell's anthems that can be attributed with confidence to his early period before 1682. He then discusses these, commenting on the influences of Humfrey, Blow and Locke, respectively. This is an interesting article, although proof of chronological placement is lacking and analytical descriptions are somewhat vague and too narrowly based solely on the English tradition.

Dent, Edward J., ed. *Purcell's The Fairy Queen as presented by the Sadler's Wells ballet, and the Covent Garden opera;* a photographic record by Edward Mandinian, with the preface to the original text, a preface by E.J. Dent, etc. London, 1948. 96 pp. The book also contains articles by Constant Lambert and Michael Ayrton.

Dent, Edward J. *The foundations of English opera.* New York: Da Capo Press, 1965. Pp. 177-234.

This is a concise but thorough survey of early English opera, with perceptive commentary on Purcell's *Dido and Aeneas, Dioclesian, King Arthur,* and *The fairy queen.*

Donington, Robert. "Further seventeenth- and eighteenth-century evidence bearing on the performance of Purcell's works." *Henry Purcell (1659-95): essays on his music.* Edited by Imogen Holst. London: Oxford University Press, 1959. Appendix B, pp. 122-26.

Additional advice on authentic stylistic interpretation of accidentals, ornaments, rubato, rhythm, phrasing, articulation, tempo, and dynamics in Purcell's music, as drawn from contemporary and near-contemporary sources. A valuable addition to the next item.

Donington, Robert. "Performing Purcell's music today." *Henry Purcell (1659-95): essays on his music.* Edited by Imogen Holst. London: Oxford University Press, 1959. Pp. 74-102.

The author makes an impassioned, convincing case for romantic expression in the interpretation of Purcell's music, continues with very good advice on various techniques for completing Purcell's actual notation, which by modern standards, seems a kind of shorthand. A very thorough and useful exposition of some of the more problematic aspects of Purcell performance.

Downes, John. *Roscius Anglicanus, or an Historical Review of the Stage: After it had been suppres'd by means of the late unhappy civil war, begun in 1641, till the time of King Charles the IIs. Restoration in May, 1660. Giving an account of its rise again; of the time and places the governours of both the companies first*

erected their theatres. *The names of the principal actors
and actresses, who perform'd in the chiefest plays in
each house. With the names of the most taking plays;
and modern poets. For the space of 46 years, and
during the reign of three kings, and part of our present
sovereign Lady Queen Anne, from 1660, to 1706, Non
Audita narro, sed Comperta,* edited by Montague
Summers. London: The Fortune Press, n.d. 213 pp.

An important contemporary source for stage music,
Roscius Anglicanus is weakened by a failure to specify
exact dates.

Downes, Ralph. "An organist's view of the organ works."
Henry Purcell (1659-95): essays on his music. Edited
by Imogen Holst. London: Oxford University Press,
1959. Pp. 67-73

The author considers Purcell's organ works as
trifling, although he speaks of the G major verse as "a
little gem of its kind." Neither analytical nor
comparative statements are offered to support such
opinions.

Duckles, Vincent Harris. "English song and the challenge of
Italian monody." *Words to music; papers on English
seventeenth-century song read at a Clark Library
Seminar, December 11, 1965, by Vincent Duckles and
Franklin B. Zimmerman.* Introduction by Walter
Rubsamen. Los Angeles: University of California,
1967. Pp. 3-42.

Professor Duckles's exploration of the influence of
Italian monody on English poetry and music, during the
reigns of Charles I and Cromwell is most illuminating.
His excellent preparation of a first-rate edition of
Nicholas Lanier's *Hero and Leander,* one of the most

perspicuous of the early English monodies, only adds to the value of the article.

Duncan, Edmonstoune. "The songs of Henry Purcell." *Monthly Musical Record,* vol. 33 (1903): 84-85.

In this short but interesting article, the author discusses about a dozen of the eighty songs which are to be found in *Orpheus Britannicus I.* It is a thoughtful essay on Purcell's art of songwriting.

Dupré, Henri. *Purcell,* par Henri Dupré. (*Les maîtres de la musique*). Paris: F. Alcan, 1927. ii, 191 pp.

List of dramatic works in which Purcell collaborated; bibliography. (See next item.)

Dupré, Henri. *Purcell.* Translated from the French by Catherine Alison Phillips and Agnes Bedford. New York: A. A. Knopf, 1928. iv, 208 pp. List of dramatic works for which Purcell composed the music with approximate dates of composition; frontispiece, illustrations (music), facsimiles and bibliography. The translation also includes a section on religious music.

Beginning with a frontispiece portrait erroneously identified as a portrait of Henry Purcell, and including a facsimile from *The fairy queen,* said to be autograph and is not, the author labors in frequent error. Discussions of Purcell's music proceed more convincingly, at least until the author begins to make wild assertions about Purcell's direct influence on such distant figures as César Franck and Richard Wagner. The book should be used with caution. The translation is an expanded edition of the French original, with additional commentary, notes and bibliographical entries.

Elkin, Robert. *The old concert rooms of London.* London: Edward Arnold, 1955. 167 pp.

This study of early concert life in London devotes only the first two chapters to "musick houses," taverns, and other musical establishments. Although there is only one brief reference to Purcell (p. 34), these first two chapters provide a useful background to musical life in his time.

Espinós, Víctor. "Las realizaciones musicales del Quijote: Enrique Purcell y su 'Comical History of Don Quixote.'" *Revista de la biblioteca, archivo y museo,* tomo 10 (Madrid, 1933): 34-62.

This study, rather general in nature from a musical point of view, is interesting in its sound literary approach to the subject.

Evelyn, John. *Diary.* Edited by E.S. de Beer. 6 vols. Oxford: Clarendon Press, 1955.

Though concerned with the half century before Purcell came to maturity, Evelyn's diary, like that of Samuel Pepys, provides invaluable eyewitness accounts of musical life in England during the Commonwealth and Restoration periods.

Favre-Lingorow, Stella. *Der Instrumentalstil von Purcell.* Bern: P. Haupt, 1950. (*Berner Veröffentlichungen zur Musikforschung* heft 16.) 116 pp., plus an Appendix of musical examples of 20 pp.

This monograph provides a thorough and highly technical discussion of Purcell's forms and techniques within the context of a historical study of his instrumental music. The author holds that Purcell's canzonas established one of the more important stages of fugal writing before the advent of J.S. Bach, but does not develop this point as fully as she might have done. Her treatment of Purcell's canzonas, fantasias, suites, sonatas, and ostinato forms is instructive as well as informative, though at times somewhat lost in detail. She did not comment on cyclical thematic usages in Purcell, nor on some of the interesting *canti prius facti* which appear throughout his works. In this regard her work study does not quite come up to the level achieved by Michael Tilmouth in his study of Purcell's instrumental music. In sum, Favre-Lingorow's methodology is sound and impressive, but her grasp of the principles of Purcell's composition not as full as it might have been.

Ferguson, Howard. "Purcell's harpsichord music." *Proceedings of the Royal Musical Association,* vol. 91 (1964-65): 1-9.

A carefully researched study based on the author's new edition of Purcell's harpsichord music, this article furnishes the most recent, comprehensive, and up-to-date information on the subject at this time.

Ferguson, Howard. "Two Purcell discoveries." *Piano Quarterly,* vol. 66 (Winter 1968-9): 18-19.

The author writes of his discovery of alternate preludes to Purcell's Suite for Harpsichord in g-minor (Z661), in B.L. Add. MS 31,403; and to the Suite for Harpsichord in a minor (Z663), Chr. Ch. Mus. MS

1177. He has edited these for inclusion in his Eight Suites. (See Selective List of Editions, *infra*.)

Fiske, Roger. "The Macbeth Music." *Music and Letters,* vol. 45 (1964): 114-25.

This article makes it clear that Purcell had nothing to do with *The Tempest.*

Flood, W.H. Grattan. "Irish ancestry of Garland, Dowland, Campion, and Purcell." *Music and Letters,* vol. 3 (1922): 59-65.

Flood, W.H. Grattan. "Purcell's Dido and Æneas; who was Lady Dorothy Burke?" *Musical Times,* vol. 59 (1918): 515.

The author in this article posed the question that eventually led to accurate chronological placement of this opera, even though he was uninformed.

Ford, Anthony D. "A Purcell service and its sources." *Musical Times,* vol. 124 (1983): 121-22.

Discussing twenty-seven MS sources for Purcell's *Service in g minor,* the author comments on the circumstances under which Thomas Roseingrave's setting of the *Magnificat* came to be associated with this work. A very detailed and well-reasoned investigation of important archival material, this article sheds valuable light on the growth of a Purcellian repertory throughout England.

Ford, Robert. "A sacred song not by Purcell." [Full of wrath, his threat'ning breath.] *Musical Times,* vol. 125 (1984): 45-47.

Ford, Robert. "Purcell as his own editor: the funeral sentences." *The Journal of Musicological Research,* vol. 7 (1986): 47-67.

Scrutinizing early manuscript sources of Purcell's *Funeral Sentences,* the author re-evaluates these and provides a very detailed analysis of their readings. As a result, he is able to demonstrate convincingly that the "authentic" versions of the sentences represented in the Purcell Society Edition need to be carefully re-examined. This study also points up the need for careful analysis of the hands of various copyists represented in early Purcell sources. Clear identification of the handwriting styles of Stephen Bing, John Blow, Jeremiah Clarke, William Croft, John Gostling, Henry Hall, and a few others, including Purcell himself, would shed much new light on questions of chronology and authenticity in the Purcell canon.

Ford, Wyn K. "The Chapel Royal in the time of Purcell." *Musical Times,* vol. 100 (1959): 592-93.

The article offers nothing new or useful.

Fortune, Nigel. "A new Purcell source." *Music Review,* vol. 25 (1964): 109-13.

Providing an inventory of four folio volumes of manuscript music in the Library, Tatton Park, Knutsford, Cheshire, Dr. Fortune points out that most of the copies from Purcell are in the hand of Philip Hayes (1738-1797), Professor of Music at Oxford. One new ascription to Purcell, "The noise of foreign wars," brings to light a possible new ode by Purcell, which may have been commissioned for the celebration of the English forces having gained victory at the Battle of La Hague in 1691.

Fortune, Nigel.. "The domestic sacred music [of Henry Purcell]." *Essays on opera and English music,* edited by F. W. Sternfeld, Nigel Fortune and Edward Olleson. Oxford: Blackwell, 1975. Pp. 62-78.

Writing a companion piece to Peter Dennisons's article, Dr. Fortune concentrates on the contents of Purcell's autograph, British Library Add. MS 30930, consulting also Bodleian Library MS 518 and Barber Institute MS 5001 for individual works and readings. He discusses the Psalm settings and sacred part songs as chamber music, in which he finds only the insular influences of Pelham Humfrey. No mention is made of either French or Italian influences, which were so demonstrably important in the stylistic development of both Humfrey and Purcell.

Fortune, Nigel, and Franklin B. Zimmerman. "Purcell's autographs." *Henry Purcell (1659-1695): essays on his music,* edited by Imogen Holst. London: Oxford University Press, 1959. Appendix A, pp. 106-21.

Given the extent of knowledge at the time of publication, this was a complete and accurate list of known sources in Purcell's handwriting. The list now needs to be updated.

Foster, Myles Birkit. *Anthems and anthem composers: an essay upon the development of the anthem.* London:

Novello, 1901. 225 pp. No musical illustrations; has portrait plates, lists of works, index.

Study of Purcell's anthems is limited to Chapter Twelve, a cursory summary of Purcell's accomplishments in this genre. However, his teachers and predecessors are discussed in Chapters 10 and 11, and the author has compiled lists of anthems by all major English composers of the period. The list for Purcell is flawed by inaccuracies, both of omission and commission. The study has only limited value.

Fuller-Maitland, J.A.   "Foreign influences on Henry Purcell." *Musical Times*, vol. 37 (1896): 10-11.

Fuller-Maitland, J.A. "Purcell's 'King Arthur.'" *Studies in music*, edited by Robin Grey. New York: Charles Scribner's Sons [A.M.S.], 1976. Pp. 185-98.

Gooch, Bryan Niel Shirley. *Poetry and music in England, 1660–1760: a comparison based on the works of Dryden, Purcell, Pope and Handel.* Ph.D. dissertation, University of British Columbia, 1962. 196 pp.

The author shows rare talent, seeming equally at home with discussion and analysis of both poetry and music, in which he finds many points of resemblance, particularly in the works of Purcell and Dryden, and in those of Handel and Pope. Dealing with both secondary and primary sources, as well as with various poetic and musical works, Dr. Gooch has given the reader many an interesting insight into intricate relations between poetry and music. Throughout, his style is refreshingly clear of clichés and of jargon.

Gordon, Lewis W. "The odes of Henry Purcell." *The American Choral Review,* vol. 26 (1984): 33.

This is a good short study, discussing principal features of Purcell's odes and providing copious musical examples. The subject calls for a much longer, more detailed study, such as that done by George Leininger, but this first published monograph on the subject is certainly a step in the right direction.

Gray, Alan. "Purcell's dramatic music." *Proceedings of the Musical Association,* session 43 (1916-17): 51-62.

A short article, filled with misinformation and badly formed musical judgements. It has no real value today.

Greenhalgh, Michael J. *The music of Henry Purcell: A guide for librarians, listeners and students.* Eastcote (Middlesex, England): M. J. Greenhalgh, 1982. 40 pp. Index.

The author states his purpose at the outset: "This booklet sets out to provide a guide to the music of Henry Purcell, concentrating upon the readiest means today of experiencing his music: sound recordings." Live performances therefore receive no attention in this study, which the author has limited to critiques of scores and recordings of about two dozen works.
These are discussed in three separate groups, presented in no particular order, with some duplication, since different performances of the same works are critiqued. There is brief commentary on biographies by Westrup and Zimmerman, on Robert Moore's monograph on Purcell's music for theatre, on the thematic catalog, and on John Harley's *Music in Purcell's London.* These are fairly superficial.

Griffiths, David. "The music in York Minster." *Musical Times,* vol. 123 (1982): 633-37.

A useful history of this important MS collection, and of its catalogs and catalogers. See also the letter from Brian Crosby in *Musical Times,* Nov., 1982. p. 746, which identifies an earlier related MS in the Bambrough Music MSS, since 1958 housed in the Durham Library.

Guy, Henry (ed. John Y. Akerman). *Moneys received and paid for secret services of Charles II and James II from 30th March 1679 to 25th December, 1688.* London, 1851. 240 pp.

A detailed account of financial transactions relating to musical and other performances. This is a valuable early source.

Halfpenny, Eric. "Musicians at James II's coronation." *Music and Letters,* vol. 32 (1951): 103-14.

Mr. Halfpenny discovered that Sandford's illustrations, showing musicians present at the coronation of James II, represented the principals, at least, in portraiture. This discovery enabled him to write a stimulating, very convincing article on the various musicians he was able to identify. He has provided a valuable addition to our knowledge of the music and musicians of Purcell's period.

Ham, R. G. "Dryden's dedication for the music of 'The Prophetess.'" *Publications of the Modern Language Association of America,* vol. 50 (1935): 1065-75.

Ham's deduction that Purcell's dedication appears in Dryden's hand in British Library MS Stowe 755, f. 43 is correct. However, that fact in itself does not constitute positive proof that Dryden actually composed the dedication. He may merely have made a transcription.

Harley, John. *Music in Purcell's London: the social backgrounds*. London: Dobson, 1968. 189 pp. Bibliography, 9 plates, illustrations, facsimile, music, portraits.

The author, whose researches have produced significant new data, presents a clear picture of music against the cultural, political, and social backgrounds of London during the Purcellian period. A cardinal study in the historiography of English music.

Hawkins, Sir John. *A general history of the science and practice of music*. London, 1776; reprinted, New York: Dover, 1963. An unabridged reprint of the edition published by J.A. Novello in 1853. 2 vols., 486, 477 pp. Appendix of music, index, music illustrations; illustrations; footnotes, and a separate volume of plates.

Hawkins's approach was that of an enlightened amateur, and his enthusiasm for Purcell's music seems to have produced a fairly complete summary of Purcell's life and works. The result is an account rich in anecdote, but not altogether reliable in factual accuracy.

Hawkins, Sir John. *Musical biography. Ancedotes and characters of Corelli and Handel [and others] from Sir John Hawkins History of music, embellished with engravings*. London: Printed for T. Wright, 1777. 26-32; 169-76: 505-509: 564-569. Biography. Excerpted in *Westminster Magazine* for Jan., Apr., Oct., Nov. 1777.

Highfill, Phillip H., Kalman A. Burnim, and Edward A. Langhans. *A biographical dictionary of actors, actresses, musicians, dancers, managers and other stage personnel.* Carbondale: Southern Illinois University Press, 1973-82.

A very useful compilation of records relating to persons active in the theater during this period.

Hogwood, Christopher. *The trio sonata.* BBC Music Guides. London: British Broadcasting Corporation, 1979. 128 pp. Music examples, short bibliography, index.

Chapter 5, on the trio sonata in England, is devoted principally to Henry Purcell's twenty-two sonatas. This is one of the most succinct, lucid, and comprehensive of the brief essays on Purcell's trio sonatas that have appeared to date.

Hogwood, Christopher. "Thomas Tudway's History of Music." *Music in eighteenth-century England: essays in memory of Charles Cudworth.* Cambridge: Cambridge University Press, 1983. Pp. 19-47.

Although covering the history of music from the the early Greeks to the Handelian period in English music, Thomas Tudway included in his history several of the earliest critical appraisals of Purcell's music that have been recorded, including a unique comparison of Purcell's music to that of Handel. Mr. Hogwood sets this jewel of early music history most admirably.

Holland, A.K. *Henry Purcell, the English musical tradition.* London: G. Bell and Sons, Ltd., 1932. 248 pp. Short bibliography, index. history, crititicism.

After brief but informative summaries of "Antecedents" and "The Restoration Scene," Holland draws an interesting, well-founded, though at times uncritical account of Purcell's life and works. Analysis tends to deal with surface characteristics, easily understandable by the layman, not with deeper theoretical or technical concepts. Holland's scholarship is impeccable and his scholarly views and judgements are balanced. There is a great deal of good common sense.

Hollander, John. *The untuning of the sky: ideas of music in English poetry 1500-1700.* Princeton, New Jersey: Princeton University Press, 1961. 467 pp.

A study of beliefs about music as expressed in English poetry, this book provides an excellent approach to relationships between word and tone during the sixteenth and seventeenth centuries. There is only brief reference to Purcell, however.

Holman, Peter "The trumpet sonata in England." *Early Music,* vol. 4 (1976): 424-29.

Summarizing the history of the English trumpet sonata and providing a complete inventory of its repertoire, Mr. Holman pays only scant attention to Purcell's compositions in this genre. His reason is simple, as he explains in an excellent critique: Professor Don Smithers has provided a full and complete account of Purcell's compositons for trumpet in his book, as listed below.

Holst, Imogen. "A note on the Nanki collection of Purcell's works." *Henry Purcell (1659-1695): essays on his music*, edited by Imogen Holst. London: Oxford University Press, 1959. Appendix C, pp. 127-30.

   A very brief description, without inventory but with a partial summary of catalog entries for the Nanki collection, representing the remainder of W.H. Cummings's collection, as sold in 1917 to the late Marquis Tokugawa. This is the richest collection of western manuscripts in the Orient, and its Purcellian holdings are quite extensive and significant.

Holst, Imogen. "Purcell's librettist, Nahum Tate." *Henry Purcell (1659-1695); essays on his music*, edited by Imogen Holst. London: Oxford University Press, 1959. Pp. 35-41.

   A sensitive study of Tate's contribution to the opera, this article perhaps gives Tate more credit than is due him.

Holst, Imogen, ed. *Henry Purcell (1659-1695): essays on his music*. London: Oxford University Press, 1959. 136 pp. Portrait, facsimile, musical illustrations. Essays by Benjamin Britten, Robert Donington, Ralph Downes, Nigel Fortune, I. Holst, Jeremy Noble, Peter Pears, Michael Tippett, E.W. White and F. Zimmerman.

   An enterprising series of essays by experts on various aspects of Purcell's life and music. The most important essays are listed elsewhere in this bibliography.

Howard, Michael. "An anthem by Henry Purcell." [My song shall be alway] *Monthly Musical Record*, vol. 83 (1953): 66-69.

Hughes-Hughes, A. "Henry Purcell's handwriting." *Musical Times*, vol. 37 (1896): 81-83.

This pioneer study opened a subject that still needs research and development. Hughes-Hughes's analysis has not been surpassed, but several new autographs have come to light, and these should be studied and analyzed with the same careful scrutiny that characterizes the work of Hughes-Hughes.

Husk, William Henry. *An Account of the musical celebrations on St. Cecilia's Day.* London: 1857. 236 pp. Notes, appendix of ode texts.

A thorough survey of the literature, music, and performances of the St. Cecilia tradition in England, with full treatment of Henry Purcell's four works in this genre. Husk's monograph is a basic reference work for the study of English St. Cecilia traditions.

Hutchings, A. *Purcell.* BBC Music Guides. London: British Broadcasting Corporation, 1982. 87 pp. Music examples, index.

A very compact review of Purcell's life and works, designed as a guide to the uninitiated or inexperienced listener. The book is well written, factually accurate, and interesting.

Illing, Robert. *Henry Purcell's sonata in g minor for violin and continuo: an account of its survival from both the historical and technical points of view.* [Monograph.] Flinders University, 1975. 80 pp. Musical examples; facsimiles of several earlier editions; new edition of the sonata; appendix containing facsimiles of sales documents relating to mss. sources.

Castigating all prior studies of the the solo sonata, the author presents a great deal of evidence supporting his approach. Although presented with great bombast, his arguments are not convincing. His musical judgement, as reflected in a new edition he proposes, is, however, less questionable.

Jensen, H. James "English Restoration attitudes toward music." *Musical Quarterly,* vol. 55 (1969): 206-14.

The author examines the decline of native music during the last two decades of the seventeenth century, when continental music was preferred over the domestic art. Much of his evidence is drawn from play-texts, particularly those of Shadwell, and for this reason some of his conclusions must be taken with a grain of salt. Nevertheless, the study is valuable for anyone interested in cultural backgrounds in Purcell's time.

King, A. Hyatt. "The first complete edition of Purcell." *Monthly Musical Record,* vol. 81 (March-April 1951): 63-69.

A. Hyatt King's first essay on the subject discussed in the next item.

King, A. Hyatt. "Benjamin Goodison and the first 'Complete Edition' of Purcell." *Musik und Verlag: Karl Vötterle zum 65. Geburtstag.* Kassel: Bärenreiter, 1968. Pp. 391-96.

Goodison's original plan, as shown in his subscription proposals, was to publish all of Purcell's works. In fact he published only a few, then abandoned the project, probably because of financial difficulties.

Klakowich, Robert. "Harpsichord music by Purcell and Clarke in Los Angeles." *The Journal of Musicology*, vol. 4 (Spring 1985-6): 171-90.

Exploring two new mansucripts now housed in the William Andrews Clark Memorial Library in Los Angeles, Mr. Klakowich identifies several Purcell pieces in "The Wild Court Volume" and in the "Powell Volume." This study of the two manuscripts, formerly belonging to Theodore M. Finney of the University of Pittsburgh, provides a useful inventory of each, and a careful study which greatly advances our knowledge of the sources and chronology of Purcell's keyboard music.

Klenz, William. *The church sonatas of Henry Purcell.* Ph.D. Dissertation, University of North Carolina, Chapel Hill, N.C., 1948. 286 pp.

Though unpublished, this study is one of the best available studies of Purcell's formal, stylistic, and technical usages in the trio sonatas. Dr. Klenz's comprehensive treatment of Purcell's forms and formulas, and wide variety of movement styles establishes his study as one no Purcellian scholar or performer interested in the trio sonatas should overlook. His careful evaluation of the influence of the English fantasia, along with those of French and Italian masters, lends great weight to his study, which compares favorably with studies by Hogwood and Tilmouth listed elsewhere in this bibliography.

Koeltzsch, Hans. "Purcells Gambenfantasien." *Musica*, vol. 9 (Kassel, 1959): 364-66.

Krummel, D.W. *English music printing, 1553-1700*. London: The Bibliographical Society, 1975. 188 pp.

   With index and many musical illustrations and textual examples in facsimile. An authoritative study of the history of printing, with particularly useful information on the period of Purcell.

LaFontaine, Henry Cart de. *The King's Musick: a transcript of records relating to music and musicians (1460-1700)*. London: Novello, 1909. xi, 522 pp. Notes and index.

   Accurate, though selective reproduction of records from the Lord Chamberlain's office. This archival compilation is supplemented by similar publications by Ackerman, Ashbee, and Rimbault, q.v.

Lamson, Roy. "Henry Purcell's dramatic songs and the English broadside ballad." *Publications of the Modern Language Association of America*, vol. 53 (1938): 148-61.

   This is a useful article, which provides the basis for understanding the means by which Purcell became known even to that part of London's general population for whom concerts would not have been accessible. While furnishing statistics on the number of new texts set to some of Purcell's tunes by broadside balladeers, the study leaves ample room for further study of this interesting method for appraising Purcell's popularity among the *hoi poloi* of his own time.

Langbaine, Gerard. *An account of the English dramatick poets; or, Some observations and remarks on the lives and writings, of all those that have publish'd either comedies, tragedies, tragi-comedies, pastorals, masques, interludes, farces, or operas in the English tongue.* Oxford, 1691; facsimile edition, University of California, Los Angeles [William Andrews Clark Memorial Library]: Augustan Reprint Society, 1971.

An alphabetical listing of English dramatic poets from William Alexander through Robert Yarrington, this compilation also provides lists of "supposed authors," anonymous plays, and an alphabetical listing of all plays mentioned in the account.

Laurie, Margaret. "Did Purcell set The Tempest?" *Proceedings of the Royal Musical Association,* vol. 90 (1963-64): 43-57.

With an extensive network of arguments based on contemporary sources and reports, publication information, orchestration, and stylistic analysis, Dr. Laurie makes it very clear that only a little of what we know as "Tempest music" was actually written by Purcell. She provides some evidence for an alternate hypothesis that John Weldon may have composed most of the music in what Dr. Laurie refers to as the "Harrison setting" of *The Tempest,* i.e., that published in 1786.

Laurie, Margaret. "Purcell's extended solo songs." *Musical Times,* vol. 125 (1984): 19-25.

This summary of one of the most interesting classes of Purcell's compositions for solo voice displays the acumen and excellence one has learned to expect from this outstanding Purcellian scholar, who has done so much for modern Purcell research. Her need to cover twenty-eight songs in less than six pages has limited some of her discussions too severely, however, and it is to be hoped that she will return to this subject, with adequate space to display her welcome erudition in Purcellian music.

Laurie, Margaret. *Purcell's stage works*. Dissertation, Cambridge University, 1962.

This work redefined the field and set the foundation for great progress in research on Purcell's dramatic music that has taken place over the last two decades. An excellent study for its time, it is still valid.

Lawrence, W.J. "Foreign singers and musicians at the court of Charles II." *Musical Quarterly*, vol. 9 (1923): 217-25.

Mr. Lawrence explores the various foundations for the poor showing that English composers made in the field of opera. In his view, English efforts along these lines were too little and too late in the making. He compares Purcell rather unfavorably to Lully and, bolstered by that audacious opinion, proceeds to analyze the actions and musical creations of Purcell's immediate predecessors and contemporaries. His work is thorough and informative so far as it goes—which is to 1669—but subject to the bias revealed in the above-mentioned comparison of Purcell to Lully.

Legàny, Dezsö. *Purcell*. Budapest: Gondolat, 1959. 265 pp.

General biography, with illustrations, chronology, selective list of works, short bibliography, but without footnotes or musical examples. Nearly half of the book is devoted to a brief history of English music. The remainder is devoted to a biography of Purcell, with commentary on main genres of composition and specific discussion of a few major works. Useful only for the general reader who would not be troubled by an otiose style.

Leininger, George. *The odes of Henry Purcell: a stylistic survey*. Ph.D. dissertation, University of Pennsylvania, Philadelphia, 1976, 606 pp.

Close worked analytical descriptions of nine odes by Purcell: Swifter Isis (1683), Fly, bold rebellion (1683), Laudate Ceciliam (1683), Ye tuneful muses (1686), Of old when heroes thought it bold (1690), Welcome, glorious morn (1691), Hail, bright Cecilia (1692); Come ye sons of art away (1694); Who can from joy refrain (1695). The study includes complete statistics on harmonies and progressions.

Lewis, Anthony. "Notes and reflections on a new edition of Purcell's 'The fairy queen.'" *Music Review*, vol. 25 (1964): 104-08.

Paying tribute to J.A. Shedlock, who edited the first modern print of Purcell's *The fairy queen* for the Purcell Society in 1903, Professor Lewis discusses new sources that had come to light in the interim. He paid particular attention to the partial autograph score in the Royal Academy of Music Library, to a manuscript in the British Council Library, and to the Gresham College autograph of songs. This is a very useful study.

Lewis, Anthony. "Purcell and Blow's 'Venus and Adonis.'" *Music and Letters*, vol. 44 (1963): 266-69.

Commenting on the significance of the relationship between Henry Purcell and John Blow, in his view one of the most important in English music, Professor Lewis explores stylistic, formal and technical links between Purcell and his teacher, John Blow. Bar by bar structural comparisons show that Purcell, even in his youth actually provided a model which Blow followed, later taking up the same model to compose again when he had reached maturity. The article affords several clear insights into this relationship between and older master and his ingenious younger contemporary, reminding one forcibly of the relationship between Mozart and Haydn.

Lewis, Anthony. "The language of Purcell: national idiom or local dialect?" Inaugural lecture delivered in the University of Hull, 1968. 22 pp.

With just a few precisely relevant quotations from the music of Purcell, Bassani, Corelli, and others, Lewis brings concise evidence to bear on the question posed in the title to his study. But his answer goes beyond either alternative, to indicate that Purcell's style was in fact supranational.

Long, Kenneth R. *The music of the English church.* New York: St. Martin's, 1971. 479 pp.

A succinct and perceptive summary of the main features, techniques and forms of Purcell's anthems, Latin sacred pieces, and services.

Luckett, Richard. "'Or rather our musical Shakespeare': Charles Burney's Purcell." *Music in eighteenth-century England: essays in memory of Charles Cudworth.*

Cambridge: Cambridge University Press, 1983. Pp. 59-77.

Scouring early memoirs, histories, and other publications of Roger North, John Oldham, Henry Playford, Tom Brown, Trajano, Pepusch, Arne, and Christopher Smart, among a few others, the author has reclaimed a great many hitherto unknown references to Purcell. From these, together with various gleanings from Michael Tilmouth's "A calendar of references to music," Dr. Luckett has woven a remarkable tapestry, showing Purcell's reputation to great advantage in a new perspective. This is an excellent piece of scholarly work, and a fine presentation.

Mangeot, André. "The Purcell fantasias and their influence on modern music." *Music and Letters*, vol. 7 (1926): 143-49.

Like J. Frederick Bridge (see above), Mssr. Mangeot settles on the *Fantasia in c minor* (Z738) as sufficient basis for his fairly penetrating, at times inspired analysis and description. Enthusiastic about the expressive beauty of various passages in this fantasia, he compares Purcell's piece to quartets by Haydn and Fauré.

Manifold, J.S. "Music in Purcell's theatre." *The music in English drama from Shakespeare to Purcell*. London: Rockliff, 1956. Pp. 106-37.

Examining Purcell's theatre music through analysis of his instrumentation, Manifold explores each section of the modern orchestra, developing Purcell's applications, with a few notes pertinent to the history of English orchestration. On the basis of this information,

Manifold describes various usages of music in Purcellian theater.

Marco, Guy. "The variety in Purcell's word-painting." *Music Review,* vol. 18 (1957): 1-3.

According to the author, Purcell's word-painting does not involve many of the predictable clichés which characterize most Baroque musical illustrations. His musical figures may be divided into two broad categories consisting on the one of hand of those which represent physical states, and on the other, those which are of an emotional nature. Restricting his investigation to Purcell's anthems, Dr. Marco finds frequent and varied illustrations of both kinds of musical imagery. This a thought-provoking, well-executed study, the method of which might profitably be applied to other Purcellian genres.

Mayer, George L. "The vocal works of Henry Purcell; a discography." *The American Music Lover.* New York: The American Music Foundation, 1959. Pp. 588-91, 670. Bibliography, discography, illustration, portraits.

A model of what any single-composer discography should be, this detailed discussion and complete listing should be brought up to date as soon as possible. It is much more than a simple discography.

McDonald, Jennifer. "Matthew Locke's *The English Opera* and the theatre music of Purcell." *Studies in Music* 15 (1981): 62–75.

Comparing Locke's music for *Psyche* and *The Tempest* with Purcell's theatre music, the author produces a very useful analytic guide to musical influence of Locke on Purcell.

McGuinness, Rosamond. *English court odes 1660-1820.* London: Oxford University Press, 1971. 249 pp. Copious music examples, select bibliography, index.

The study examines the history and stylistic development of the royal ode, a new musical and poetic form appearing after the restoration of Charles II. Written for royal birthdays, for New Year's celebrations, for returns from vacation travels, or for progresses, the court ode reached its zenith in the works of Henry Purcell and his teacher, John Blow. An excellent, detailed, well-reasoned study. This work is the outgrowth of the author's earlier dissertation written for the degreee of Doctor of Philosophy at St. Anne's College, Oxford.

McGuinness, Rosamond. "The ground-bass in the English court ode." *Music and Letters*, vol. 51 (1970): 118-40.

Although his name does not appear in the title, Purcell is the main subject of this essay. Dr. McGuinness, while not neglecting the technical aspects of Purcell's ground-bass movements in her description, certainly does not allow these to obscure the expressive value of such movements, of which she gives a very good account. Somehow she captures the liveliness of Purcell's imagination in the use of this form which he made so uniquely his, and at the same time gives a very good account of his formal ingenuity and technical virtuosity. Replete with an appendix presenting in chronological order a generous sampling of Purcell's grounds from all periods of his life, this study is a model of its kind.

McLean, Hugh. "Blow and Purcell in Japan." *Musical Times,* vol. 99 (1958): 249-61.

A brief history of the "Nanki Library," formerly the "Library of Kishu," this article also provides descriptions of several compositons by Purcell and Blow in the collection.

McManaway, J.G. "Songs and Masques in *The Tempest.*" *Theatre Miscellany: Six pieces connected wtih the seventeenth-century stage.* Oxford: Luttrell Society Reprints, 1953. Pp. 70-96.

Although it pertains to the generation before Purcell, this is an excellent study of the *Tempest* libretto. It is a unique document that provides the original texts to the many settings of these songs and masques which appeared during the last three decades of the seventeenth century.

Meffen, J. "A question of temperament: Purcell and Croft." *Musical Times,* vol. 119 (1978): 504-06.

Musical temperaments in use in England before the second half of the nineteenth century were neither standardized nor established. This article clarifies the usage at least where Purcell and Croft were concerned, establishing the old mean-tone temperament as belonging particularly to Purcell.

Mellers, Wilfred. "Purcell and the Restoration theatre." *Harmonious Meeting.* London: D. Dobson, 1965. Pp. 215-25.

Meyer, E.H. *English chamber music: the history of a great art from the Middle Ages to Purcell.* London: Lawrence and Wishart, 1946; reprint ed., New York: Da Capo, 1971. xiv, 318 pp. Copious musical examples; appendix of unpublished fantasia scores; index.

Though somewhat colored by sociopolitical theories, this valuable study presents valid musical views and solid musical analysis. The section on Purcell, though inaccurate in biographical details, presents several useful generalities. However, there is little detailed commentary on individual works. This remark applies also to the German translation of this work, *Die Kammermusik Alt-Englands vom Mittelalter bis zum Tode Henry Purcell's* (Aus dem Englischen übersetzt von Gerda Becher). Leipzig, VEB Breitkopf & Härtel, 1958.

Milhous, Judith. "Opera finances in London, 1674-1738." *Journal of the American Musicological Society*, vol. 37 (1984): 567-92.

Scrutinizing financial accounts available for five opera companies, the author covers Purcell's period in the first section of the article. Her study reveals that the semi-operas could only be presented by underwriting from profits generated by plays.

Miller, Hugh M. "Henry Purcell and the ground bass." *Music and Letters*, vol. 29 (1948): 340-47.

Commenting on the significance of basso-ostinato throughout the Baroque, the author points out that 87 of Purcell's compositions employ this procedure. Of these, 65 are vocal compositions and the rest instrumental. His approach to Purcell's use of the ground as an art form involves only statistical statements such as these, along with some commentary on external features and technical devices. It is a useful article, the chief value of which may have been to pave the way for another article dealing with the expressive quality of Purcell's ground basses, and with the extraordinary climaxes he was able to achieve through their use in his music.

Moore, Robert Etheridge. "The music to Macbeth." *Musical Quarterly*, vol. 47 (1961): 22-40.

Advancing the claims of various other composers from Robert Johnson to Richard Leveridge, Moore definitively proves that Purcell had nothing to do with the music for *Macbeth*.

Moore, Robert Etheridge. *Henry Purcell & the Restoration theatre*. London: Heinemann, 1961. xv, 223 pp. Foreword by Sir Jack Westrup. 5 plates (including portrait), music, discography.

Discussing English compromise theatrical forms of the seventeenth century against the backdrop of Italian and continental musical theater, Professor Moore analyzes the 'ambigue,' the semi-opera, and a more general type, the dramatic opera, along with Purcell's one true opera, *Dido and Aeneas*. He discusses both intellectual and aesthetic qualities of these kinds of entertainment, and describes the manner in which Purcell brought recent French and Italian innovations into the native English masque. Thus does Moore identify and explain principal features of *Dido and Aeneas, Dioclesian, King Arthur, The fairy queen*, and *The Indian queen*, although he does not always clarify the value of practical realization of this seventeenth-century art form before modern audiences. His monograph emerges as a valuable study of relationships of words, music, and of the dramatic impulse that should animate performances of these works. No one researching Purcell's theatrical music will progress far without taking into account the crucial issues which Professor Moore identifies and clarifies in this excellent study.

Nelson, Everett. *An introductory study of the English three-part string fancy.* 2 vols. Ph.D. dissertation, Cornell University, 1960. 798, 292 pp.

Classifying the variation techniques of the period in question in four categories, Dr. Nelson deals first with late Renaissance techniques before taking up the later seventeenth century. In this latter period, he discusses the Italian influence and shows the importance of five basso ostinato techniques as he discusses variations in the middle and late Baroque periods. An excellent, highly analytical and closely reasoned study.

Noble, Jeremy. "Purcell and the Chapel Royal." *Henry Purcell (1659-1695): essays on his music,* edited by Imogen Holst. London: Oxford University Press, 1959. Pp. 52-66.

A thorough discussion of the Chapel Royal roster, as recovered from *The Old Cheque-book*, with detailed commentary on some of Purcell's principal soloists.

North, Roger. *An essay of musical ayre. Tending chiefly to shew the foundations of melody joined with harmony.* Br. Mus. Add MS 32536.

Although understandably lacking in terminology of modern music theory, this essay explains many of the concepts of the common style era, then in process of formulation. "Musical ayre" emerges as an omnibus term denoting concepts we now refer to as "melody," "harmony," "key," and "tonality."

North, Roger. *Memoires of musick by the Honourable Roger North, Attorney General to James II*. London, 1846.

This is a sketch of the history of music written by a well-informed, enthusiastic musical amateur. Historical anecdotes, gleaned from classical Greek and Latin scholars, Greek scales and ancient instruments make up the first third of the book. The second third deals with the history of music of the early church up to the period of Charles I and Cromwell, and the last third with post-Restoration music. Copiously noted, this is a primary source and is of great signficance to Purcell research.

North, Roger. *Roger North on music*. Edited by John Wilson. London: Novello, 1959. xviii, 372 pp.

A compilation of Roger North's perceptive views on the musical art of his time, this is a very important source document, representing ideas and opinions on music recorded by North over a lifetime of thoughtful musical activity.

Pears, Peter. "Homage to the British Orpheus." *Henry Purcell (1659-1695): essays on his music*, edited by Imogene Holst. London: Oxford University Press, 1959. Pp. 1-6.

Sensitive, if somewhat fanciful interpretive commentary by a talented vocalist.

Petre, Robert. "A new piece by Henry Purcell." *Early Music*, vol. 6 (1978): 374-79.

From a rare copy of *The Harpsichord Master,* as published by Walsh & Hare in 1697, Dr. Petre has edited a newly discovered "Prelude for ye fingering by Mr. Henry Purcell." Along with this there are also harpsichord transcriptions of "I come to sing great Zempoalla's praise" (from *The Indian Queen,* Z630/6); "Mr. Purcell's new Cibell" (ZT678); and various pieces by Clarke and Barrett. This is a valuable study of an important addition to the Purcell *oeuvre* and to the study of relevant sources.

Playford, John. *An introduction to the skill of musick, in three books. The first contains the grounds and rules of musick, according to the gam-ut . . . The second, instructions . . . The third, the art of descant, ed. H. Purcell.* London, 1694. 144 pp. 9 plates, frontispiece, portraits, illustrations.

Undoubtedly one of the most popular and influential English handbooks of music ever printed, Playford's "Introduction" was actually a compendium of methods, whose individual components kept changing with each of the nineteen successive editions that appeared between 1654 and 1730. Thus, the instructional set was continually adjusted to the needs of each new generation, keeping abreast with most recent developments in music both at home and abroad. [For a more complete analysis of the contents of the first fourteen editions, see the introduction to the facsimile edition listed below.]

Playford, John. *An introduction to the skill of musick, in three books.* Facsimile edition by F. B. Zimmerman,

New York: Da Capo Press, 1973. 282 pp.
Introduction, glossary, index, and appendix.

As a facsimile of the twelfth edition of Playford's
Introduction, this publication presents Purcell's first
effort as a music theorist, and discloses actual examples
of some of the techniques of Italian musicians which he
had found attractive. This modern edition is provided
with helpful additions, including an historical summary
of Playford's many editions and impressions, a
glossary of seventeenth-century musical terms, an index
and an appendix of title pages from all the editions
discussed in the introduction.

Pohlenz, Michael. *A performance analysis of 'Come ye
sons of art' by Henry Purcell.* D.M.A Dissertation,
University of Oklahoma, 1983. 110 pp.

The level and quality of this study are clearly shown
in the author's summary statement: "No greater assets
need be cultivated than those of technique and
imagination."

Prendergast, Arthur H.D. *Masques and early operas,
English music [1604-1904] Being the lectures given at
the music Loan Exhibition of the Worshipful Company
of Musicians . . .* London: Walter Scott, 1906. Pp.
257-63.

A brief summary of the history and significance of
Dido and Aeneas that is remarkably up to date,
considering its provenance. Virtually all the old
misconceptions about the early origin of this opera are
cleared away.

Price, Curtis A. *Henry Purcell and the London stage.* Cambridge: Cambridge University Press, 1984. 380 pp. Plates, music examples, bibliography, index.

A well-integrated and wittily written set of essays describing and analyzing the principal genres of English theatre music, including the serious dramas, the tragic extravaganzas, the comedies, and the operas, with a brilliant introduction to the subject and excellent summaries. In sum, the author has provided an illuminating and comprehensive answer to his own key question in the preface: "What is English opera?"

Price, Curtis A. *Music in the Restoration theatre; with a catalogue of instrumental music in the plays 1665-1713.* Ann Arbor: UMI Research Press, 1979. 302 pp. Notes, general index, index of song titles, index of stage works.

A very careful and thorough study of all sources of theatre music extant during and just after the lifetime of Henry Purcell. The author sheds new light on all the principal genres of theatrical life in England during the post-Restoration period and provides important new data on songs, dances, entertainments, and various instrumental forms. Imaginatively written and well documented.

Price, Curtis. "Political allegory in late-seventeenth-century English opera." *Music and theatre: essays in honour of Winton Dean,* edited by Nigel Fortune. Cambridge: Cambridge University Press, 1987. Pp. 1-29.

Discussing Louis Grabu's *Albion and Albanius,* William Davenant's *The Siege of Rhodes,* James Shirley's *Cupid and Death,* Pierre Perrin's *Ariadne, ou le mariage de Bacchus,* Thomas Shadwell's and

Matthew Locke's *Psyche,* and John Crowne's *Calisto,* the author demonstrates fully that opera had been used throughout the early seventeenth century as a vehicle for various kinds of political propaganda. With Purcell's *King Arthur* and *Dido and Aeneas* topicality is still present, although to a lesser degree in the latter, and certainly not so openly as in the works discussed earlier. For reasons not readily apparent, neither *Dioclesian* nor *The Indian Queen* are discussed in this light, which is a pity, since there is much to be dealt with in these works.

Price, Curtis, and Irena Cholij. "Dido's Bass Sorceress." *Musical Times,* vol. 127 (1986): 615-18.

The authors present their case persuasively, even though the evidence to support it is slender. Prompt notes contemporary with the first professional production of *Dido & Aeneas* seem to show that one Mr. Wilshire, a baritone, may have sung the part of the Sorcerer. The reasoning is inconclusive, however, and further evidence and further argument will be necessary before the thesis can be accepted.

Price, Curtis A. "Purcell's theatre music on Record." *Early Music,* vol. 12 (1984): 85-90.

Dr. Price describes the new Florilegium Series, as performed for recording by Christopher Hogwood. The series will include all of Purcell's music for plays, when complete. The critical analysis of performance practices and interpretative level is excellent, with a plentiful sprinkling of this writer's bright, sometimes salty wit. This attribute, together with a rich and well controlled depth of background material—qualities all too rare in professional musicological writing—sets this brief article on a very high level of excellence.

Price, Curtis. "Restoration theatre music restored." *Musical Times*, vol. 124 (1983): 344-47.

Announcing the publication of a new series of facsimile publications, "Music for London Entertainment," this article explores interrelationships between theatrical plays and music in London from 1660 to 1714. Locke's stellar position in the development of theatrical music during the first twenty years of Charles II's reign is traced through his main works, *The Tempest, Cupid and Death*, "The Masque of Orpheus" in Settle's *The Empress of Morocco,* and *Psyche.* Professor Price then turns to the works of Purcell, who was the stellar figure throughout the next two decades, even though he died halfway through the second of these. Given the extent of Purcell's music for theatre, there was room for no more than bare summary in this article, which also brings excellent commentary on the works of Purcell's primary successors, John Eccles, Daniel Purcell, Jeremiah Clarke, and William Croft. Readers familiar with Dr. Price's two books on the London theatre music will not be surprised to find a wealth of information packed into these few pages.

Pulver, Jeffrey. *A biographical dictionary of old English music.* London: Kegan, Paul, Trench, Trubner & Co., 1927. 537 pp. Frontispiece [a portrait of Henry Purcell], index.

Relevant articles include those on Daniel Purcell (pp. 376-79), Edward Purcell, Henry Purcell I (pp. 379-82), Henry Purcell II (pp. 382-400) and that on the latter's uncle, Thomas Purcell (pp. 400-02). All five articles are informative, up to date, and well-written summaries of these four members of that remarkable musical family. The fourth, on Henry Purcell II, is an excellent essay on the warmth and dramatic spontaneity of his music. Pulver shows unusual understanding of

Purcell's imaginative inventiveness, of the depth of his musicianship, of the curious balance of ultra-modern and traditional elements in his music, and, in short, of all the reasons that Purcell, as he put it, "must occupy the foremost place in the history of English music." This understanding finds expression in every part of this excellent essay, which is one of the best summaries of the life and works of Purcell that can be found.

Quervain, Fritz de. *Der Chorstil Henry Purcells: Studien zu seinen Anthems.* Bern and Leipzig: P. Haupt, 1935. 117 pp. Illustrations, music, brief bibliography.

After a brief but quite thorough sketch of the history of English choral forms, the author discusses first the various styles and techniques utilized by Purcell in the anthems. Relating these to the styles of Renaissance English masters, he then presents a close-worked and highly technical analysis of Purcell's imitative and homophonic settings, with special emphasis on word-tone relationships and harmonic usage. The result is an imaginative, wholly dependable study that will be quite useful to anyone who wishes to apply similar analytical techniques to classes of Purcell's music other than the anthems.

Ravenzwaij, G. van. "Henry Purcell's muzikale synthese in Engelands Restauratie-periode." *Miscellanea musicologica Floris van der Mueren.* Ghent, 1950. Pp. 201-07.

Ravenzwaij, G. van. *Purcell.* Gottmer, Haarlem and Antwerp, 1954. 259 pp. Eight illustrations, musical examples, index.

The author begins with a potted history of England, closely coordinated with the version of Purcell genealogy advanced by J.A. Westrup. Indeed, apart from historical commentary, there is little in Ravenzwaij's account of Purcell's life and times that cannot be found in Westrup's book. Curiously organized, the study returns to historical forerunners after the account of Purcell's death, then proceeds genre by genre through the anthems, services, hymns, psalms, canons, odes, sacred songs, cantatas, catches, songs, instrumental pieces, and theatrical music. Layout and contents indicate that the lists came straight out of Westrup's Appendix B: Catalogue of Works. However, for the new insights into cultural and social relationships between England and Holland, and for some careful work on archival sources, this biography is valuable enough to be listed in this compilation, despite its eclectic make-up.

Rendall, E.D. "The influence of Henry Purcell on Handel, traced in 'Acis and Galatea.'" *Musical Times*, vol. 36 (1895): 293-96.

This is a very good presentation of Handel's ability to absorb the content of another composer's invention, without seeming to copy directly. Here we have a very thoughtful and well-executed article on the Handelian *Entlehnungsfrage,* an endless subject.

Rendall, E.D. "Some notes on Purcell's dramatic music, with especial reference to the Fairy Queen." *Music and Letters*, vol. 1 (1920): 135-44.

Deriding Purcell for not having appreciated Shakespeare's genius sufficiently to set any of his verses to music, Mr. Rendall deals mainly in generalities. Indeed he never quite gets around to discussing what was essentially dramatic about Purcell's setting of *The Fairy Queen*, or any other dramatic music. This is neither an inspired nor very helpful study.

Rimbault, E.F., ed. *The old cheque-book or book of remembrance of the Chapel Royal from 1561 to 1744.* New York: Da Capo, 1966. 250 pp. With an Introduction by Elwyn A. Wienandt, notes, indexes of names and places.

Though incomplete, and flawed by a gap in the records from 1640 to 1660, this remains one of the most important source documents for Purcell research now available in print. Rimbault 's notes and comments should be used with caution.

Rohrer, Katherine Tinely. *The energy of English words: a linguistic approach to Henry Purcell's methods of setting texts.* A dissertation presented to the faculty of Princeton University. Ann Arbor, 1980, 267 pp. Music examples, appendix, selected bibliography.

A very important study of Purcell's text-setting methods with a new and interesting approach to analysis of the relationships between words and music, based on recent theories of phonology. Backgrounds to the understanding of these problems provided from various English sources which are contemporary or nearly contemporary with Purcell. The musical analysis is clear and well reasoned.

Rose, Gloria. "A new Purcell source." *Journal of the American Musicological Society*, vol. 25 (1972): 230-36.

The author identifies and inventories an interesting manuscript song-book collection, Ms. 9 in the Osborn Collection at Yale. The manuscript, which dates from 1692, contains nine pieces by Purcell, all anonymous. The song book is well ornamented, though possibly to excess, and serves as a useful document for contemporary vocal practices as well as a new source.

Rose, Gloria. "Purcell, Michelangelo Rossi, and J.S. Bach: problems of authorship." *Acta Musicologica*, vol. 40 (1968): 203-19.

Citing the various ascriptions of the Toccata in a minor (Z229) to Purcell, Michelangelo Rossi, and J.S. Bach, the author chooses the last as most likely. On similar stylistic arguments, she suggests that the trio sonata in C major (BWV 1037) is by Bach rather than by J.G. Goldberg; that the song "Bist du bei mir" (BWV 508) is by J.S. Bach rather than by G.H. Stölzel, and that BWV 824 is probably by Telemann.

Rumery, L.R. "Choral music in Purcell's dramatic works." *American Choral Review*, vol. 26 (1984): 5-11.

This article consists of sketchy descriptions of three passages from choruses from *King Arthur* and *The fairy queen*. It does not live up to the promise of its title.

Runciman, John F. *Purcell*. London: Bell, 1909. 78 pp. Musical examples.

Making use of a rather poetic, or at least personal, approach, the author sketches Purcell's life briefly in the first three chapters. Then he turns to the music, discussing it in rather general terms, genre by genre. For its time, it was an adequate book, which now has value mainly in revealing the perceptions of those former times.

Rylands, George, and Anthony Lewis. "The tempest, or the enchanted island." *Musical Times*, vol. 100 (1959): 320-22.

The play, a galamaferie, is given great relish by the music, according to the authors, who found nothing problematical in attributing all of the music to Henry Purcell. Compare their views to those of Laurie and Covell, above.

Savage, Roger. "Producing Dido and Aeneas: An investigation into sixteen problems." *Early Music*, vol. 4 (1976): 393-406.

With well-reasoned answers to sixteen questions of his own devising, Dr. Savage suggests that: *Dido and Aeneas* should always be programmed with another work because of its shortness; needs re-editing whatever modern source is used; requires considerable preliminary study of the libretto, but not necessarily a return to Vergil's version. Scenery and costumes might well be kept chronologically and geographically vague, and the use of a double chorus is a luxury. The witches should be portrayed as purely evil, not comic, and the work as a whole should be limited to four scenes. Aeneas need not be portrayed as a complete booby— *pace* Joseph Kerman. Indeed, Purcell may have intended an aria for him: "Direct me, friends." The opera should be choreographed, and Queen Dido should die by dagger. A comprehensive approach to the production of *Dido and Aeneas,* this article should be required reading for any one contemplating a staged performance of the opera.

Savage, R. "The Shakespeare-Purcell Fairy Queen: a defense and recommendation." *Early Music*, vol. 1 (1973): 200-21.

The author draws parallels between Purcell's *Fairy Queen* and Weber's *Oberon*, both of these being "ambigue entertainments" fashioned for English audiences. He disagrees with Mellers and Tippett in their not bowing to Shakespearean bardolotry, and believes that for the most part *The Fairy Queen* should be performed just as the anonymous revisers prepared it for Purcell's productions. This is an excellent defense of the work, with a marvelous set of suggestions and instructions for performance, carefully and thoroughly reasoned out.

Schjelderup-Ebbe, Dag. *Purcell's cadences*. Oslo: Oslo University Press, 1962. 66 pp. Musical illustrations.

Basing his terminology and analytical procedures on Roger Sessions's *Harmonic Practice*, the author presents an anachronistic view of Purcell's harmonies, analyzing and discussing the development of these accordingly.

Scholes, Percy A. "Purcell in praise of princes." *Musical Times,* vol. 56 (1915): 591-94.

A useful discussion of the texts of Purcell's odes, with a list of all the pieces Purcell wrote for royal occasions.

Shaw, Watkins. "A collection of musical manuscripts in the autograph of Henry Purcell and other English composers, c. 1665-85." *The Library,* ser. 5 vol. 14 (1959): 126-31.

Until recently, this article provided the definitive inventory and provenance of the works preserved in this collection. The detailed discussion is sound, and still useful. But some of the author's conclusions have been opened to question as a result of Margaret Laurie's researches.

Shaw, Watkins. "Eight concerts of Henry Purcell's music; commemorative book of programmes, notes and texts, with a foreword by Ralph Vaughan Williams, and eight essays by Denis Arundel, and others." London, 1951. 93 pp. Illustrations, (inc. music).

Shaw, Watkins. "Purcell's 'Bell' anthem and its performance." *Musical Times,* vol. 100 (1959): 285-86.

This is a very closely reasoned article on interpretation of Purcell's time signatures as a guide to appropriate tempi, and on the use of ornamentation. The suggestions are excellent.

Shaw, Watkins. "Purcell sonatas: [a review of Roger Fiske's new edition]." *Musical Times,* vol. 120 (1979): 495-96.

Praising the edition as 'impeccable,' Mr. Shaw provides a thorough analysis of the sonatas and an excellent evaluation.

Shaw, William A. "Three unpublished portraits of Henry Purcell." *Musical Times,* vol. 61 (1920): 588-90.

Although the portraits reproduced seem authentic, they cannot be established as genuine in the absence of the originals. Even the blocks from which these were reproduced by the editor of *Musical Times* have disappeared, and all efforts to trace them have been in vain.

Siedentopf, H. "Eine Komposition Purcells im Klavierbuch einer Würtemburgischen Prinzessin." *D i e Musikforschung,* jahrg. 31 (1978): 446-50.

Curiously, a copy of Purcell's "If love's a sweet passion" is to be found in a newly discovered "Clavierbuch" dating from 1697, now housed in the Badisches Landesbibliothek in Karlsrüh.

Sietz, Reinhold. *Henry Purcell; Zeit, Leben, Werk.* Leipzig: Breitkopf und Härtel, 1955. viii, 236 pp. List of printed works, 9 plates, music examples, bibliography.

With regard to life and times, this study offers nothing that cannot be found in Westrup and other earlier monographs. However, the musical analyses are presented in depth, and bring interesting facets of Purcell's style to light.

Smith, Alan. *An index of the works of Henry Purcell, as published by the Purcell Society.* London: Novello, (1970?). 48 pp.

A simple and tidy alphabetical list of Purcell's works, with "Z-numbers." The order differs somewhat from that of the catalog due to a different method of alphabetizing entries. The list is accurate for its time.

Smithers, Don. *The music and history of the Baroque trumpet before 1721.* London: Dent, 1973. 323 pp.

The chapter on Purcell provides the definitive statement on this subject. It is an excellent study.

Squire, William Barclay. "An elegy on Henry Purcell." *Zeitschrift der Internationalen Musik-Gesellschaft,* jahrg. 2 heft 8 (1900-01): 267-69.

The first volume of Robert Gould's works, published in London in 1709, contains an elegant funeral elegy "On the Death of the Famous Musick-Master Mr. Henry Purcell." Gould, a servant of Charles, Earl of Dorset, was also a friend of Purcell, and ended his days at the Oxfordshire home of James, Earl of Abingdon, as did Henry Purcell's elder brother, Edward Purcell. It is a moving, personal tribute to his great contemporary, with whom, incidentally, Gould had collaborated in the play *The Rival Sisters* (Z609).

Squire, William Barclay. "Purcell's dramatic music." *Sammelbände der Internationalen Musik-Gesellschaft,* jahrg. 5 (1903-04): 489-564.

For the first half of the twentieth century this study and listing existed as the main reference in any study of Purcell's dramatic music. It continues to be a basic reference article.

Squire, William Barclay. "An unknown autograph of Henry Purcell." *Musical Antiquary*, vol. 3 (1911): 5-17.

With thematic index. An inventory, with commentary on the Gresham MS, now Guildhall Library MS LGC VI.5.6, this article provides expertly marshalled evidence as to the value and provenance of this important MS. It contains also a full copy of the song, "Bell Barr, I love and I must," with full discussion of the possible meanings of the title.

Squire, William Barclay. "Purcell as theorist." *Sammelbände der Internationale Musik-Gesellschaft,* jahrg. 6 (1904-05): 521-67. Music examples.

This is a study of Purcell's edition of the third book of Playford's *Introduction to the skill of music,* which proceeds detail by detail to provide a comprehensive picture of Purcell's musical theories, as projected against the theoretical thought of the time.

Squire, William Barclay. "Purcell's music for the funeral of Mary II [with composition, printed for the first time]." *Sammelbände der Internationale Musik-Gesellschaft,* jahrg. 4 (1902-03): 225-33.

The author here discusses the second of two discoveries of Thomas Taphouse: the sonata for violin and the funeral music for Queen Mary II. The latter was discovered in the Oriel College Library in MSS books donated by Lord Leigh. Squire provides also a detailed description of the funeral ceremonies.

Squire, William Barclay. "Purcell's 'Fairy Queen.'" *Musical Times*, vol. 61 (1920): 25-29.

Statham, Heathcote D. "Purcell's church music." *Musical Times*, vol. 65 (1924): 419-20 and 535-38.

Statham, Heathcote D. "The influence of the Elizabethan composers on Purcell." *Musical Times*, vol. 64 (1923): 419-20.

Stevens, Denis. "Purcell on the gramophone." *Music and Letters*, vol. 40 (1959): 166-71.

A very thorough critical inventory of Purcell recordings available in 1959, this review is worth bringing up to date. As it stands, it serves as a useful guide to the lore of Purcellian performance as well as to available recordings.

Stevens, Denis. "Purcell's art of fantasia." *Music and Letters*, vol. 33 (1952): 341-45.

Under this imaginative title, Dr. Stevens has produced a lucid account, and clear definition of the fantasia art as Purcell practiced it. He has also skillfully traced compositions once contained in Purcell's autograph score volume, British Library Add Ms 30930, and has established the provenance of those still extant. It is an excellent study, elegantly written, which might well pave the way for a fully detailed monograph on Purcell's 'art of fantasia.'

Swalin, Benjamin F. "Purcell's masque in Timon of Athens." *American Musicological Society Papers*. Oberlin, 1941. Pp. 112-24. Illustrations, music, bibliography.

Theile, Eugen. "Die Kirchenmusik Henry Purcells." *Musik und Gottesdienst,* jahrg. 12 no. 5 (Zurich, 1958): 97-105.

Thiemann, Susan. *The works of Henry Purcell: an index to the Purcell Society Edition.* New York: Music Library Association, 1963. 22 pp. Includes index of first lines, titles, and subtitles.

Tiggers, Piet. "'King Arthur' van Henry Purcell." *Mens en melodie,* jaarg. 9 no. 2 (Utrecht, 1954): 47-51.

Reporting on a performance of King Arthur by the Brabant Chamber Chorus on January 19, 1954, Piet Tiggers provides a brief summary of Purcell's life, with commentary on four excerpts from the opera. The article does not add greatly to either our store of knowledge about Purcell, nor increase our understanding.

Tilmouth, Michael. "A calendar of references to music in newspapers published in London and the provinces (1660-1719)." *Royal Musical Association Research Chronicle,* no.1 (1961).

Dr. Tilmouth has provided a very thorough calendar of musical events throughout London and England. His main concentration was on the Burney Collection in the British Library, but he covered the provinces as well. A very useful pioneering effort.

Tilmouth, Michael. "A calendar of references to music in newspapers published in London and the provinces (1660-1719)." *Royal Musical Association Research Chronicle,* no. 2 (1962).

This, an index to the foregoing, shows a very healthy scattering of allusions to Purcell and his immediate family. For most musical interests in the seventeenth century, a very useful index.

Tilmouth, Michael. "English chamber music (1675-1720)." Ph.D., Cambridge University, Cambridge, 1960.

Tilmouth, Michael. "Henry Purcell, assistant lexicographer." *Musical Times*, vol. 100 (1959).

Tilmouth points out that Purcell assisted with musical terms in Edward Phillips's *The New World of Words*. In his opinion, the new musical terms are not very helpful.

Tilmouth, Michael. "The techniques and forms of Purcell's sonatas." *Music and Letters*, vol. 40 (1959): 109-21.

One of the most significant borrowings from the Italians, according to Tilmouth, was the technique of extended recapitulation. This had begun in Italy as early as G.B. Fontana, and turned up in England in Blow's *Overture to Awake my lyre* (1678) and Purcell's *Laudate Ceciliam* (1683), *Hail, bright Cecilia* (1692), and *Come ye sons of art* (1694), etc. Tracing this kind of influence and also showing in similar detail other aspects of Purcell's fascinating art of chamber composition, Tilmouth has created a model study for anyone approaching the analysis and evaluation of this highly imaginative, subtle music.

Van Tassel, E. "Two Purcell Discoveries-1: Purcell's Give Sentence." *Musical Times,* vol. 118 (1977): 381-83.

The author has found the remaining portions of the hitherto incomplete anthem, "Give sentence with me." In this article he describes the new edition and traces some of the influences which it reflects with special emphasis on that of Pelham Humfrey.

Wailes, Marylin. "Four short fantasias by Henry Purcell." *The Score and I.M.A. Magazine,* no. 20 (1957): 59-65. 1 plate, music examples.

This article presents scores of the short fantasies, with brief commentary on their source, British Library MS Add. 33236.

Walker, F.H. "Purcell's handwriting." *Monthly Musical Record,* vol. 72 (1942): 155-57.

Warlock, Peter. "Purcell's fantasias for strings." *The Sackbut,* vol. 7 (1927): 281-85.

Wesley-Kropik, H. "Henry Purcell als Instrumental-komponist." *Studien zur Musikwissenschaft,* bd. 22 (1955): 85-141.

Westrup, Jack Allen. "Church music at the Restoration." *Monthly Musical Record,* vol. 71 (1941): 131-35.

Westrup, Jack Allen. "Das Englische in Henry Purcells Musik." *Musica,* jahrg. 13 (Cassell, 1959): 170-73.

Accompanying his article with a portrait of the wrong Purcell—the man represented is probably Daniel Purcell—Professor Westrup wrote a brief summary of Purcell's life. Then he dedicated something less than a page to the discussion of Purcell's English quality. However, he did not define this quality, except to say that Purcell was more than a typical English composer and also more than a mere imitater of French and Italian musical styles. The article does not represent this excellent Purcellian at his best.

Westrup, Jack Allen. "Fact and fiction about Henry Purcell." *Proceedings of the Musical Association,* 62nd session (1935-36): 93-115; discussion, 112-115.

In this paper, his first venture into Purcell research, Sir Jack Westrup clarified several misconceptions that had somehow crept into the field. At the same time, unfortunately, he planted a new error, arguing that Henry, the famous composer, was the son of Thomas, and not of Henry the elder. It was a brilliant move for upsetting the apple cart, but not helpful in separating fact from fiction. This new fiction, perpetuated in all but a few recent editions of Westrup's biography of Purcell, clouds our approach to the story of Purcell's early years. No great harm is done here, for we have so little other direct information about these years that the damage is only hypothetical. Otherwise, this study was a significant milestone in Purcell research.

Westrup, Jack Allen. "Foreign musicians in Stuart England." *Musical Quarterly,* vol. 27 (1941): 79-80.

In this excellent article there is no reference either to Purcell or to his works. But the author has amassed an impressive roster of foreign musicians whose works and activities were influential throughout the reigns of the Stuarts. This is an indispensable study for anyone wishing to map out the bewildering skein of foreign influences that affected post-Restoration musical style in England.

Westrup, Jack Allen. *Purcell.* London: J.M. Dent, 1937; 8th ed., 1980. xii, 325 pp. Plates, musical examples, calendar, catalog of works, personalia, bibliography, genealogy, list of songs in the plays and operas, index (latest edition).

A concise, thorough and elegantly written account of the life, times and musical works of Henry Purcell. Assigning Henry Purcell to the wrong family tree—i.e., that of Thomas Purcell—is not a serious flaw, since all of Purcell's brothers and sisters were assigned along with him, in due course. Musical judgements, often expressed in rather general terms, are less impressive, given the consistent tendency to downplay the affective quality of the music, and to avoid 'musicology' like the plague. All other discussions, along with the reasoning behind them except that connected with Purcell's genealogy, are praiseworthy.

Westrup, Jack Allen. "Purcell and Handel." *Music and Letters*, vol. 40 (1959): 103-08.

Characterizing the two men as "heavenly twins, about whom we know little" Westrup thought Purcell's influence on Handel was minimal except in a very general way, particularly in the Chandos anthems, which in his view show purely continental influences. Direct borrowings from Purcell, as in the fourth Chandos anthem and frequent use by Handel of the principal motive from "Rejoice in the Lord alway" might be advanced to show that Purcell's influence on Handel may be more direct than Sir Jack supposed.

Westrup, Jack Allen. "Purcell's music for 'Timon of Athens.'" *Festschrift für Karl Gustav Fellerer,* edited by H. Huschen. Regensburg: G. Bosse, 1962. Pp. 573-78.

Westrup, Jack Allen. "Purcell's parentage." *Music Review*, vol. 25 (1964): 100-03.

To explain away hard facts from contemporary records relating to Purcell's parentage, the author shores up his early innovative family tree by creating new branches. Inventing several brothers, cousins, uncles, and aunts, he reconciles facts to his theory, also denigrating testimony of contemporary witness such as John Hawkins, Charles Burney, Thomas Ford, and Anthony à Wood, not to mention several modern authors.

Westrup, Jack Allen. "Purcell's reputation." *Musical Times*, vol. 100 (1959): 318-20.

Westrup comments on the loss of interest in Purcell's music during the course of the eighteenth century in England. He then traces the rekindling of interest and assumption of responsibility for Purcell's music during the nineteenth and twentieth centuries. In this useful, though brief article he praises the pioneer efforts of Vincent Novello, Gerald Cooper, The Musical Antiquarian Society, and the Purcell Club and comments on the bicentennial anniversary of Purcell's death in 1895 and the tricentennial of his birth in 1959.

Westrup, Jack Allen. "Royal music under the Stewarts." *Festschrift für Ernst Hermann Meyer zum sechzigsten Geburtstag*, edited by Georg Knepler. Leipzig: Deutscher Verlag, 1973. Pp. 189-96.

A thorough study of public records of Purcell's time. This essay mainly makes clear the economic difficulties which all musicians suffered throughout the reigns of the Stuarts. The comments on Purcell's difficulties are interesting, but do not greatly increase our understanding of him either as man or musician.

White, Eric Walter. "Early theatrical performances of Purcell's operas, with a calendar of recorded performances, 1690-1710." *Theatre Notebook*, vol. 13 (Winter 1958-59): 43-65.

White, Eric Walter. "New light on 'Dido and Aeneas.'" *Henry Purcell (1659-1695): essays on his music*. Edited by Imogen Holst. London: Oxford University Press, 1959. Pp. 14-34.

A masterful treatment of the subject of musical and textual sources of Dido and Æneas, with commentary on lacunae that opens the way to new research even after 30 years have elapsed.

White, Eric Walter. *The rise of English opera*. London: J. Lehmann, 1951. 335 pp. Illustrations, three appendices, index.

The first chapter, "Early Representations (The Seventeenth Century)" is a succinct and thorough account of first operatic attempts in England, and a valuable introduction for anyone seeking to research Purcell's own efforts in the operatic field.

Whittaker, William Gillies. "Some observations on Purcell's harmony." *Musical Times*, vol. 75 (1934): 887-94.

Discussing Purcell's harmonic style, his modulations, his chromaticism and general disposition to use startling harmonic clashes, the author has left one of the best pieces available on this subject.

Wienandt, Elwyn A., and Robert Young. *The Anthem in England and America.* New York: Free Press, 1970. Illustrations, musical illustrations, bibliography, index.

A complete history of the anthem, the work is solidly conceived and well executed. Only a few pages are devoted to the works of Purcell, and to those of his teacher, John Blow, but the analyses are keen, the musical judgements sound.

Wood, Anthony à. *The life and times of Anthony Wood, antiquary, of Oxford, 1632-1695, described by himself; collected from his diaries and other papers.* Edited by Andrew Clarke. 4 vols. Oxford, 1894.

A remarkable source for backgrounds of musical life in the seventeenth century, these volumes provide an excellent source for the Purcellian period, even though Purcell's name, unfortunately, does not appear in the index. It is unfortunate also that the journal ends on November 12, 1695, just ten days short of Purcell's death.

Wood, Bruce. "Two Purcell discoveries; 2. A coronation anthem lost and found." *Musical Times,* vol. 118 (1977): 466-68.

Arguing from circumstantial evidence, the author assumes that a setting of "I was glad," which is attributed to John Blow by its copyist, James Hawkins, was actually composed by Henry Purcell. The strength of his thesis is such as to cause the author to leap over the stylistic incongruities of the piece, to the conclusion that, given the circumstances, Purcell must have written it.

Wood, Bruce. "A newly identified Purcell autograph." *Music and Letters*, vol. 59 (1978): 329-32.

Inventorying the musical repertory of the English Chapel Royal between 1660 and 1688, Bruce Wood examines full scores and "fowle originals" of the music, which contains Purcell's autograph string parts for *My song shall be alway,* a new identification of what appears to be a genuine autograph.

Young, Percy M. *Henry Purcell (1659-1695)* [Aus dem Englischen übertragen von Gerda Becher]. *Musik und Gesellschaft,* jahrg. 9 heft. 8 (1959): 2-7.

Young, Percy M. *A history of British music.* London: Benn, 1967. xi, 641 pp.

In a subsection of a chapter on the English Baroque, Mr. Young devotes thirteen pages to a summary of Henry Purcell's life and works. Though somewhat tinctured by political dialectic, the discussion is succinct, the insights original and valid, and the coverage is good.

Zimmerman, Franklin B. "A newly-discovered anthem by Purcell." *Musical Quarterly*, vol. 45 (1959): 302-11.

Article, with edited score of the anthem. Discusses the provenance of Purcell's setting for solo bass and chorus of the eighteenth Psalm, "I will love thee, O Lord." Evidently, the anthem was composed as a test piece for John Gostling's entry into the Chapel Royal in 1679.

Zimmerman, Franklin B.   "Air, a catch-word for new concepts in seventeenth-century English music." *Studies in musicology in honor of Otto E. Albrecht,* edited by John Walter Hill. Kassel, Basel, London: Bärenreiter, 1980. Pp. 142-57.

   Baroque English theorists used the word 'air' with a constellation of meanings. These shed light on various aspects of the developing sense of tonality and modulation among theorists, which may also be traced in the music of the time. This article traces the 'road to major-minor' as it was traversed by English music masters such as Thomas Morley, Thomas Campion, Charles Butler, Christopher Simpson, Matthew Locke, John Playford, and Henry Purcell. In the process one sees such terms as 'air,' 'key,' 'harmony,' 'transfer of accord,' and 'base notes silenced,' or *'basses suposées'* as Rameau was to label this phenomenon.

Zimmerman, Franklin B.   "Anthems of Purcell and contemporaries in a newly rediscovered Gostling mansucript." *Acta Musicologica,* vol. 41, fasc. I-II (1969): 59-70.

   Provides a complete inventory, history, and analysis of this valuable manuscript, which had disappeared in England some thirty years before its rediscovery in Austin, Texas, just prior to the publication of this article.

Zimmerman, Franklin B.   "Handel's Purcellian borrowings in his later operas and oratorios." *Festschrift for O.E. Deutsch,* edited by Walter Gerstenberg, Jan LaRue and Wolfgang Rehm. Kassel: Bärenreiter, 1963. Pp. 20-30.

The article explores the significance of a number of direct borrowings, along with subtler connections between Handel's works and those of Purcell. Some of the latter kind now seem somewhat inferential.

Zimmerman, Franklin B. *Henry Purcell, 1659-1695: an analytical catalogue of his music*. London: Macmillan, 1963. xxiv, 575 pp. Music incipits, commentaries, apparatus (including lists of manuscript and early printed sources and literature), 6 appendices; 4 indices.

As a fairly complete list of Purcell's complete works and their main sources, the catalogue has proved useful to persons interested in Purcell's music. Cross-references between individual works and the manuscript and printed source lists in appendices 3 and 4 have been helpful, as have incipits for inner movements and sections for all works.

Zimmerman, Franklin B. *Henry Purcell: 1659-1695: his life and times*. First edition, London: Macmillan, 1967. vii, 429 pp. Illustrations (incl. 16 plates), notes, documents, genealogy, bibliography, index of Purcell's music, and general index.

A detailed account of Purcell's life, as seen against the historical and cultural backdrop of his times. Fully documented, with a study of Purcell's genealogy, securely returning to traditional theories concerning the identity of his father. The study uncovered new documentary evidence to add to the store of knowledge about Purcell, including Purcell's Sacrament Certificate, evidence on his trip to Holland, and a great number of new facts relating to his family relationships.

Zimmerman, Franklin B. *Henry Purcell, 1659-1695: his life and times.* Second, revised edition, Philadelphia: University of Pennsylvania Press, 1983. xxxi, 473 pp. Documents, genealogy, iconography, notes, bibliography, index, and illustrations.

A detailed account of Purcell's life, as seen within the historical framework of his times. Fully documented, with new evidence on Purcell's trip to Holland, and further support of the genealogy presented in the first study (see above).

Zimmerman, Franklin B. *Henry Purcell: 1659-1695: melodic and intervallic indexes to his complete works.* 2nd edition. Philadelphia: Smith-Edwards-Dunlap, 1975. 133. 31-tone nomenclature, index of pitches, index of intervals, foreword.

A detailed thematic index of 3,000 themes representing each movement and section of Purcell's complete works, including doubtful and spurious ascriptions.

Zimmerman, Franklin B. "Jeremiah Clarke's trumpet voluntary." (Written in collaboration with Charles Cudworth.) *Music and Letters*, vol. 41 (1960): 342-48.

Explores in detail the sources of "The Trumpet Voluntary," proving beyond doubt that it was composed by Purcell's pupil, Jeremiah Clarke. The same sort of proof was provided for another trumpet piece, the "Trumpet tune in D Major." This also seems to have been written by Jeremiah Clarke, although proof is not so definite here.

Zimmerman, Franklin B. "John Playford's *Introduction to the skill of music,* 12th edition." New York: Da Capo Press, 1972. 282 pp. Introduction, 6 appendices, presenting sections from earlier editions, along with facsimiles, glossary, and index.

A facsimile edition, with introduction, glossary, index, and plates reproducing title pages of all 19 editions and various impressions of Playford's popular handbook.

Zimmerman, Franklin B. "Musical borrowings in the English Baroque." *Musical Quarterly,* vol. 52 (1966): 483-95.

Tracing the historical background for musical borrowing, the author provides interesting comparative examples of Purcell's and Handel's borrowings from their contemporaries and predecessors.

Zimmerman, Franklin B. "Musical styles and practices in Purcell's anthems. Part I." *American Choral Review,* vol. 4, no. 3 (1962): 1-4.

Discusses evidences in Purcell's anthems of an older layer of influence on Purcell's anthem composition, deriving from earlier English masters, in combination with more recent influence from the second practice of Monteverdi and his Italian contemporaries and followers.

Zimmerman, Franklin B. "Poets in praise of Purcell." *Musical Times,* vol. 100 (1959): 526-28.

This reproduction of eight poems on Purcell, as written by his contemporaries, shows that his significance as a musician was not lost on his fellow citizens. They took pride in his preeminence, comparing him favorably with Bassani and Corelli.

Zimmerman, Franklin B. "Purcell and Monteverdi." *Musical Times*, vol. 99 (1958): 368-69.

Presents and discusses a new autograph source advancing Monteverdi as one of the "most fam'd Italian masters" whom Purcell professed to imitate in the preface to his Sonatas of III Parts, 1683. The article opens the way for broader discussion, which may be found in the author's second revised edition of *Henry Purcell, 1659-1695: his life and times*.

Zimmerman, Franklin B. "Purcell and the Dean of Westminster—some new evidence." *Music and Letters*, vol. 43 (1962): 7-15.

The article shed new light on Purcell's quarrel with the Dean of Westminster over money he had collected for seats in the organ loft at the coronation of Willam and Mary in 1689. The new evidence was collected from the reverse sides of leaves devoted to financial records from the reigns of the Georges. There it had lain for two and a half centuries, virtually hidden. This, along with other evidence, shows that Purcell, in accepting money for seats in the organ loft, was merely claiming a perquisite of long established tradition among organists.

Zimmerman, Franklin B., and Nigel Fortune. "Purcell's autographs." *Henry Purcell (1659-1695): essays on his music,* edited by Imogen Holst. London: Oxford University Press, 1959. Pp. 106-21.

A complete listing, with locations of Purcell's works in autograph sources, together with works by other composers which he copied, supposititious autographs and a selective list of other important manuscript sources.

Zimmerman, Franklin B. "Purcell's family circle, revisited and revised." *Journal of the American Musicological Society,* vol.16 (Fall 1963): 373-81.

This article restates the case for accepting Henry Purcell the elder as father of the famous composer, and explores new evidence that greatly weakens any argument that Thomas Purcell may have been the father.

Zimmerman, Franklin B. "Purcell Portraiture." *Hinrichsen's 10th Yearbook* (1958): 135-49.

A complete list of Purcell portraiture, including several lost items. The article was offered as the beginning of a Purcell iconography, which more properly would be researched and published by an art historian.

Zimmerman, Franklin B. "Purcell's Service Anthem 'O God, Thou Art My God' and the B-flat Major Service." *Musical Quarterly,* vol. 50 (1964): 207-14.

Analyzing the main melodic motiv in the anthem, the author shows that this incipit relates directly to a predominant motiv in the Service. The relationship between the two reflects the older continental custom of relating motets to masses through sharing of motivs, and provides an interesting instance of Purcell's use of Renaissance musical techniques in his works.

Zimmerman, Franklin B. "Purcell's concerted anthems: new aesthetic concepts." *American Choral Review*, vol. 5 no. 2 (1963): 8-13.

   The subject of this article is the style of the late anthems with orchestral accompaniments, which prefigure the great choral-orchestral compositions of G.F. Handel in this genre.

Zimmerman, Franklin B. "Purcell's polyphonic anthems." *American Choral Review*, vol. 4, no. 4 (1962): 1, 3-6.

   Devoted to earlier unaccompanied anthems as well as to some later examples, this article discusses Purcell's stylistic and technical characteristics in light of the influence of earlier English composers of sacred music.

Zimmerman, Franklin B. "Purcell's Handwriting." *Henry Purcell (1659-1695): essays on his music,* edited by Imogen Holst. London: Oxford University Press,1959. Pp. 103-05.

   A brief, inconclusive, and somewhat simplistic treatment of the subject.

Zimmerman, Franklin B. "Purcellian passages in the compositions of G.F. Handel." *Music in eighteenth-century England: essays in memory of Charles Cudworth,* edited by Christopher Hogwood and Richard Luckett. Cambridge and New York: Cambridge University Press, 1983. Pp. 49-58.

   After a summary analysis of Handel's various kinds of borrowing techniques, including direct borrowings from Purcell, the author turns to the more subtle borrowings from the works of the latter. These include motivic reworkings to achieve a certain affect, choral affect passages, and veiled borrowings from instrumental accompaniments.

Zimmerman, Franklin B. "Restoration music manuscripts at Lincoln Cathedral." *Musical Times*, vol. 101 (1960): 24.

Discusses and provides a brief inventory of important seventeenth- and eighteenth-century manuscript copies of works by Purcell and near contemporaries at Lincoln Cathedral.

Zimmerman, Franklin B. "Sound and sense in Purcell's single songs." *Words to music; papers on English seventeenth-century song read at a Clark Library Seminar, December 11, 1965, by Vincent Duckles and Franklin B. Zimmerman.* Introduction by Walter Rubsamen. Los Angeles: University of California, 1967. Pp. 45-90. Music, illustrations, tables.

This article relates Purcell's art of song-setting to some of the principles of Thomas Morley and Thomas Campion and also to a theory of rhythmic affects advanced by Isaac Vossius. More significantly, it makes clear Purcell's sensitive ear as concerns subtle inflexions and accentuations of the English language in poetic dress.

Zimmerman, Franklin B. "The anthems of Henry Purcell." *American Choral Review*, vol. 13, nos. 3 and 4 (1971): 65.

A brief, but comprehensive study of Purcell's styles and practices, forms and techniques, and compositional development in his anthems. The study ends with a list of all Purcell's anthems, arranged by form and performing media, and a selection of modern editions.

Zimmerman, Franklin B.,ed. *The Gostling manuscript* (compiled by John Gostling). Austin, Texas, and London: University of Texas Press, 1977. xiii, 205 and 213 pp., in reverse-ended format.

Foreword, facsimiles of the entire manuscript. A complete facsimile of this very important English source for the sacred music of Henry Purcell and contemporaries in full facsimile, with brief description of its contents. The manuscript had lain hidden for nearly half a century prior to this publication.

Zimmerman, Franklin B. "The social and political functions of the Restoration anthem." *Report of the International Congress for Musikforschung*. Kassel, 1962.

This article examines the political and social topicality of the Restoration anthem, which had not been a subject of serious research at the time this article was written. The propagandistic bent of several anthems of Purcell, along with those of predecessors and contemporaries, makes it clear that this is a subject worthy of closer examination. Its relationship to the music is of course germinal.

Zimmerman, Franklin B. "Thematic unity in Purcell's grand concerted anthems (I)." *American Choral Review*, vol. 5, no. 4 (1953): 10-13.

This study reveals that Purcell began writing "motto anthems" fairly early in his career, developing a very interesting set of works in this category. Here is another instance of his reviving an old Renaissance practice. (See above.)

Zimmerman, Franklin B. "Thematic unity in Purcell's grand concerted anthems (II)." *American Choral Review,* vol. 6, no. 1 (1963): 3-4, 8-12. (See above.)

INDEX

adagio, 77
affect or affections, musical,
  66, 68
Akeroyd, Samuel, 83, 134
Albion and Albanius, 44,
  50, 111
Aldrich, Henry, 117
allegro, 77
Altisidora, 53
Amphion, 119
Amphitryon, 102, 109,
Anne, Princess of Denmark,
  and Prince George, 41,
  146
Anne, Queen of England,
  137 (Her Majesty's
  Army)
Anon., *Laudamus te
  Dominum* , 98
Apollo, 117
Apollo's Banquet, 96, 105,
  109, 122
Argyll, 44
Aristophanes, 97
Aristotle, 68
art of descant, The, 92, 124
Arundel St., 74

Arundell, Denis, 54
Ayliffe, Mrs., 116
Aylmer, Brabazon, 136,
  138-39

Bacchus, 121
Baldwin, 82
Baldwin, Richard, 115,
  122, 127
Banister, John, 67, 147 (n.
  5)
banquet of music, The, 100
  (2), 101, 104, 105,
  110, 115
Baptist, Signor, 83, 121
bass viol, instructions on,
  92, 124
Bassani, Giovanni B., 39,
  120
"Battle of the Organs," 58
  (n. 31)
Beaumont, F., 106
Beda (Bede), 112
Belk, Dr. and Lady, 56 (n.
  10)
Bell Yard, 97, 101
Benskin, T., 78